NOW THAT I'M *Married,* WHY ISN'T EVERYTHING *Perfect?*

ALSO BY SUSAN PAGE

If I'm So Wonderful, Why Am I Still Single?

NOW THAT I'M *Married,* WHY ISN'T EVERYTHING *Perfect?*

THE 8 ESSENTIAL TRAITS OF COUPLES WHO THRIVE

Susan Page

LITTLE, BROWN AND COMPANY

BOSTON NEW YORK TORONTO LONDON

FIRST EDITION

Library of Congress Cataloging-in-Publication Data

Page, Susan.
    Now that I'm married, why isn't everything perfect? : the eight
essential traits of couples who thrive / Susan Page. — 1st ed.
    p.   cm.
    Includes bibliographical references.
    ISBN 0-316-68837-1
    1. Marriage.   2. Married people—Psychology.
3. Communication in marriage   I. Title.
HQ734.P17   1994
646.7'8—dc20   93-33149

10 9 8 7 6 5 4 3 2 1

MV-PA

Published simultaneously in Canada by Little, Brown & Company
(Canada) Limited

PRINTED IN THE UNITED STATES OF AMERICA

For Mayer

From studies of various age and population groups in the United States and abroad, [psychologists] have reached some objective conclusions on the makings of happiness. What comes up consistently at the top of the charts is not, as many might expect, success, youth, good looks or any of those enviable assets. The clear winner is relationships. Close ones. Followed by happy marriage.

Newsweek, May 24, 1993

Contents

Part One

THE 8 ESSENTIAL TRAITS OF COUPLES WHO THRIVE

Part Two

THE CHALLENGE

Preface

The seed for this book was planted in my mind when the hundredth person approached me after I published my first book to declare, "Susan, I have the perfect title for your next book: *If I'm So Wonderful, Why Am I Still Married?* Ha, ha, ha!"

I chuckled to be polite, but inside I didn't understand why this was supposed to be funny. After hearing it dozens of times, I began to feel downright sad. I wanted to say to these people, "If you aren't happy with your marriage, why don't you do something about it?"

I began to search the literature for books about happy marriage — but they all turned out to be about how to drag your awful relationship up out of the gutter and make it tolerable. The more I read and the more gallows humor I heard, the more determined I became to tell the world that I was extremely happy with my husband, and that I thought people were making attaining a happy marriage more complicated than it needed to be.

At first I began to tell the story of Mayer and me and all that we have learned in our eventful twelve years together. But I didn't want negative thinkers to dismiss us as an aberration. And I kept writing things like, " . . . and this isn't unusual. Our friends Bob and Jeanne had a similar experience." When I began sharing my ideas with Bob and Jeanne and others, we had such an exciting time talking about our relationships that I quickly realized I had much to learn from other thriving couples. And when I set about finding happy couples to interview, I was faced with an avalanche.

The major points in this book are also the result of my more than twenty years of professional involvement with couples. In 1970, when my colleague Roseann Packard and I founded one of the nation's first university-based human sexuality programs, at the University of California in Berkeley, I learned from the young couples I counseled the importance of letting go of preconceived ideas about how sex ought to be and of accepting what it actually was *for them*. And I quickly saw that letting go of preconceived ideas about how relationships and life in general "should be" was an important basic prescription for a good life and a sense of well-being.

In my work as a Protestant campus minister and as the director of a domestic violence prevention agency, I continued to gain experience and insights about the way some couples resign themselves to a lackluster marriage. It was the sense that I had an unusual view of relationships that led me to begin my workshops in 1980.

All of my work was supported by extensive training in Gestalt psychology and Bioenergetic therapy. As I explained in my first book,

> The theory behind Gestalt (a German word meaning, roughly, "whole") is that through the process of ordinary living, most individuals become fragmented; that is, they become alienated from certain aspects of themselves. For example, a woman who grew up in a family where anger was severely punished and politeness was maintained at all costs may be completely unaware of her buried anger. Or, a man who was taught never to cry and always to maintain an "in-control" attitude may be altogether unconscious of his soft, vulnerable feelings. Using a variety of techniques, Gestalt, which was developed by Fritz Perls, assists individuals to reclaim lost aspects of themselves and, thereby, to become more integrated, more "whole," and more fully functioning human beings.

Much of what I learned in my workshops over the years is presented in the pages that follow. I have also drawn heavily on the experiences of the thirty-two happy couples I interviewed in depth as well as my own odyssey from an eight-year first marriage, through a painful but ultimately enlightening divorce, six years of singlehood, and now twelve years of experiencing life's joys and challenges together with my wonderful husband.

*   *   *

Mayer and I met when we were both thirty-seven. Both of us had been married before and were looking, deliberately and systematically, for new marriage partners. When I met Mayer, I dismissed him as a nice guy, but not at all my type. I was in the market for a university professor or minister or politician, someone who had a Ph.D. and lots of public recognition. When Mayer told me he was a studio potter, I thought it was a polite way of saying that he was a hippie dropout who made mugs in his garage and sold them at flea markets. I had three two-hour dates with him (lunch, breakfast, or coffee), for I had a policy of holding off on evening dates with a person until I felt the relationship was something I might want to pursue. Our fourth date was for breakfast, but it lasted all the way to dinner and beyond, and we have rarely been apart since.

I soon learned that there really is such a thing as a career studio potter. Mayer had been making his living as one for twenty years and was quite well known. He opened up an exciting new world to me of decorative and craft arts.

We faced several challenges early on. To begin with both of us were in career transition when we met. I had just left a position as the executive director of a child-abuse prevention agency in order to give more attention to my relationship workshops and my writing. Mayer was determined to move away from functional pottery so he could work full-time creating ceramic art. We encouraged each other to pursue our true desires, even though this meant that our financial situation was unstable, causing us periods of real anxiety.

Mayer's son, Gabe, who lived with Mayer full-time, was eleven when they "adopted" me. I was thrilled to be a part of this sweet boy's life, but was naive about how hard it might be for Gabe to accept me, uninvited competition for his dad's attention. Because I believe strongly in the value of professional help in matters like these, we went into family therapy almost as soon as we got married. It was enormously helpful. For example, Mayer felt torn between his loyalties to Gabe and to me, and didn't know how to handle Gabe's attempts to exclude me. The therapist made it clear to us that what Gabe needed most was limits and consistent messages, and that Mayer had to make it absolutely clear to Gabe that I was now part of the picture. For my part, it was difficult for me not to take Gabe's rejection personally. I had to be reassured over and over that the problem wasn't me. I could be a fairy godmother and still be seen by Gabe as unwelcome. Both of these were insights we would not have seen so clearly if we had tried to chart a course without help.

If we had predicted when we got married what would happen over the ensuing twelve years, we would have been right about some things, but way off the mark about others.

We guessed that we would grow in our knowledge of each other and our feeling of closeness and unity. This has been true. When we celebrated our twelfth anniversary in Hawaii, we could not imagine feeling more relaxed and compatible — or more passionately in love with each other. While we were there, we each took a quiz about our personal values, attitudes, and habits. Then I answered the questions as I thought Mayer would answer them for himself, and vice versa. We were amazed — but then not so amazed — that with the vast majority of the questions, our views of each other exactly matched our own and we were never more than one point apart.

But many things turned out very differently from what we had anticipated twelve years ago. We predicted another child in our lives. We never guessed that I would spend five years involved with Mayer's business — corresponding with galleries, writing articles for magazines, and traveling with him to trade shows and gallery openings. And we certainly didn't predict that, five years later, when my travel schedule with workshops and lectures around the country became heavy, Mayer would take over the managerial aspects of my business and travel with me, giving him the opportunity to turn his antique hobby into a business.

You, dear reader, will get to know us — and our own marriage — better in the pages that follow. What I regret is that I can't know more about you and your partner. For, even though we have never met, you and I have a relationship. I have been thinking about you for many months as I wrote. It has been a challenge and a great pleasure for me to express what I so fervently believe about what marriage can be. My fondest desire is that you will find what I have written to be genuinely helpful. I welcome your comments.

SUSAN PAGE
Berkeley, California
June 1993

$\mathscr{A}cknowledgments$

My extraordinary husband, Mayer Shacter, is my most important partner in this book, for I couldn't write about thriving marriage if I weren't a part of one. Our marriage gave me the concept for the book and provided its framework. Mayer supports my writing with all manner of material and spiritual nourishment — from his sensational meals awaiting me when I come home from the computer to clever ideas and long conversations in which I clarify my thinking. My love and gratitude know no earthly limits.

All writers know the agonizing search for the perfect book title. This time I was spared. Toni Sciarra suggested the title of this book to me several years ago, for which I remain extremely grateful. She was prodded by my agent, the indefatigable Sandra Dijkstra, my cheerleader, wise critic, coach, and friend. Sandy envisioned this book before I did and steered me away from lesser projects I was tempted to undertake. She is a brilliant literary and business partner who gives me both guidance and support. I cannot imagine writing without her.

I am deeply indebted to the couples I interviewed for allowing me to ask all manner of personal questions and for responding with great enthusiasm and thoroughness. This book could not have been written without their cooperation, and I am deeply appreciative.

My administrative assistant, Alice Vdovin, has gone miles beyond the call of duty many times. Her resourcefulness, humor, generosity, support, and friendship are a true blessing. Michelle Madhok was a most reliable and enthusiastic research assistant.

Psychotherapist Harriett Sage and editor Dorothy Wall became valued advisors in the latter stages of the project.

My wonderful, loving family read all or part of the manuscript and made suggestions that have been included in the final text. Big thank yous to Bonnie Davis, Helen Hammock, Jan Hammock, and Paul Hammock. Important contributions were also made by Warren Greshes and Shelley Nelson. I am grateful to Naomi Epel, David Garfinkel, Dick Roth, Michelle Murphy, and Susan Woodring for their special support.

Working with Fredrica Friedman, my editor at Little, Brown, her associate, Jordan Pavlin, and her assistant, Eve Yohalem, has been a true pleasure. Her belief in this book buoyed me all along, and her work on the page and off gently coaxed me to my true potential. She is a gifted editor.

NOW THAT I'M
Married,
WHY ISN'T
EVERYTHING
Perfect?

Introduction

A BRAND-NEW IDEA ABOUT
MARRIAGE

TWO KINDS OF people will read this book.

Happy couples will read it — so they can read about themselves. Welcome. You'll find this book a pleasure and an inspiration.

Unhappy or mildly happy couples will read it — to see if *this* book will give them the secrets they seek to becoming happier and more fulfilled in their relationship. If you are one of those readers, you are in for the surprise of your life, because this book does hold secrets to happiness — but not in the forms you are used to seeing them. It will not tell you how to change your spouse. It will not give you techniques you can use to paper over limitations in your own character and to patch up your relationship. It won't give you a course of therapy that has worked for other unhappy couples. It won't tell you what to *do* to have a better marriage; rather, it will tell you how to *be* to have a better marriage.

This book is about the kinds of people who have thriving marriages. They didn't all have happy childhoods; some of their early families were quite miserable. They aren't all superachievers. They don't all have charmed, lucky lives. They don't all have "perfect" partners. What they do have in common is that they are people who are guided by deep and timeless principles — the ones you will discover as you read on.

The German painter Max Ernst once said, "Our fear of ideas is probably the greatest dike holding back human knowledge and happiness." Welcome to the exploration of a brand new idea. First let's look at the old idea we will be replacing.

The Old Idea

The old idea — the one that most of us are still dragging around, long after its usefulness and validity have evaporated — is that there is no such thing as a really great marriage — or at least, that joyfully happy marriages are so rare that they are unattainable to most of us normal, somewhat neurotic folks. Marriage never really delivers on the romantic images we continue in vain to cultivate. How could reality ever match up to such unrealistic visions? In fact, if you expect too much from marriage, you are bound to be disappointed. After all, fully half of all marriages end in divorce.

The old idea about marriage is that it is hard work. Even if you are willing to do the hard work, you are bound to be disappointed, for the very nature of marriage requires that you make major sacrifices. In the real world, being married involves compromise and disillusionment:

He's not as romantic as he was at first.

She's more demanding than I thought she'd be.

We aren't close and romantic any more. We're getting along okay, but we need lots of space.

We're just like everyone else: the passion and heightened excitement of the early stages of our love have faded. This is normal and natural.

All marriages go through stages, the old wisdom goes. After the honeymoon phase ends, a couple will begin to be annoyed by the very qualities that attracted them to each other in the first place. Inevitably, they will go through a frustrating power struggle with each other. Ultimately, marriage is a vehicle we use to work through unresolved issues from childhood, and this will, of course, be painful.

With babies, "failure to thrive" is a cause for alarm. In marriage, it is considered normal.

One of the best measures of a society's fundamental beliefs is its sense of humor. Black humor about marriage is rampant in our culture. Blondie Bumstead and Maggie Briggs nagging their husbands and chasing them with rolling pins is supposed to be hilarious. Apparently thousands of people find it funny to see "The Lockhorns'" utterly miserable relationship portrayed day after day in cartoons that depict their thoughtless, selfish, and mean-spirited behavior toward each other. Endless variations of the classic, "My wife left me ten days ago—but I'm going to wait two weeks before I start to celebrate," are still common fare in comedy clubs. An updated version was circulating recently: Q: "What is the difference between herpes and true love?" A: "Herpes is forever."

A joke anthology chosen randomly from the public library offered 249 jokes in the marriage category. Virtually all of them based their humor on the common belief that marriage is a trap. For people who are delighted with their marriages, jokes like this aren't funny: "Matrimony isn't just a word, it's a sentence." The jokes build on the idea that marriage will destroy any hint of happiness that might have been there before: Q: "You seem to like his attentions, why don't you marry him?" A: "Because I like his attentions." Most of them are sexist as well. Q: "Do you know who the greatest living dictator in the world is?" A: "Know her? I married her!" Of course, such jokes not only build upon negative stereotypes about marriage but also they perpetuate them.

Large numbers of the single men and women I have worked with over the past twelve years hold the following sentence to be true: "If I get into a committed relationship, I'll be giving up more than I will gain." Many agree that they have never known of a marriage that really works. When I tell acquaintances about my project of interviewing couples who describe their marriage as genuinely happy, I frequently hear comments like, "It shouldn't be too hard to interview all three of them," or "Where in the world do you find such anomalies?"

Disparaging beliefs about marriage are deeply imbedded in our collective psyche. At best, many would agree, marriage is a mixed bag. To be sure, some marriages "survive," but are any long-term couples truly happy? No — only in teenage romance novels and "Kodak moments," says conventional wisdom. Some couples might think they are happy, but they are in denial. We still *want* marriage to be wonderful, but deep inside, we fear that happy marriage is unrealistic.

WHY WE BELIEVE THE OLD IDEA

Let's look for a moment at how the belief that marriage is doomed from the start has become so widespread.

One significant reason is that virtually all experts on marriage are psychologists or marriage counselors who are trained for and interested in not marriage, but marital *pathology*. These people spend all of their time with couples who are experiencing high levels of dissatisfaction, and then write books about how they have helped these couples. Most of our literature about love and marriage is written by clinicians, who see a skewed portion of the general population, namely, couples whose marriage *is* hard work.

Many of these books are helpful — even for happy couples. The clinicians who write them are indeed experts, and I would never suggest that they not share their wisdom with us. But it is inappropriate for us to derive our ideas about what is "normal" in marriage from these books and studies. They are not about love; they are about the inability to love or the absence of loving. Yet they inadvertently convey that weak marriages are the norm in our society.

Sociologists and journalists also perpetuate the impression that marriage is a fundamentally flawed institution. "Conflict and ambivalence," writes Arlene Skolnick, the author of a popular college text on marriage, "are as intrinsic to the family as intimacy and love." It is in the very nature of marriage, she would have us believe, that it must be riddled with conflict. In her bestseller about marriage, *Intimate Partners, Patterns in Love and Marriage,* journalist Maggie Scarf looks almost exclusively at dysfunctional patterns in love and marriage, implying throughout that there are no functional patterns to describe. Her chapter titles betray her conclusions: "The Intimate System: The Caretaker and the Wounded Bird"; "What Marital Problems Are Made Of: Couples in Collusion"; "A Classic System: The Silent Husband and the Hysterical Wife." Why would anyone who reads such a book ever voluntarily join an "intimate partnership"? Indeed, books like this one abet singles in justifying their continued solo status, whether or not it is genuinely in their best interest. "The problems of marriage don't make it worth doing," they tell themselves. "The real fun lasts only a couple of months." Everything they read about marriage reinforces this discouraging picture.

But it is not only psychologists and journalists, writing almost exclusively about the negative aspects of marriage, who reinforce in us the belief that marriage is hard work. We perpetuate the idea ourselves, for when we believe something, we see the world through the lens of that belief. We quite naturally focus on people and events that validate the belief. And we create the kinds of marriages that we believe are possible.

DOES THE OLD IDEA ABOUT MARRIAGE
SERVE US OR CHEAT US?

The belief that mediocre marriage is a social reality might not be so insidious if we believed it mostly about other people's marriages. But the worst part of this popular American myth is that we personalize it. "If 50 percent of all marriages end in divorce," the thinking goes, "then my own chances of success are only fifty-fifty. Since no one really has a good marriage, why should I expect to have one myself?"

In fact, the popular 50 percent statistic has recently been challenged. In a 1987 *San Francisco Chronicle* article entitled "Marriage Is Holding Up," pollster Louis Harris called it "one of the most specious pieces of statistical nonsense ever perpetrated in modern times." He says that government figures and his survey show that only one of eight marriages will end in divorce, and that in any single year only about 2 percent of existing marriages will break up. And even if the 50 percent figure were accurate, statistics about a population are irrelevant to your own individual odds. Your "odds" of staying married are what you make them — as we shall see in upcoming chapters — based on what you believe about your marriage and whether or not you choose to be a loving, proactive spouse.

We need beliefs in order to justify our behavior. A friend of mine has an idea for a book, but she believes that she does not have the discipline to write it. This belief will serve her if she never writes the book. It will comfort her, and relieve her guilt. But if she would really like to write the book, the belief will not serve her.

The prevailing belief about marriage endures because it allows us to feel normal if our marriage is unexciting. We willingly cling to the idea that marriage is not supposed to be joyful because it helps us to rationalize our own ho-hum marriages.

"People will not want to read about thriving couples," a friend cautioned me. "It will make them uncomfortable and anxious. People would rather read about couples who are worse off than they are so that they can feel good about themselves."

My friend is right only about people who want to keep their marriage exactly where it is — people like my friend who *wants* to believe that she can't write a book. If you generally fear that any change will be for the worse, then this book, this new idea about marriage, will not serve you.

But if you are willing to challenge the old idea that marriage is supposed to be routine, and if you are willing to suspend — even for a few hours as an experiment — your beliefs about your own marriage, then you are in for a pleasant surprise.

The chapters ahead will show that the primary difference between thriving couples and troubled ones is that thriving couples *want* to thrive and *believe* they can be extremely happy together. Thriving couples simply don't buy the current wisdom about marriage; they are quietly pursuing their own reality. I believe that looking closely at happy couples will take the mystery out of happiness for the rest of us. Happiness in marriage is not so elusive. It starts with being willing to hold in abeyance for a while the old belief about marriage — that, because of its very nature, it is basically doomed from the start — and to entertain an altogether different belief, that marriage can be joyful for large numbers of people including you.

The New Idea

What this book will tell you is that in order to have a joyful marriage you have to change not your marriage but your mind-set. That is the new idea we will explore in depth. Many, many people are enjoying abundant, auspicious marriages, and many more people could be — if they could but make an inner shift.

"But look at how busy marriage counselors are," you say. "Besides, I don't know any really happy couples!" Right. It's the old belief again. Persistent, isn't it?

Instead, believe you and your partner can become a thriving, joyful couple who are genuinely enthusiastic about your relationship and thrilled to be together.

"What if I really am with the wrong partner?" you may ask. "What if we have already tried everything?"

The more you have "tried," the more entrenched you have become in the belief that your marriage is hopeless. This book will suggest a completely different approach, what I call a "second-order change." That is, simply making small changes while retaining your present ideas about marriage will not result in any meaningful change. What has to shift is your entire concept of marriage. This is an internal shift, and if you can make it, you will be able to change your marriage dramatically. This book will show you how.

There are some circumstances in which a marriage should be terminated, in which a change of partners is in fact an appropriate solution. After I have presented my initial case for transforming marriage,

I will explore this question thoroughly and identify those limited situations.

THRIVING MARRIAGE

This book is not a scientific study. I have interviewed at length thirty-two couples who describe themselves as flourishing and exceptionally happy, and I have spoken with forty others. (Their names have been changed in the text.) These couples were not randomly chosen, nor are they statistically significant. For what I have attempted in this book is to present a *gestalt*, a whole that is greater than the sum of its parts. Happy marriage is not just a certain belief or a set of behaviors; it is a combination of beliefs, feelings, behaviors, and attitudes that make up the whole. As you get inside the experience of thriving couples, your own belief system may begin to shift without your even realizing it. As C. S. Lewis says in *The Four Loves*, it's like the dawning of day or the warming of a room: by the time you notice it, the shift will already have occurred.

By observing real thriving couples, I hope to present a believable *gestalt*. For if you believe that your marriage can be more joyful, you will be motivated to make it so. It has not been your methods that have held you back so far, I submit, but your motivation. And you can't be motivated to improve your marriage if you don't believe any improvement is possible. Once you believe in thriving marriage, you will want one for yourself.

So, why isn't everything perfect? The short answer is, because you don't yet believe it can be.

THERE IS NO BEAUTY IN PERFECTION

"But perfect?" you ask. "No marriage is really perfect, is it? Do you really mean 'perfect'?"

I mean perfect, but I do not mean flawless; I mean just right. I mean beautiful.

Recently, I was in a conversation in which a woman who has been married for thirty-five years announced that she has the perfect marriage. Predictably, there was a strong reaction against her statement. "There's no such thing," people said. "No relationship is perfect — it's just the nature of human beings." "You must be an extremely tolerant person," one woman said.

Obviously, these people were making statements about their own relationships — and their own beliefs about relationships. If you believe there is no such thing as a perfect relationship, you'll never see one, and you'll certainly never have one.

The woman's claim reminded me of a passage I love from a book by Soetsu Yanagi about Japanese folk pottery, called *The Unknown Craftsman*:

> True beauty cannot lie either in the perfect or the imperfect, but must lie in a realm where such distinctions have ceased to exist. . . . The precise and perfect carries no overtones, admits of no freedom; the perfect is static and regulated, cold and hard. We in our own human imperfections are repelled by the perfect, since everything is apparent from the start and there is no suggestion of the infinite. Beauty must have some room, must be associated with freedom. Freedom, indeed, is beauty. The love of the irregular is a sign of the basic quest for freedom.

Folk potters, Yanagi tells us, are not striving for a flawless pot. For it is in the imperfections, the infinite variations on a theme, that true beauty is achieved.

The same is true of marriage. A "perfect" marriage is not a marriage without challenges, but a marriage that has the strength to manage the challenges that arise.

There is still more wisdom to be learned from Japanese folk potters. American potters make a pot knowing exactly what they want it to look like when it emerges from the kiln, and they judge the finished product according to the ideal they planned for that pot. By contrast, Japanese potters love to anticipate what the mysterious, powerful fire will do to the piece, which they have participated in creating but cannot control. They judge the finished product on its own merits. They ask not "Does it look like it is supposed to?," but "Do I like it? With all its imperfections and unique characteristics, is it beautiful?"

In a similar way, we must learn to embrace the flaws and imperfections that the fire of life has cast upon us. Maybe you don't share her passion for sailing or you have to have separate bedrooms because he snores. Like a free-form Japanese tea bowl, your relationship is the more lovely because of its little idiosyncrasies. They should not be merely tolerated, but embraced with real joy. They are a part of what makes your marriage what it is.

In other words, we must learn to judge our marriages on their own merits. The perfect marriage is not one that conforms to a set of standards set by anyone else, but rather a marriage that both partners experience as fulfilling.

Japanese potters also do not compare one beautiful tea bowl to another. They would not say, "This one is more beautiful than that." Rather, each has its own presence, just as each thriving marriage has its individual beauty. Comparison and competition bring nothing but unhappiness, for someone must always come out the loser. As you read through this book, and as you see other couples in real life, resist the temptation to compare your own relationship to others. Yours is unique. It is yours. This is what the fire of life has produced for you. What is the most you can do with what you have?

The question should not be "What is a perfect marriage?," but "What is *your* perfect marriage?," for one person's definition of perfect may differ greatly from another's. Whatever works for the two of you is what is right for you. A marriage does not have to conform to any of the common stereotypes of marriage in order to be perfect for the two people who are in it.

I'll never forget the sparkle in his eyes when one man I interviewed told me this: "If a genie came up to me and said, 'You may have any partner in the world and exactly the marriage you would most like to have,' you know what I would say to the genie? I would tell him, 'Genie, get back in the bottle. I already have it.'"

That man has a "perfect" marriage. It may not be without its rough spots and trade-offs, but he feels absolutely wonderful about it. He is happy. Like a Japanese tea bowl, casually glazed and warped by the fire, his marriage, with all its idiosyncrasies, is perfectly beautiful, richly satisfying to behold in its irregularity.

The Couples

It was not difficult to find thriving couples eager to be interviewed for this book. Far more volunteered than I could speak with at length. These were people who felt they had a lot to contribute to a book about great relationships, and who took the time to do so with sincere pleasure. It was quite common for them to call me after the interview with anecdotes or points that had occurred to them later that they wanted to be sure I included.

My only regret is that you could not be there for these interviews, for try as I might, I will never be able to describe adequately the delight these people took in each other; the trust and respect that was completely self-evident; the obvious affection; the openness between them, no matter what I asked; the great care and thoughtfulness with which they responded to my questions. If only there were a way I could convey the unmistakable pleasure I saw: the little winks and jokes flying around the room; the way the couples sat with their legs intertwined or their arms casually around each other or their hands in each others laps; the respectful, easy manner in which they disagreed with one another; the fun they poked at each other. The atmosphere surrounding the couples revealed as much about the relationship as their words.

With one exception, all the couples have been together at least seven years, many of them far longer. Five of the couples are childless, and the rest have children ranging from six months to thirty-five years old. The couples represent a wide variety of backgrounds and professions and include one lesbian and two gay couples. I know you will enjoy meeting them.

Again, welcome to the adventure of exploring a new idea: a wonderful marriage!

Part One

THE 8 ESSENTIAL TRAITS OF

COUPLES WHO THRIVE

$\mathcal{C}hapter$ 1

TRAIT 1: DESIRE, BELIEF, AND

COMMITMENT

EXACTLY HOW HAPPY would you like your marriage to be? On a scale of 1 to 100, with 100 being as happy as the happiest couple on earth, what number would you like to strive for? (Go ahead, choose a number.)

Do you believe you and your spouse can ever be that happy together?

If you knew you could achieve 100 on the scale, would you do whatever was required to get there?

Your answers to these questions will be a strong indication of your potential to thrive as a couple. Let me explain.

It has become a cliché in these times to say that the vast majority of marital problems result from poor communication. In fact, there is a much deeper cause of marital unhappiness. Because most couples are unaware of it, they follow quick-fix pathways that turn out to be dead ends, or consign potentially rich relationships to the scrap heap.

It is this: though they may not realize it, many couples are deeply ambivalent about each other — and about their relationship.

Couples who thrive show no evidence of ambivalence. Their happiness and all the other beautiful qualities in their relationships derive from their unmitigated *desire* to be together, their total *belief* in the rightness of their relationship, and their absolute *commitment* to their life together. They are not driving through their marriage with their brakes on.

"But they must be among the lucky few who found nearly perfect partners," you might say, or, "They must not be crippled by dysfunctional childhoods," or again, "Couples who thrive can glide through their marriage with no brakes on because they are so happy with each other! It's easy for them!"

That's the way it looks to outsiders, but in fact, it is the other way around: couples who thrive are happy together *because they choose* to drive without their brakes on. They throw themselves fully into their marriage and embrace what they have together.

For too long, couples — and even practitioners in the marriage-support business — have been missing this critical distinction. Most of us think that happy couples are just more compatible than the rest of us. But happy couples have stresses on their marriage, they have disagreements, they have pet peeves about each other, they get angry and depressed, they disappoint each other. They start with the same raw ingredients the rest of us have. But they don't let these potential roadblocks to happiness dominate their whole relationship. They are always aware of a bigger picture: their *desire* to be happy, their *belief* that they can be happy, and their unswerving *commitment* to each other.

And their happiness flows naturally out of their desire, belief, and commitment. If these are present in a couple's relationship, the couple is likely to thrive even if they don't have a lot of other relationship skills. And if desire, belief, and commitment are not present, all of the other skills and insights are not likely to make a critical difference in their relationship.

For example, it is true that couples who thrive communicate very well with each other. But they communicate well not because they were born with "good communication skills" or because they went to a workshop to learn them. They are able to communicate well because of their deep, unambivalent desire to do so.

For couples who harbor hidden ambivalence, learning "communication skills" will only paper over this fundamental deficit in their relationship.

Desire, belief, and commitment form the essential foundation on which couples who thrive build their "house." With such a foundation, a couple can withstand the hurricanes, tornadoes, earthquakes, and floods that assault them as they go through life.

"But," you might argue, "desire, belief, and commitment are complicated issues! For one thing aren't they just either there or not there? These aren't qualities we can simply will to appear, are they?"

How do you discover whether you have hidden ambivalence? And what do you do about it if you really are ambivalent? How do you "get" desire, belief, and commitment if you don't have them?

To find the answers to these questions, we must look at desire, belief, and commitment separately. For although they are related, they are also entirely separate matters. Let us begin, then, by looking at the *desire* to have a thriving relationship.

Desire

In order to achieve any worthy goal, you have to want it with a burning passion. Otherwise, you will probably let yourself be defeated by the many obstacles that will almost certainly present themselves to you on your way to the goal.

It is a driving passion to succeed that keeps the entrepreneur persevering through the first three years of losses and mistakes on her way to a thriving business. If she were ambivalent, the first hint of trouble could deter her, could make her ask, "Is this worth it?"

Couples who thrive do not ask themselves, "Is this worth it?" They are not beset with questions like, "Do I really love being in this relationship? Do I really want to be in any relationship at all? Is this really the person I should be with?" Because they already have the answer.

They want each other and they want their relationship with a passion. They are excited to be together. They often say things like "How did we get so lucky? Where would I be without you? If I weren't me, I would envy me, getting to be with you." Couples who thrive say these things to each other, not just in the first year after they meet, but for decades. They are like the man who told the genie, "Get back in the bottle. I already have exactly what I want."

I interviewed a woman who had fallen in love with a man just two months previously and was already looking forward to her wedding. She was thirty-seven, had been married to her first husband for seven years and then single for seven. I asked her, "How do you know this is the right person?" Here is what she told me:

> A big part of the ecstasy we feel is the *mutuality* of our love. We both know beyond any doubt that we want to be married, and we are both very excited about each other. I realize only now that we have met that what I was dreaming of and hoping for all these years was precisely this: that I would find someone I felt no hesitation about who felt exactly the same way about me. I mean that mutual desire, that total lack of pulling back or caution — *that* is the pleasure!

Couples who thrive are enthusiastic about each other. And they maintain this enthusiasm over the many years of their relationship. A woman who is seventy-nine and has been married for fifty-six years to a man who is eighty-three told me, "I still brighten up when he walks into the room. When he has been away playing bridge all afternoon, I feel excited about kissing him when he comes home and about getting a report of his game."

The opposite of a clear, burning desire to be together is ambivalence — doubts, hesitations, fears.

I love David, but I feel too lonely too much of the time in this marriage.

I love Sarah, but I'm furious that she won't do her share of the housework.

I love Bill, but I can't stand the way he yells at the kids. I just hate that.

I love Judy, but about half the time, I feel it was a mistake to get married at all. I feel trapped.

Yet to a certain degree, ambivalence is a natural and normal response to the very confusing world that we face today. The variety of lifestyle options, the apparent ubiquity of divorce, the financial constraints placed on marriages, the competing options for our time, and the disagreements and compromises that beset most marriages all make it quite difficult *not* to be ambivalent from time to time — or even much of the time — in a marriage.

And remaining ambivalent has many apparent advantages: You get to keep all your options open. You never have to give up fantasies about other relationships or other lives you might be leading. You never have to feel that you have made a final decision.

Olivia, a homemaker in her forties, told me, "As long as I can keep the option of divorce open, it serves as a kind of safety net for me. I don't feel I actually have to do it, but the idea gives me a sense of power when I'm feeling the worst." Ambivalence, that is, failing to throw herself totally into making her marriage thrive, was serving a purpose for Olivia.

Sugar, a twenty-nine-year-old model already in her second marriage told me,

I'm in this marriage to stay. My husband is a wonderful provider, and we both want kids. But to be perfectly honest, I think I might have acted a little hastily in marrying him. We had a lot of spark at the beginning of our relationship, and now he is a lot more interested in golf than in me. I wouldn't be at all surprised if I have an affair someday. I do think about it. I'm positive he'd never find out, and I can't imagine suppressing my need for passion for the rest of my life.

Sugar was keeping her options open as a way to empower herself. But she was already giving up on her marriage. Her desire was moving in other directions. She didn't believe she could get what she wanted from her marriage, and she had no commitment to it. Her ambivalence was serving her, but she was paying a big price for it: a mediocre marriage.

"But I can't fake enthusiasm!" you may say. "What if I really do feel ambivalent? What if I have hesitations and doubts and areas of discontent? What if we just can't get along all the time?"

Ah! This is the heart of our discussion. You are quite right: it is not realistic to assume that you can reverse your hesitations by an act of will. Your ambivalence is there for perfectly good reasons. It is genuine, and it is based on real issues. It won't disappear because you wish it away.

So if unmitigated desire to be together with your spouse is so fundamental to happy marriage, and you just don't have it, what can you do?

The answer, it turns out, is quite simple: you have to learn to act in the presence of ambivalence. Acknowledge your ambivalence, but don't be governed by it. Turn down the volume. Make a decision to move toward what you truly want, and don't let your ambivalence deter you.

For example, most couples who want to have a baby are ambivalent. They want a family, but they are hesitant about the responsibility and the disruption to their lives. But every couple makes a decision. If they have a baby, they may still be ambivalent about the big change in their lives. If they don't, they may still worry about what they are missing. But they take action in spite of their ambivalence.

So how exactly do you "act in spite of your ambivalence" when you are in a marriage that you are less than totally enthusiastic about?

You have to modify your *behavior*. Even if you don't feel like it, *act as if* you have a passionate desire to be with your spouse and to have a wonderful relationship together. Find some small way to *behave* the way an enthusiastic spouse would behave. Very often, new feelings will follow new behavior.

What I am suggesting here is that you act differently intentionally, that you try on a new and more positive role. It may require a great deal of effort, for it will be a major reversal of your usual practice — namely, dwelling upon the things you don't like about your marriage — but you could end up much happier.

Let's say that your main problem with your spouse is that he or she is simply a workaholic. The two of you virtually never spend any time together, and you feel like a second priority to all the work demands. (Substitute your own real complaint, if you prefer.)

You are right about this analysis. It's obvious to everyone.

But look. You are paying a big price for clinging to your analysis. You get to be right about what the problem is, but you don't get to be loving. You don't get to be forgiving. You don't get to be understanding. You don't get to be appreciated for your patience. You don't get to see how your partner would respond if you let go of your judgments, if you shifted to a more open attitude. You don't get to experiment with different potential solutions to the problem because if anything changed, you might have egg on your face. You wouldn't be right about your analysis of the problem anymore.

Maybe you really are right. But *who cares?* As long as you remain invested in proving you are right about your spouse's faults (or your own limitations, if that is what you are focusing on), you preclude the possibility of changing these things.

Of course, being right does serve a purpose. Being right keeps you safe. It keeps you from having to risk making any change in yourself.

Here is a little experiment that may surprise you. Ask around. With a genuinely open attitude, ask a few people who know both you and your spouse whether they agree with your analysis of the problems in your marriage. You may be absolutely certain that you are right, but if reasonable people disagree with you, maybe there are other legitimate analyses. Maybe you aren't totally right. Maybe you are only half right.

See if you can let go of your position. Just as an experiment. It will be a little scary because your position has defined your whole world and your identity. But, as you may begin to see now, your definition of the problem and the energy you put into proving you are right are a defense mechanism for you. They are behavior you engage in so that you won't have to look at the real issues and feelings beneath your tough, clear exterior.

Carolyn had been divorced for seven years after an eighteen-year marriage when I spoke with her. She had five grown children and was an elementary school teacher. She reflected upon her marriage:

> I really didn't love my husband. I'm not sure I ever did. I was in a hurry to get married so I could start my family, and I didn't have very high self-esteem back then. He seemed like a good provider and a nice guy. But I was critical of him from the very start. He had a temper. He was very controlling and ordered me around. He yelled at the kids. I used to go on for hours with my friends about all the awful things he did. People agreed he had some difficult qualities, but some of my friends liked him a lot. What I see now is that I blamed him for every-thing, but the truth is, *I was not a loving wife!* I thought I was not a loving wife because he was such a jerk, but I now think that if I had been loving toward him, he might have been willing to work on some of the problems. Why *should* he have given anything to me? I was so cold to him. I didn't see his good qualities, and I never asked him to change the ones I didn't like. I was stuck in proving that he was awful. I saw no other alternatives.

Lorinna got the booby prize: she got to be right about how con-trolling and unreasonable a person her husband was.

Suppose she had been able to make a shift. Suppose she had been able to behave as if she wanted to have a good marriage. Even if she acted this way for only a day, she might have been able to get the insight she has today. If even for only one hour, she had suspended all her judgments, and had behaved in a loving manner toward her part-ner, something might have begun to shift.

Without the *desire* to have a thriving marriage and to adjust your behavior to make such a marriage possible, all the communication skills and negotiations, all the discussions — even all the couples therapy in the world — won't make a difference. Desire, belief, and commitment are not the only things you need to have a happy mar-riage, but they are an essential foundation.

"But isn't 'acting' dishonest?" you ask. "Isn't it important to be real, to be true to your feelings?"

Striving to make a change in your feelings and deliberately experi-menting by acting as if you feel the new way is quite different from wittingly or unwittingly deceiving yourself or another person. When you act as if you are enthusiastic about this marriage and this person, you are creating an experiment, not an illusion or deception.

The beauty of an experiment is that you can never fail, because the purpose of an experiment is to gather data. So if you pretend that you are enthusiastic and you find that you just can't bring it off — you would rather think about all the problems in your marriage — then you haven't failed. Rather, you have succeeded in learning that you are not ready for this experiment right now, that at some level you actually prefer to dwell on your problems. That is very important and interesting data for you. Take a look at it. What does it tell you about what you truly want — or what you are ready for?

An experiment is wonderful also because you truly cannot know in advance what you will discover by doing it. Let's say you pretend for one week that you are genuinely enthusiastic about your marriage. Maybe you will discover that some part of you really is. Maybe you will feel sad. Maybe you will find yourself laughing. Maybe you will become extremely angry. Maybe you will experience relief. Maybe you will . . . who knows? You might think you know how you will feel, but until you do the experiment, you can't know. Very often people who do these experiments end up experiencing something they could never have imagined before they did them. That's why experiments are such a gift.

Relating to your partner with enthusiasm will result in new behavior. New behavior will bring new results. New results may bring new feelings or new insights — or at least new material for discussion, with your spouse or with a friend.

One of the thriving couples I interviewed, Ben and Ruthie, discovered on their own the value of pretending. They have been married for twenty-four years. He is a corporate vice-president, she is a history professor, and they have two teenagers. Ben told me this story:

> When Ruthie decided to go back to graduate school in history, I went to pieces. I tried to be a good sport about it, but I really hated it. I was worried about our finances, our schedules, our child care — I didn't believe we could do it.
>
> It was a crisis: I felt abandoned; Ruthie felt hurt and unsupported. We got into several real fights, and that was extremely unusual for us. After one such fight, after we had had a couple hours to cool down, I got an idea. I realized that I felt guilty that I didn't feel better about Ruthie's decision. In my ideal image of myself, I would be proud of her, and I would be a "feminist" man who would be willing to pitch in and cook and clean the house. I did not feel that way, but I thought I could

try pretending that I did. I said I would continue to talk to Ruthie about my feelings, but that I would try to behave as though I felt good and was behind the project. What happened amazed me. I found I was actually proud of the little meals I prepared. When talking to other people, I faked how proud I was of Ruthie and how pleased I was for her, and I found there was lots of truth in this. The further we got into it, the more I saw we really could do it, and the more my feelings changed.

Couples who want to thrive — or who want to want to thrive but are deeply ambivalent — can move toward happiness simply by behaving as though they want to be happy together.

To begin cultivating and nurturing your desire, act as if you have it. Pretend — for an hour, a day, a week. You can be sure that something will happen, but exactly what happens will be a total surprise.

Throughout this book, I will suggest "experiments" you might want to try. As I said, since the purpose of an experiment is to gather data, it can never fail. If you try one, you will find out something about yourself, and that is the spirit in which I suggest them. In my personal life, whenever I find myself at an impasse, I devise an experiment as a way to move beyond this block and get a new perspective. Often I am very surprised and could never have predicted what I end up discovering. But it is always enlightening.

You may wish to get a little notebook or journal in which to do your experiments, since many, though not all of them, require some writing. That way you can keep them together and refer back to the ones you found useful. Also, whenever you do an experiment, date it. One of the most educational ways to use an experiment is to repeat it after several months or years.

Experiment #1

---

1. Now that you are married, why isn't everything perfect? In other words, to the extent that your marriage is less fulfilling or happy than you would like, what are the reasons? Take a few minutes to brainstorm, and list whatever comes to mind.
2. Next, rate each item on your list 1 to 5 as follows:
   1 = I am not very invested in holding on to this reason. I could let go of it. I think we could change it.

5 = I am absolutely certain I am right about this, and it would be virtually impossible for me to change my mind about it.

3. On a scale of 1 to 100, with 100 being as happy as the happiest couple on earth, how happy would you like your marriage to be? Write down your number. Now, write a paragraph describing your marriage exactly as it would be if you were at that number.

Belief

Couples who thrive believe that they can achieve the happiness they seek. They believe that joyful marriage is a possibility theoretically, and they believe it is possible for them.

Most couples don't believe this.

What most people believe is that what they want from marriage is not available in this world — that a really great marriage is just an anomaly, not something the vast majority of us can expect to experience in our lifetimes. Most of us reading this book about couples who thrive will be reading about other people's experiences. We should never expect to have their experiences ourselves, for we will certainly be disappointed.

But wait. It is common knowledge that what you believe can affect your experience — even if what you believe is not true. If Sally believes she is a slow learner, she will perform poorly, even if she has a high IQ. What Sally believes about herself determines what she experiences about herself. A doctor tells a patient he'll never walk again, but the patient believes he will — and he does. If he really believed he couldn't walk, he wouldn't even try.

Beliefs about relationships work in exactly the same way. If you believe all the negative messages about relationships you hear from all the people who are in mediocre ones, your expectations for your own relationship will not be very high. Then, because it is human nature to behave in a manner consistent with what you believe, you will pay attention to the times you feel lukewarm or discontented, and minimize the times you feel happy, and then your belief that marriage is ho-hum will be reinforced. You will see that you were right about marriage being difficult, and you will continue to believe this. Your belief system may be so strong that it can supersede your actual experience.

Most of this belief reinforcement goes on at a subconscious level.

Because you aren't always aware of what you believe, you aren't always aware that you have any choice about what you believe.

But you do.

And if you want to be a couple who has a happy marriage, you have to find a way to believe that happy marriages are possible, and that one is possible for you — even if there is evidence that seems to contradict this idea.

If you don't already believe in happy marriage, it may not be easy for you to switch.

Why? Because, as we have seen already, our culture is rife with negativity about marriage. Our culture believes that happy marriages are rare and virtually impossible to achieve, that marriage is hard work, and that most couples can expect to be only reasonably happy together. This cultural bias may be difficult for you to overcome.

But not impossible.

Let's simplify the task. You don't have to believe that every couple can be happy; in order to be a happy couple yourselves, you need to believe only that you and your partner have the potential to be happy. And not just reasonably happy — extremely happy to be together and very much in love.

I am saying a rather radical thing here, namely that if you can change your belief, you can change your experience. But it isn't a new idea. For example, in 1902 the great American psychologist William James said, "The greatest revolution in our generation is that human beings, by changing the inner attitudes of their minds, can change the outer aspects of their lives."

Let's look at the alternative. What if you go along with all the seemingly incontrovertible evidence that marriage is so difficult that only modest results should ever be expected? When you discover that your marriage is difficult and is giving you as much grief as joy, you will simply take this as evidence that the belief is accurate. Even if you take measures to improve the marriage, you will not even try to improve it beyond a certain point, because you accept that your belief about marriage is the truth, and therefore, that effort would be an exercise in futility.

You will not see possibilities if you are convinced there are no possibilities.

When Barbara began to look at the beliefs that were governing her behavior with men, she discovered that because her father had always subtly belittled her, she felt inferior to men. She put on a good act with them when she dated, and men were attracted to her intellect, her sense of humor, and her varied interests. But underneath Barbara feared every man who tried to get too close. She was subconsciously afraid they would put her down and make her feel bad about herself.

Barbara's internal belief was that she was inferior to men and could never make a man happy. So she didn't *believe in* happy marriage for herself. She *desired* it, but she didn't believe it could happen. Since people behave in a manner consistent with what they believe, Barbara unwittingly undermined her marriage by focusing on her husband's faults. If she had believed she could have a good marriage and that she could make a man happy, she might have been more accepting and tolerant of her husband's shortcomings, and this would have made a world of difference in their marriage.

By contrast, couples who have beautiful relationships make allowances for each other's shortcomings:

CRAIG: David is so absentminded. The other day I found a coffee mug in the refrigerator! I used to get so annoyed with him. But now I realize he is just being David. If he's late getting home, I've learned now, I just need to call him. I know he gets so absorbed, he forgets to call. I don't take it personally. If he weren't spaced out half the time, he wouldn't be David. And his absentmindedness has a real up side, too. He gets an enormous amount done when he gets so absorbed. At times like that, the rest of the world doesn't matter to him.

Of course, changing your beliefs is not a trivial matter. But it is possible, and it is the most essential key to making your relationship flourish. If you are dragging around negative beliefs about your marriage, you simply won't be able to move beyond them. In fact, you will fulfill them.

So how do you change your beliefs?

First, you have to figure out exactly what it is you believe and where you got your beliefs. Some of them, like Barbara's, may be a result of experiences in your family. Or you may have simply tapped into our culture's pervasive negativity about the potential of marriage.

Second, you have to get some distance from your beliefs. You need perspective. It is very difficult to change a belief when you are in the middle of the consequences of believing it. You have to recognize that your beliefs do not represent an objective reality; they are a combination of your own personal cumulative experience and your attitudes.

Third, you must feel the pain of your negative beliefs. For example, suppose you believe, "My spouse is not romantic (and never will be)." Spend some time thinking how you would feel if your spouse *were* romantic, as you would like. Now think about how much you miss this. The point of this exercise is not for you to be masochistic, but rather for you to be motivated to make a change in your belief system. Your spouse may or may not in fact be romantic. But if you are locked into the idea that there is no romance in your marriage, then there will certainly never be any.

You can take this even further. Imagine how you will feel ten years from now if there has been no change and you are still in a romance-less marriage. Does this make you want to try to believe that if you do something about it you *can* bring romance into your marriage — and into your spouse?

Most people are more highly motivated to avoid pain than to experience pleasure. So if you can associate pain with your negative beliefs, you may be more highly motivated to change them.

Fourth, you must suspend your old beliefs and try some behavior that results from a new belief. Then observe your experience. For if you can change your experience, your beliefs will change automatically.

Begin with this simple experiment.

Experiment #2

1. Make a list of beliefs you have about your marriage that limit what your marriage can be. Consider them carefully.
2. Now, for each of these beliefs, write an opposite statement to that belief. For example, if your limiting belief is "I will never feel good about my spouse's behavior toward the children," you might write as a new belief "If we work together, my spouse can alter the behavior toward the children, and I can feel great about this effort and the resulting behavior."

Here are some self-limiting beliefs I have heard from couples who have done this exercise, along with a positive belief that could be an alternative:

I can't be intimate because I grew up in a dysfunctional family.
I am not limited by my past. With perseverance and support, I can learn to be intimate.

There is no way my husband will ever change to become someone who cares about intimacy and communication.
I can stop demanding and can be lovingly persistent. We can be intimate, and he can use good communication even if he doesn't admit that he's using it. I will enjoy seeing him change.

I can't be who I really want to be and still be in this relationship.
I can be who I really want to be and still be in this relationship.

I'll never be as happy again as I was with my first wife, who died.
My next partner will be different from my wife but just as wonderful in a new way. I know I will be happy again.

Too much damage has already been done between us for us ever to feel good about each other again.
Life presents endless opportunities to begin anew. If we both want to, we can put the past behind us.

I can't be a good marriage partner; my self-esteem is too low.
I can learn to love and accept myself fully.

Beliefs represent decisions. You have the ability to choose beliefs that will enhance, enrich, and empower your life. Couples who thrive believe that they can be wonderful for each other, and that they can have a charmed marriage.

Commitment

Couples who thrive are unswervingly committed to each other and to their relationship. They have joyfully cast their lot with each other, and they don't spend time looking back, wondering if they did the right thing, or casting about for an escape route.

Being fully committed to a relationship means that you have no doubts that this is the right place for you to be. It doesn't mean that you have no challenges within the relationship. Remember, we are talking about beauty — with all its irregularities — not perfection.

But commitment does mean that you have no hesitations whatsoever that your life is now together with this other person, this intimate partner whom you have chosen.

To see why commitment is essential to a truly happy marriage, let us begin by looking at how the lack of commitment inhibits intimacy, and prevents the full flowering of a relationship.

If I am in a relationship with you but I am not fully committed to it, I am telling you one or more of the following things: "I have hesitations about whether I can be truly happy with you." "I don't love you quite enough." "I sometimes think other options might be better." "I'm worried that I might change my mind." "I don't like the feeling that I'm tied down."

These hesitations, doubts, and fears construct limitations for us. It is dangerous for you to become completely vulnerable and honest with me if you know that at some point I might disappear — emotionally or physically. If I offer you love the way a cuckoo in a clock hops out but then disappears behind his door, how can I expect you to give your heart to me?

People in relationships in which the commitment is tentative have to spend part of their energy protecting themselves from hurt and preparing for the part of their lives that does not include the other partner. There can be no complete release into a full intimate bond. Lack of commitment is withholding, and withholding is antithetical to intimacy.

Lack of commitment also makes it difficult for couples to fight because every time they do, the relationship itself is at stake. They have no safe context within which they can work out their conflicts. This means they will be less likely to work them out and more likely to withhold things that are bothering them. And withholding erodes closeness. Moreover, couples who are not committed are not highly motivated to work out problems since they may eventually break up anyway. They will spare themselves the hassle and live with what annoys them. But this undercurrent of annoyance creates distance and inhibits intimacy.

Living in a relationship where the commitment is tentative or intermittent is like living in a rented house. You don't like the color of the walls, but you don't want to put the time and money into painting them because you may be in another house soon enough. It's just not worth the investment.

In many relationships, the absence of full commitment causes more conflict than any other single thing. If the partners could make a real commitment, their biggest problem would disappear. Yet they would rather argue about their future and discuss their relationship than either break up or commit fully to being together.

Relationships that are without the cement of wholehearted commitment suffer from a vicious circle: the lack of commitment causes stress and problems, and then the stress and problems reduce the likelihood of commitment. This pattern is reflected on a cultural level as well: few people are willing to make serious commitments because they see that relationships are in such bad shape, and relationships are in bad shape precisely because there is such a widespread aversion to commitment.

A relationship without commitment is entirely different from a relationship in which the two partners have chosen to commit to each other. The difference goes far beyond the potential duration of the relationship; the entire nature and quality of the experience between the two people involved are affected.

When commitment happens, a shift takes place — a shift in the energy of both partners and in their whole psychological system. They are no longer driving with their brakes on. They are no longer asking, "Is this right?"

For several years I had a running debate with a friend of mine over the issue of commitment. Her position was this:

> I am not going to make a commitment to Karl until I feel totally ready. And when I do, then the commitment won't make any difference; the relationship will already be what it is. In other words, commitment is useless. By the time you are ready to make it, it becomes academic.

Then my friend got a job in a distant city, and Karl had to decide whether to move there with her. After they had decided to move and were making their plans, my friend told me,

> Susan, you were right. I never dreamed how much closer we could be. This commitment has made a big difference. There is a whole new quality to our relationship. I didn't realize it before, but I didn't quite believe that Karl loved me. Now that he is committed enough to move with me, I "got it" that he does! But I didn't realize this quality was missing until it wasn't missing any more! We didn't know that we were holding back, but suddenly now we have relaxed in a way that lets a lot

more energy flow between us. It's not just that we know we won't leave each other. It's that we've let go of our struggle and we are just totally there for each other. There has been a big shift, and I love it.

Part of the shift that takes place when two people make a commitment to each other is a shift from conditional to unconditional love. If I make a commitment to you, I am making a statement that I am not going to disappear the first time something that I don't like happens. I love you for who you are — not for what I wish you were. That is the nature of my love. It is unconditional — or at least that is what I would like for it to be and what I will strive toward.

Another shift that occurs with commitment is a shift in a couple's sense of time.

Closeness and realness require time to develop. The most ecstatic moment of openness and love with a new acquaintance is multiplied a thousandfold when it occurs between two people who for years have been growing and sharing their lives together. In any relationship, there is simply no substitute for time and the depth of closeness it can bring. Commitment lets two people know that they will have the time to let their intimacy deepen. They can relax into a leisurely rhythm with each other, knowing they will have the pleasure of time together, and the opportunities for knowing each other that only time can make available. In this way, commitment makes a relationship more likely to last.

When my good friend Cathy told me that her lover of six months, Terry, had left her because he couldn't get along with her daughter, I felt a jolt of recognition. The initial stages of my own relationship with my stepson had been extremely painful for me (and, I dare say, for him). But whereas Terry had chosen to leave the situation in spite of a lovely relationship with Cathy, the idea of leaving Mayer never even crossed my mind. I'm sure it would have had I not felt deep inner commitment because the problems seemed insurmountable, and I remember thinking, "Life is too short. I can't live this way." But I shudder when I think about what I would have missed if I had left! We all got through our painful adjustment, and the process taught us a lot and strengthened our relationships. What have Cathy and Terry missed? They'll never know.

A widespread misconception about commitment is that it means you can't ever change your mind. "What if things change?" people say. "What if it turns out I didn't know everything I needed to know, and I end up changing my mind?" "I can't make a commitment because I might be wrong." This idea prevents many people from making commitments, but it is based on an error.

A commitment is a statement about the quality of the relationship now, not about how long the relationship will last. Commitment means "Right now I am fully and totally with you. Right now I want to build my life with you and right now my intention and desire is to stay with you forever."

People and circumstances do change, and these changes can affect commitment. But recognizing that a commitment might change some day is no reason to avoid making one now. All anyone can be expected to do is to make the best decision he or she is capable of making, taking into consideration all the data available at the time the decision is made. Most decisions have to be made on the basis of insufficient data. If we waited until we had perfect data, we would not have to make decisions; they would make themselves. In other words, every commitment requires a leap of faith.

A second misconception people have about commitment is that it is a way of tying oneself down.

Quite the contrary: commitment is a way of letting go. Commitment requires a willingness to trust, not only in the other person, but in the forces that brought you together and that keep you together. Commitment represents a willingness to let go of total control. Rather than holding the horse back to a walk, you commit yourself to the ride, let go of the reins, and let the horse gallop freely.

Les had been with Katie for five years and had been married for two. He told me,

> I was the original fear-of-commitment type. But when I was faced with the idea of losing Katie, I realized I felt committed to her *inside*. I didn't ever want to be without her. One day I told her, let's not commit, but let's just say we'll always be together. I didn't expect it to be a special moment, but Katie had been waiting so long to hear this that it was magical. When I saw how happy she was, I felt elated instead of scared. That was a totally new experience for me. During the conversation that ensued, I told her that this was a risk I felt ready to take. That summed it up for me. It still felt like a risk — not because of anything to do with Katie, but only because of the unknowns — especially the other women I might meet. But I wasn't going to let fear stop me anymore. The amazing thing is, that is the last day I felt anxiety about this. I still get tan-

talized by other women, but I find it an enormous relief that I don't have to — in fact that I *can't* — do anything about it. . . . Commitment was the last piece missing from our relationship. It made a huge difference. But I didn't decide to do it; I discovered it was there.

Commitment has two pleasurable aspects to it. One is the joy of loving the other person. The other is the joy of giving up your ambivalence. Now one aspect of your life is "nailed down." The feeling of complete certainty is the feeling of commitment, and that certainty is a great pleasure to experience — especially when it is shared with another who is equally certain.

Commitment does bring a kind of security with it. But when you commit yourself to something, it does not stop changing. What two people commit themselves to is a process of discovery, a journey, the adventure of exploring life's road together. They may discover lions on the road, but as Peter Matthiessen warns in *The Snow Leopard*, "the lions never get out of the road of the person who waits to see the way clear before starting to walk."

Chapter 2

TRAIT 2: GOODWILL

S HOWING GOODWILL MEANS giving your partner the benefit of the doubt. It means being on your partner's side and knowing that your partner is on your side. When two people have goodwill toward one another, their spirits are open to each other. They will experience a mutual feeling of fair play. Even when they are angry or out of sorts, they will ultimately behave in a reasonable manner because beneath all of their emotions lies a foundation of goodwill.

Having goodwill means being as concerned about meeting your partner's needs as you are your own. It means you have empathy with your partner's point of view. Even when you disagree, you assume your partner means well. You never impugn your partner's motives.

The happy couples I interviewed had an abundance of goodwill toward each other, and this fundamental quality was the basis for the freedom and ease they felt with each other. Whenever I encounter couples who are not doing well together, this spirit of goodwill is conspicuously absent.

Gail and Jeff told me about a tense exchange they had one evening. Their two children were getting on their nerves, Jeff was late for a meeting, and, in the midst of all this, Gail was in a delicate negotiation with her son, whom she was trying to toilet train. At the end of her patience, she asked Jeff to come in and help. Jeff gladly did, but it was not at all the type of help Gail had in mind, so as soon as Jeff started helping, she became furious with him. They were both so angry that Jeff simply walked out the door.

Gail was in tears, and she told me she had horrendous fantasies of having to raise two children on her own, even though she knew that was absurd. But about five minutes after he left, Jeff phoned her. He just said, "I love you, and we will talk about this soon and work it all out. Don't worry."

Jeff's gesture was goodwill in action. Even though his angry emotions had not yet abated, his basic thoughtfulness did not allow him to leave Gail stranded with the children feeling furious, unsupported, and alone.

If these two people had not had goodwill toward each other, that is, if they had become invested in blaming each other, if they had gotten caught up in defending their own position, the fight could have escalated. It would not only have caused them both a lot of pain, but it would also have further eroded any spark of goodwill that might have been there to begin with.

When two people first fall in love, they feel and sometimes say that they will do anything for each other. Couples who experience goodwill toward each other retain that feeling. It doesn't mean they really will do anything for their partner; they will spend a lot of time negotiating to achieve a balance between meeting their own and each other's needs. But the feeling is still there. I want to make you happy. I want you to have what you want.

Exhibiting feelings of goodwill is not exactly the American way. From the beginning of our history, we have emphasized individualism and self-sufficiency. In the competitive workplace, a spirit of goodwill is considered dangerous. We are often wise to suspect each other, withhold information, and assume that other people's motives are not pure and selfless. We are taught to take care of ourselves. Our tendency toward narcissism and self-involvement makes it hard for us to experience genuine goodwill toward very many other people.

Yet goodwill is a critical ingredient in any good relationship. It is the soil in which all the other qualities are planted and grow. In his book *Getting the Love You Want*, psychologist Harville Hendrix, who works with troubled couples, says that the first step in helping even the most unhappy of couples is to reestablish their feeling of goodwill toward each other. He suggests that they begin doing kind and generous things for each other as a way of recovering their basic goodwill.

Goodwill incorporates several critical qualities, all of which will naturally be present if genuine goodwill is there. It includes a willingness to focus on positive qualities; an attitude of gratitude; mutual tolerance and acceptance; respect; trust; and the ability to give.

A Willingness to Focus on Positive Qualities

Couples who thrive focus on what they love about each other and their relationship, and pay less attention to what they don't like. They recognize instinctively that, as psychologist George Pransky puts it, "Problems are like goldfish; the more you feed them, the bigger they get."

One man told me, "We figured out a long time ago that there are problems that have a solution and problems that don't. We solve the ones we can solve, and ignore the ones we can't." I asked him for some examples. He replied:

> Ellie was into Scottish Country dancing when we met. We both just assumed that I would get involved too. But too many of the rehearsals were times I had to work, I wasn't very good, and I just didn't like it that well. I tried, but I couldn't get into it. It was sad for both of us, but I couldn't make myself into someone I wasn't. Once we accepted that Ellie would dance and I wouldn't, and that's the way it would be, that was it. We were fine with it. It was a problem without a solution. Just go with it. We never talk about it anymore. But we get to see the difference between our approach and the opposite, because there is another woman who dances whose husband doesn't dance who does nothing but complain about her husband. According to her, his not dancing is the least of his sins. There are a lot of nice things about this guy, but all she looks at is what she doesn't like.

You have a choice about what you focus on, what you think about. You are not at the mercy of your thoughts. When a thought comes into your head, you can decide to think about it, dwell upon it, and let it consume you. Or, you can decide to think about something else.

A woman I know who is a corporate trainer always asks for evaluations at the end of her workshops. One time when I was with her, she received eleven glowing evaluations and two rather negative ones. She was quite upset. She focused all her attention on the negative evaluations and none on the positive ones. She let her whole afternoon be spoiled because she did not exercise her option to focus on the positive evaluations. She couldn't see that she had a choice.

I have a friend who often complains that her husband doesn't see what needs to be done around the house. The irony is that this man is very handy. He does lots of little jobs, he does them well, and promptly. I keep telling my friend to look at the positive side of this, but all she will see is that she has to tell him to do every job.

Of course, issues like this one can be negotiated with lots of room for giving on both sides, as we shall see in the chapters that follow. But the point here is that my friend is making her own life miserable just by choosing to think about what her husband does not see instead of what he does do.

Couples who thrive are in the habit of focusing on the positive aspects of their relationship. One woman said to me, "People tell me my husband is conceited, but I just tell them, 'He deserves to be.'" I thought her comment was a delightful way of telling him, "I'm on your side. I love you exactly the way you are."

Focusing on the positive is a skill that can be learned. This experiment will get you started.

Experiment #3

---

1. List all the things you don't like about your spouse.
2. Now list all the things you like about your spouse.
3. Now, make a pact with yourself that you will not mention anything in list number one to your spouse or to anyone else for two full weeks. Mark this on your calendar.
4. Be certain that you mention at least five things on the second list to your spouse every day for the next two weeks. Think of original ways to compliment your spouse. In addition to simply telling him or her, you might write a note and leave it on a mirror. You could write a little rhyme or give him or her a little gift as a thank-you. But however you do it, be sure you mention five positive qualities every day.

An Attitude of Gratitude

"Every morning, the first thing I do is to thank God for three things: my life, my health, and my wife," Bruce told me.

Virtually every happy couple I spoke with mentioned how grateful they are to be with each other. They behaved as though they were grateful, and they told me that they mention this to each other often.

When I asked this simple question, "How often do you talk about your relationship, and of what does that usually consist?," these are the responses I often heard:

We are always telling each other how lucky we are to be together and to have the life that we have.

I really feel that Lisa saved my life. I mean she did. I thank her for it every day.

We probably mention our relationship every day, just saying things like, "I'm so grateful to be with you. We're so lucky to be together."

If anything comes up that we need to talk about, we do it right away. But we're always saying how much we love each other — if that's talking about our relationship.

One of our favorite things to say is "We deserve each other." We probably say that at least once a week.

Among many of these couples I could detect a slight feeling of awe that they had found each other. Even after many years, they felt their being together was a little miracle. As one man said, "After thirty-two years, I have finally gotten used to the idea of being happy and of having this extraordinary woman by my side, but it doesn't mean I'm not still extremely grateful."

What are you grateful for in your life? Make a list. How often do you focus on these things? Are you grateful to be with your spouse? How often do you say so?

To cultivate an attitude of gratitude in your marriage, spend as much time talking about the good things in your life together as you spend complaining about your problems. This is not hard work; feeling grateful is a pleasant activity. You may find that even thinking about your blessings will bring a smile to your face. And sharing your gratitude with your partner will bring a smile to his or hers. The more you feel grateful, the happier you will be.

Mutual Acceptance and Tolerance

I was recently in a conversation with a man who was trying to convince me that "unconditional love" is only a theoretical possibility, or something that only God is capable of, not humans. The term "unconditional love" does have a ring of perfection to it, or of a goal that is worthy of working toward but that one should never expect to achieve in reality.

But I don't agree at all that unconditional love fits into that category. My husband and I love each other unconditionally, and so do the thriving couples I interviewed. Unconditional love is simply total acceptance. It means not putting any restrictions on your love for someone. When my husband does something that upsets me, I don't stop loving him. My love isn't dependent on how he performs or what he achieves or how he behaves toward me.

Imagine someone saying, "If you don't stop being anxious about your business, I won't love you any more," or, "If you don't learn to be more affectionate with me, I'll love you only partially, not fully," or, "I love you but when you get into a sour or angry mood, I don't love you."

These statements are ludicrous. I may be angry, I may feel hurt, I may feel distant. But this doesn't mean that my love is in any way diminished. In fact, it is when someone feels sad or anxious or blue that unconditional love is the most important. You need to know that you are loved *especially* when you aren't being very loving toward yourself.

If I choose to love someone, then I am saying, "I care for all of you, the whole package. I am invested in your personal and spiritual growth. I don't want to change you; I want to support you." If I choose to make a full commitment to someone, and then I fall short of it, my failure is a statement about me, not about the other person. Although I may believe you behaved in a certain way, and therefore, I can't love you, it might be more accurate to say, "I have come up against a fear in myself that makes it impossible for me to love you right now, or to love this part of you." When love is conditional, the weakness is not in the object of love, but in the lover.

Accepting something doesn't mean you have to like it; it means you stop fighting it. If you are accepting something you don't like in the person you love, you may want to ask for change. But you don't stop loving the person, even if he or she can't change.

If you try, you may be able to view a troubling quality in your mate as an endearing trait, simply a part of who the person is. I once went with a man who was very finicky about his car. Even in what seemed to me a dire emergency, he wouldn't lend it to me. He wouldn't even let me drive it when he was there. I thought his attitude was ridiculous, but I realized that it was consistent with his personality, and that it really did make sense to him. I adored this person, and that was just part of him. I remember thinking at the time, "This is what they mean when they say that you accept all of someone you love." It wasn't that I had to make up my mind to accept him and force myself to do it. Rather, I just noticed that, because I loved him, I did accept this quirk.

Accepting something in your partner that you don't love means, above all else, not judging your partner. For example:

MICHELLE: Conrad doesn't fly. He's just way too afraid of it. It's not a rational fear, but a phobia. Of course this inconveniences us a lot. I wish he did fly. I wish he wanted to get help for his phobia. But I don't blame him or judge him for it. We find ways to work it out.

MARGARET: I'm a writer. Most days, I don't see anyone but Ross and the kids. And I am not into clothes. I find one set of jeans and a sweatshirt, and I'll wear it four or five days in a row. This used to drive my first husband crazy. He kept trying to convince me I'd feel better if I put on new outfits and blah, blah, blah. I mean, I could have changed to please him, but why? He really judged me for this. He was trying to make me admit I was wrong for doing it. I see the difference so clearly now with Ross. I don't even know whether he likes it or not. He doesn't care. I'm me, and I do things my way. If I were all into clothes, I wouldn't be me. Ross accepts me.

I can well imagine that in Margaret's first marriage, her husband believed that Margaret — not he — was at fault. In his view, she wouldn't see how wrong she was not to wear different clothes each day. But when one partner is trying to change another, the *conflict is usually caused by the partner who is not willing to be accepting*, not the partner who is not willing to change.

If you are experiencing a conflict with your spouse, ask yourself, Is it your demands, your opinions, your judgments that are causing the problem, or the circumstances themselves? How attached are you to your own position on this issue? Could you be more flexible?

Of course, it is entirely appropriate in some circumstances to ask your partner to change. We will discuss "asking for what you want" in detail in the chapter on Communication. But far more important than trying to get your partner to conform to your ideas about what he or she "ought" to be is learning to accept your partner — the parts that you love as well as the parts that, because of your own personal preferences, you don't.

Bruce, the man who thanks God every day for his life, his health, and his wife, adores his wife, Jan. She is exuberant, filled with energy, and truly a delight to be around. Bruce's one complaint about her is that he feels she talks too much and tends to dominate conversations. What he needs to see is that Jan's lively conversation is an integral part of the woman he loves.

The big secret in learning to be more flexible, accepting, and tolerant toward the person you love is to make an internal shift so that you can begin to see the qualities that are less desirable to you as acceptable — possibly even endearing.

> HANNAH: Marty's frugal nature used to embarrass me sometimes — like when he would get out his calculator to divide up the bill at the end of a meal with another couple. I usually just divide it equally and throw in a little extra for tax and tip. But now I realize that our friends rely on Marty for his shopping expertise, his knowledge of bargains, his coupons for car rentals and restaurant meals, and on and on. He couldn't be who he is and just be casual about the bill. And some of our friends who are casual about the bill aren't in the greatest financial shape. So now I tease Marty sometimes, but I love his little obsessions. He has a calculator on his watch now, and everyone knows it. They may rib him, but they rely on him for it.

What is the opposite of being accepting and tolerant of your partner? Setting yourself in opposition to him or her: nagging, criticizing, belittling, putting your partner down. If you are nagging your partner about something that the person is not likely to be able to change anyway — like talking less for an exuberant woman, or not worrying about his fair share of the bill for a naturally thrifty man — then you are actually creating a problem. *Whatever you resist will persist.* For example, by resisting Jan's talking, by bugging her about it, Bruce was causing this issue to persist in their lives. After our conversation, he decided to experiment with letting go of his intensity about the whole thing. He stopped mentioning it. Whenever he wanted to get into the conversation, he would very politely say, "Could I interrupt a second?" or "Could I say something?" Jan always stopped and let him talk. When he stopped resisting and let himself go along with what was happening naturally, the problem disappeared.

In my own work with couples, I have found that a common difference between men and women is that men often have a need for "alone time," especially at the end of a busy day, whereas women are more likely to be eager for some intimate contact at that time. Misunderstandings about this difference have led many couples to monumental impasses. "He's too remote." "She's too demanding." Psychologist John Gray, in his insightful book *Men Are from Mars, Women Are from Venus*, suggests that if each partner simply recognizes these differences and is willing to accommodate the other partner, both of their needs can be met. For example, she could give him forty minutes to read the mail, change clothes, relax by himself. Then he could give her forty minutes to connect and talk.

Very few of the thriving couples I met experienced this end-of-the-day syndrome as a problem. When it did come up, the couples had naturally accepted each other's needs and had adapted accordingly. Any potential problem was nipped in the bud by their spirit of goodwill toward each other. These couples were sure enough of each other's love and devotion and they had enough close contact that they didn't take their differences in temperament personally. If one person asked for some alone time at the end of the day, the other person understood and accepted this need and gave it. Because of their ability to be flexible, tolerant, and accepting, they were able to avoid many potential problems.

Remember, though, that when two people are accepting of each other, it does not mean that they cannot ever ask for change. Quite the contrary. *A spirit of acceptance in a relationship creates a nonjudgmental, safe atmosphere that makes asking for change much easier.* It would be very hard for me to consider changing for you if I felt that your love for me depended on whether or not I changed. All successful negotiations in a relationship start with a spirit of acceptance and goodwill.

Experiment #4

---

1. Make a list of all the things that annoy you about your partner.
2. Rate each item on a scale from 1 to 5, with 1 being not at all integral to who your spouse is, and 5 being extremely integral to who your spouse is.
3. Now, with regard to each item, ask yourself if the problem would go

away if you simply became more accepting of whatever it is that annoys you.

4. If you found one or two items in #3 that you believe you could alter with your own attitude, make a pact with yourself to avoid mentioning the item for two full weeks.

Trust and Respect

Couples who thrive have learned to take their mutual trust for granted. They have stopped worrying about it, because they know each other so well.

> TOM: Of course I trust Sherry. But really, I don't think of it that way. I don't have to trust her, because I *know* she will be there for me. What is trust? I trust you not to lie to me? I trust you not to cheat on me? I trust you to be honest with me? I mean, we are way beyond that. I don't have to think about whether I trust Sherry. I don't have to do anything to trust her. I know she's a person of integrity. I know I can rely on her. Is that trust?

In some cases, trust was a problem for one partner early in the relationship. Usually this was because, as a child, the person had had unreliable caregivers and had learned early in life that it was not safe or wise to trust anyone.

> MARY: One of the most incredible gifts Wes gave me was teaching me to trust. I was so cautious and defensive after my abusive upbringing that I literally had never fully trusted anyone. It was only after a couple of years with Wes that I finally realized that I could trust him. I knew in my head that I had no reason not to. Then I had to work on getting my body to go along with this idea. Therapy helped too. But I'm extremely grateful to Wes for this. I don't actually think about it much any more. I mean, the issue hasn't come up for us in many years, but it was a big problem at first.
>
> Learning to trust was hard for me. I felt I couldn't open up to Wes because I didn't trust him. But I felt I couldn't learn to trust him unless I tried opening up. Wes was patient, and every time I took a baby step, it was a positive experience.

In much the same way, mutual respect is a fundamental component of thriving relationships.

DORIS: I once went with a man for a couple years. He was fun, but I knew all along I could never marry him, mainly because I just couldn't respect his contemptuous attitude about politics and political involvement. He never voted. And he had this whole rationale that I thought was stupid and irresponsible. I know he believed it, but I just couldn't respect where he was coming from. We were so far apart on such a basic value, I just knew I couldn't marry him. It seemed like that — and some of his other views — prevented us from becoming soulmates. We didn't see the universe through the same glasses. I don't mean you can't disagree with your spouse, but this was a matter of respect.

TIM: For me, respect and admiration go hand in hand. I not only respect Sarah, I admire her. I admire her artistic ability, her kindness to people, her cooking, her ability to teach other people how to paint, her way with words, the way she manages to keep in touch with all our friends — it goes on and on. I admire these things in her.

DONALD: When I say I respect Barbara, I mean that I value her in a way that goes way beyond all the things she does. I respect that she is a wise, old soul, that she is connected to the universe in a way far beyond what I can see. We have been put together for this sojourn on earth, and I have a great responsibility to honor her and treat her well. She's a beautiful and very special spirit.

Respect has slightly different meanings to different people. To some, respect means a kind of reverence. To some, it means believing in the integrity of others, or appreciating their values. And to others, respect means holding a person in high esteem. Whatever the nuance, when you feel respectful toward someone, you are likely to feel an outpouring of goodwill toward him or her. Respect empowers both the one who respects and the one who is respected. It is a beautiful and essential feeling to have toward your spouse if you want to have a marriage that thrives.

Experiment #5

---

1. Ask yourself if there is anything about your spouse that you do not trust. If there is, has your spouse given you a reason not to trust him or her, or is it simply hard for you to trust in general? If there is not

complete trust between the two of you, write a page in your notebook in response to this question: What would it take for me to feel complete trust with my spouse?

2. Write a love letter to your spouse listing all the specific things you respect and admire about him or her.

Giving

One of the casualties of the Me Decade and all that followed in its wake was the joy of giving. "It is more blessed to give than to receive" was replaced by "We are not here to meet other people's needs." So preoccupied are we now with avoiding being inappropriately helpful that we have become adept at saying no, at protecting our own territory, at becoming self-sufficient and encouraging others to be the same.

In gaining our cherished independence, we have forgotten how nourishing it is to give freely and generously, wanting nothing in return.

Of course there is such a thing as unhealthy giving, as we know. When you do for other people what they need to do for themselves, you are giving in a way that helps no one. But in forsaking this behavior, we need not give up generosity.

Couples who thrive know the difference. They quietly go about defying all the current caveats about helping each other and giving too much. They take great joy in giving to each other. As one woman put it, "If people would spend less time in their marriages trying to get their needs met and more time going over to rub each other's shoulders, we wouldn't have so many couples in therapy these days."

Giving freely and generously works wonders, not just for the recipient of the giving, but for the giver as well. Erich Fromm points out that "poverty is degrading, not only because of the suffering it causes directly, but because it deprives the poor of the joy of giving." In their well-researched book *The Healing Power of Doing Good*, Allan Luks and Peggy Payne document actual health improvements among AIDS patients and others who volunteer their time to other people in need. And psychologist Harville Hendrix contends that one's deepest, most instinctive self, what he calls the "old brain," doesn't distinguish between self and other, so that giving to another person is experienced as giving to oneself!

In marriage, you have the opportunity to please yourself and your partner with thoughtfulness and generosity every day. From doing the little favors your partner requests, to offering help, to giving in when your preferences differ, to thinking up lovely surprises, giving is part of the basic design of the tapestry of marriage.

One woman I worked with resented that her marriage called upon her to "make sacrifices." As a feminist, she didn't want to be in a position of having to subordinate her own needs to those of another person. But as we spoke, she realized that she had misunderstood what sacrifice really means.

A sacrifice is an offering. According to the *Random House College Dictionary*, it is "the surrender of something prized or desirable for the sake of something considered as having a higher or more pressing claim." So when you give in and go to your partner's movie choice instead of your own, you are actually gaining something you prize even more than your movie: the joy of making the person you love happy.

Needless to say, the "sacrificing" and giving between two people has to be fairly equal over the course of a relationship. But couples who thrive tend to be more concerned about whether they are giving their fair share than whether they are getting their fair share.

A more accurate and more useful term than "sacrifice" or "compromise" to describe the giving that takes place in all relationships is the term "trade-off." Because for everything you give up in a relationship, there is always something you gain. A long relationship is filled with trade-offs — big ones and little ones. Couples who thrive understand this and make trade-offs willingly — not necessarily without some negotiating, but always with an awareness of the larger benefit they are receiving from their trade-off: their prized relationship with each other. They make trade-offs in a spirit of goodwill.

Carla's story is a good example of this. She and John were car-camping through Oregon for ten days. She very much wanted to go to the beach town of Lincoln City, but John was lukewarm about going there since he had other priorities.

> CARLA: I felt like the bottom line was, Do I care? Do I care enough to give up what I need? I gave in on Lincoln City, and John was so moved that I gave up something I needed — especially me, because, you know, I usually get what I want. (She chuckled.) If I had gotten Lincoln City, I'd have won the battle but lost the war. John would have been so unhappy. I got it: John's happiness is as important as mine. If

he's unhappy, I'm unhappy. . . . John's usually the giver in this relationship. This was a good experience for me.

Carla reminded me of something Jan had said in her interview:

When we got married, the one thing my mother told me is, "Remember, now there are always two of you to consider. Before, with everything you did, you just had to see how it fit into your world. Now there are two people, and you always have to consider that other person — whether it's a job decision or whether or not to make dinner that night. There's just another person in your life now."

When I asked Barbara and Donald about the giving in their marriage, Barbara was quick to respond:

I have two friends who keep insisting that I acquiesce to Donald too much. His goals have become my goals, and I have given up some of my own in the process. They point out that I don't play bridge anymore and that I dropped out of two singing groups I was in. I spend half my time now promoting his business, making hand-crafted furniture.

But I've taken a close look at the whole picture, and I'm only giving to Donald what I want to give. I love working with him. I'm making a huge contribution, and I'm as invested in it as he is now. The whole thing has added a stimulating new dimension to my life. I enjoy it, and he appreciates it. I'm free to choose not to give to him, and I choose to. It seems to me that's what marriage is all about. If you spend all your time looking after your own needs only, you might as well have stayed single.

Giving is part of what makes us close and keeps us excited about each other. I do think I have to be vigilant to be sure my most important needs are not being papered over. But I want Donald to succeed, and I want to contribute to his success.

Carla, Jan, and Barbara were all thinking, not, "How can I get my needs met?," but, "How can *we both* get our needs met?"

Two specific suggestions about *how* to give to your partner may be helpful.

1. People tend to give what they themselves would like to receive, forgetting that the recipient of their gifts might have altogether different preferences. This is often true in sexual giving, for example, and in gift-giving as well. If you make a deliberate attempt to find out

what your partner wants and how your partner wants to be given to, your gift will be all the more appreciated.

2. The most thoughtful and often the most appreciated giving of all is the unsolicited, unexpected gift. Flowers on Valentine's Day are lovely, but they don't count nearly as much as flowers on any normal, routine day. Best of all is when you notice something your spouse could use, or you pay attention to a little hint that gets dropped, and you totally surprise your spouse with exactly what he or she most wants.

Emerson's Law of Compensation is still true: If you want more, give more.

Experiment #6

---

1. Ask your partner what he or she needs in order to feel loved, and write down the answers. This will give you a treasury of ideas for giving to your partner exactly what he or she most loves to receive.
2. Ask your partner for a wish list of items or favors that he or she would enjoy receiving spontaneously. Then, over the next month, do as many of them as you can. And now that you know what is on the list, keep giving your favorites: things that you enjoy giving and that your partner enjoys receiving. You may want to renew your wish lists with each other every few months.

I am not the first writer who has identified goodwill as the basis of successful marriage. In his "Treatise of Human Nature," the eighteenth-century philosopher David Hume, wrote of love, "'Tis plain, that this affection, in its most natural state, is deriv'd from the conjunction of three different impressions or passions, viz., the pleasing sensation arising from beauty; the bodily appetite for generation; and a generous kindness or good-will."

Thriving marriages are characterized by precisely this spirit of generous kindness, including the ability to focus on the positive aspects of your loved one; a feeling of gratitude about your life together; the capacity to accept even the things you don't like so much about your relationship; trust; respect; and the desire to give freely to your partner. These qualities both reflect the goodwill that is already present in your relationship and enable you to generate more of it.

Chapter 3

TRAIT 3: CLEAR VALUES
Part A: Time

What then shall I do this morning? How we spend our days is,
of course, how we spend our lives. What we do with this
hour and that one is what we are doing.

ANNIE DILLARD, THE WRITING LIFE

THE MOST COMMON challenge I heard about among the thriving couples I interviewed was finding a way to spend time together. It wasn't an issue for all of them, but it was the most common problem I found.

Yet even when they find it to be a major challenge, happy couples do make time for each other. These are not the couples we hear about in those studies that find married couples spending only fifteen minutes a week talking to each other. Thriving couples do not need to be told to make their relationship a high priority; they do it automatically. Their relationship is not incidental in their lives; it is central. However difficult, they find ways to spend time together consistently and in a wide variety of ways.

Exactly what hurdles did they have to leap over in order to find the time to spend with each other? I heard about workaholism; difficulty in shifting gears between work and home; overcommitment; financial constraints; and the general ongoing battles of attempting to balance work and family. Marsha, a corporate vice-president, told me she was a recovering workaholic and that she had trouble confining her disease to the office. She said she had a *New Yorker* cartoon on her refrigerator depicting a man and woman stranded on a tiny desert island. The man had just found a briefcase, and the caption was, "Thank heavens! Some work." I asked her what the secret of her recovery was:

MARSHA: Fred! He has been so patient with me, but at the same time relentless. He just keeps gently insisting that I set limits. Now I'm learning to do it myself because I am so much happier when I do. I don't think I'm really a workaholic. It's just that work could easily take all my time if I let it. . . . I'll tell you one trick I learned. I set a time when I want to leave the office. Then exactly one half hour before that — I actually set my watch alarm — I start to make a transition from work. I stop what I'm doing. I sort of get set up for the next day. Then I can really leave it, and I'm ready to be at home when I get there. At first I thought I wouldn't be able to spare the extra half hour, but now I see it makes everything much pleasanter for me.

Several other people talked about their struggle to balance work and family.

MARGARET: When I was single, I couldn't imagine how I could ever have time for a partner in my life. But after I fell in love, I found out. Then, I couldn't imagine how I would ever find time to have a baby. But then I had a baby, and I found out. You know, you make time for the things that are really important to you.

Margaret reminded me of the old Gestalt principle that at any given moment you are doing exactly what you most want to do. For example, if you are working late, you may *say*, "I really want to be home with my family," but if you really wanted that most of all, you'd be there. Bill, who is a minister, seemed to agree with this and to have learned it on his own.

BILL: Our society trains us to believe that work is most important. We just assume that it is. But when you think about it, the whole reason you work is to have a happy life. Work is important, but so is your life, your family. These days, I think there is increasing tolerance for giving work an appropriate status in your life. . . . I used to make arrangements with my wife, and then if something came up at the church, I'd break my engagements with her. Now, when I make a time with my wife, I keep it.

Several couples talked about how they begin to get restless and edgy with each other if they aren't spending enough time together.

CARLA: For the last four months, John and I [both college professors] have known that we weren't getting enough time together. Several things had interrupted our usual patterns. He was teaching three new courses and had no alternative but to work weekends. At the same time, I had several late afternoon and evening classes and often didn't make it home for dinner at all. We began to get on each other's nerves, and we knew why. But we just kept telling ourselves that the end was in sight. Then, a couple weekends ago, sure enough, we had a big blowup — over nothing really. I mean it was something we would have resolved in a flash if we had been in our usual mode of being together a lot. The time together is absolutely critical for our relationship to do well.

Even though it is a major challenge, most thriving couples find ways to spend high-quality time together. They do this not because they think they ought to, but because they want to. It is an instinctive, automatic priority for them. Like Carla and John, if their precious time together begins to disappear, they notice it right away and take immediate steps to remedy it. I heard several examples of specific changes couples made in order to get more time together. For example:

REBECCA: A couple weeks in a row lately, I was out every single night. Jonesy really put his foot down. At first, I felt he was constraining me and not being understanding and I got defensive. But then he got all soft and sweet — and I'll tell you, this was an example of good communication skills on his part. He talked about what the evenings were like all alone and how he really missed me. You know, he was making "I" statements and talking about his own feelings instead of accusing me of being a bad person. It was really hard for me to shift gears, to think about giving up anything I was doing. But once he saw I got the message, he backed off and gave me a little time to make a shift, and then I really saw he was right. And I decided to resign from the Board of a Battered Women's Shelter I'm on. I know — and he knows, too — that I am much happier and feel more joyful when I have a manageable amount to do. One night right after that we were home just hanging around. I was folding laundry, and he was out in the garage, and I said to myself, "I stayed home for this?" But I knew it was the right thing.

Seven of the couples I interviewed actually work together all or most of the time. Two were ministers, and the rest ran small businesses together. Again, these couples did not fit the stereotype of couples who spend so much time together that they get on each other's nerves. They did take time out away from each other, systematically and deliberately. But they felt blessed and lucky to be able to be together as much as they were. They loved their work and enjoyed each other's company and were thrilled to be able to combine both of those in a life that flowed together. Jeff and Gail planned their small consulting business when they were on their honeymoon. Jeff told me, "It feels so satisfying to be living out a dream we had. I never think about how much time I am or am not spending with Gail. Our life just works."

I identified at least seven kinds of time that couples who thrive spend together. They fit roughly on a continuum from brief conversations on the run at one end to weekends given over entirely and exclusively to intimacy at the other. Let's look at them in detail.

Daily Exchanges

Couples who thrive stay up-to-date with each other. They usually share the details of their day if they spent it apart. And they talk about all the other "stuff" that is going on for them: their children, phone calls with friends or family, events in the news, movies they heard about, their plans for the next week. For two-career families with children, finding enough time for even this catch-up talk can be a challenge, for as soon as they come home, the children need their attention — along with dinner and the mail and phone calls and remembering to move the car for the street cleaners, and dozens of other exigencies. But couples who thrive make time. Grandma comes over twice a week to put the children to bed, a treat for all of them, and a little *re*treat for Mom and Dad. Or the children get fed first (with Mom and Dad in attendance) and have early bedtimes. Then Mom and Dad get a leisurely meal by themselves. Or Mom and Dad sneak lunches together.

Late afternoon and early evening is a tough time for many couples. All at once both partners have a need to (at least) a) unwind and get some time alone, b) connect with each other, c) read mail and make phone calls, d) spend time with children, and e) fix dinner. Conflicts can arise when one partner wants to retreat and unwind and the other wants to connect. Many couples make the mistake of taking their differing needs personally. For example, he needs to unwind, but she feels he is being distant *from her*. Or she wants to connect, and he feels she is being too demanding. Couples who thrive tackle this late-afternoon problem and find a solution that works for them.

One couple has this regular evening routine: They both give their full attention to the children first for a full half hour. Then the children understand that Mom and Dad need some time, and they occupy themselves while Mom and Dad get a little "cocktail hour." The couple goes into the living room, which is off-limits for the kids at that time, and they talk and relax with no other distractions. They don't even take phone calls. Sometimes cocktail hour is only fifteen minutes, but often it is longer. Only then does one of them start to fix dinner.

For another couple, the woman loves to cook and finds it very relaxing to putter in the kitchen while she and her husband talk. When he comes home, he gets a half hour or more to read the mail, change clothes, and generally shift gears. Then, in accord with their agreement, he "keeps her company" while she fixes dinner. She doesn't want any help, but they both welcome the time to talk.

Still another couple routinely telephone each other in the late afternoon and talk for fifteen minutes or so, knowing that the children will take their attention when they get home. And yet another couple told me that they keep their nanny two nights a week while they are home so they can get some help with dinner and the children and some time with each other.

Adrienne found this solution:

> It may sound silly, but what has really helped us is that Clen got me a car phone. I can get so much done on the way home now. I'm not frustrated in the commute any more, and I'm ready to relax with Clen when I get home.

While many couples agreed that finding time to stay in close touch is an almost-daily challenge, they all found ways to do it. And of course, it wasn't even a challenge for many couples. But finding time was routine for all of them. As Doris said,

> When I was in grade school, I had a super-close best friend, and one year we were in different classes. Every recess we'd race to get with each other and tell every little detail that had occurred in the last two hours — mostly gossip about the other kids. Sometimes when I call

Alan just to tell him about something that happened, or I can't wait to see him at the end of the day, I'm reminded about my friend Cathy and me. Alan's a close, close part of my world.

Couples must recognize the importance of private time for each of them, as well as time together. Men tend to be better at simply retreating into themselves for periods of time to relax and recharge their batteries. They find time to read the paper, watch TV, or do little projects that are relaxing. Women often don't take this kind of time as easily, but they need it just as much. Women may "burn out" because they haven't made sure that they get enough "down time," time when no one is making any demands on them and they can be completely alone. Along with finding time for each other, couples should help each other guard their time alone as well.

Experiment #7

---

1. Each of you separately, list all the needs you have when you get home at the end of the day, or when your spouse arrives home.
2. Now, put them in the order in which you would like to do them.
3. Together with your partner, see if you can agree on a schedule that will meet all your needs.
4. As you try it for a few days, modify it as necessary.
5. Finally, figure out what is the best time every day for you to get some time to connect with each other with no other distractions. Breakfast? An early morning walk? Lunch? The last thing before bed? Try to take that time every day for two weeks.

Routines and Rituals

Daily and weekly routines around a household offer a family both comfort and security. Predictability around home is especially important for children. Also, because every couple follows different ones, routines help give a family its distinctive identity. Some family rituals go back several generations, and carrying them on becomes a way of honoring the family.

Sometimes couples who enjoy their relationship will embellish normal routines with a bit of extra thoughtfulness, such as candles on the dinner table or music every morning at wake-up time.

Rituals are one of the casualties of the hurried pace of modern living. Nevertheless, I heard about many from couples who thrive. Often they were little ways these couples have of expressing their love. One couple told me that whoever gets up first fixes breakfast for the other. Another couple cherish their Sunday morning crossword puzzles. In my own family, for fifty years, whenever my father left for work in the morning, my mother always stood at the window and threw him a kiss and they would wave to each other.

Most families have traditions and rituals surrounding birthdays and holidays. These are important because of the continuity they provide, the feeling of belonging, and the connection with the past and the future. Any special one-time event, like a promotion or reward or the completion of a major project, provides an important opportunity to celebrate and savor the victory. As the spiritual writer Starhawk says, "When we undergo a change uncelebrated and unmarked, that transition is devalued and rendered invisible."

Rituals, whether they are elaborate ceremonies like bar mitzvahs or weddings, or simple endearing routines like my mother's waving good-bye to my father every day, bring us a heightened sense of our own identity and our place in the scheme of things.

Playtime

Couples who thrive spend lots of recreational time together. Although a high percentage of these people have satisfying careers, I found very few workaholics among them. They value their playtime, and they spend much of it together.

Of course the kinds of play varied widely from couple to couple. They dance; run or work out; hike; ski; play volleyball; play bridge; eat out; go to movies, theater, or concerts; entertain friends; play parlor games, and so on. Watching TV did not count for most of these couples as playtime, unless they were watching a special program together. As one woman put it, "TV watching is for individual relaxing, like reading. It doesn't bring us together. It separates us."

One couple had set up a routine in which they alternated planning Saturday night. Sometimes it was a surprise, sometimes not, but every Saturday night was their time.

Many of the couples I spoke with were quite social and enjoyed spending time with friends.

HANNAH: When I was single, I didn't know very many couples, and the ones I knew weren't very happy. But now that I'm married, I can't believe how many couples we know whom we adore. In *When Harry Met Sally*, they said couples date other couples, and I loved that. It's definitely true of us. I feel so good about the friends we have. I feel absolutely rich to spend time with any of them. Because we are involved with each other's lives, we are invested in each other — and we can be crazy with each other. I appreciate the variety of friends we have. I always glow after an evening with any of them.

KEVIN: A woman said to me the other day that she wouldn't be able to stand it if she had to listen to her husband's Mexico story one more time. That amazed me. Miriam and I both listen to each other's stories over and over, and it's a kick. She gets all animated when she gets into her stories, and she's entertaining, and of course she's going to tell them again. Do I think she shouldn't tell a story to some other people because she knows I've heard it before? Dumb. That's one of the things husbands and wives give each other. They listen to each other's stories. It's part of getting together with friends, and we love to do that!

PAULA: When we get together with friends, I notice that Reuben and I start talking about things in a way we don't with each other. The other night we were talking with some friends about in-laws, and he said some lovely things about my parents that I had never heard before — how fortunate he feels to have such considerate in-laws. I mean I knew he liked them, of course, but I had never heard him put it in just that way. Getting together with friends is valuable because it puts new material into the system.

Virtually all the thriving couples I interviewed shared at least one interest. They worked together or had a small side business together; they collected antiques; they both danced or played tennis; they enjoyed traveling together. They often had quite separate interests as well, but they respected and enjoyed each other's concerns, and they had at least one hobby or specialty that got them both excited. These people did not live "separate but parallel" lives. Their lives were intertwined in such a way that they automatically had substantial amounts of time together.

Social scientists who have studied leisure time corroborate the conclusion I reached in my interviews: husbands and wives who spend leisure time together tend to be much more satisfied with their marriages than those who don't.

My sister-in-law once considered writing a book of creative experiences for couples entitled *There Aren't Enough Sundays.* She graciously gave me a list of the activities she had planned to suggest so that I could include some of them here. I found this a delightful set of suggestions.*

1. Make a painting or craft project.
2. Take a class together (dancing, photography, cooking, etc.).
3. With another couple, cook an ethnic dinner and dress and decorate accordingly.
4. Take an elaborate bath together with bubble bath, incense, candles, music, flowers, sake, etc.
5. Prearrange a time when you will appear at the same bar, and then pick each other up.
6. Spend an evening body-painting or face-painting each other.
7. Take a walk in a beautiful park and make up stories about the people you see.
8. Go to an amusement park together and pretend to be ten years old.
9. Make a picnic and take it to a beautiful park or woods. Try making separate lunches for each other.
10. Read out loud to each other.
11. Go to the zoo.
12. Put on your favorite music and dance freely all over the house. Or find a lake or meadow, bring a portable tape player, and dance outdoors.
13. Go to an art gallery. Pretend you are a wealthy art dealer or patron. Dress up elegantly, bring a fancy notebook, and decide which five paintings or sculptures you will buy. You have $650,000 to spend.
14. Create your own board game around the theme of your work or hobby.
15. Start a collection (shells, stamps, teapots, camels, etc.). It always makes shopping more fun.
16. Play hooky for a half day and go to an elegant restaurant for breakfast.

*I am indebted to Golda Clendenin for the list of play ideas for couples.

17. Feed each other a whole meal.
18. Build a piece of furniture together.
19. Plan a surprise day's outing for a friend.
20. Spend an afternoon at a convalescent home entertaining the residents.
21. Do an "energy exchange": I'll sew on your buttons if you'll fix the leaky faucet. Or teach each other some new skills.
22. Pamper your partner for a half day (breakfast in bed, massage, read a story, put on favorite music, etc.).

If you can't find a play activity here that inspires you, make up one of your own that does. For if you rarely make time for fun together, your relationship will suffer, though you may not realize why. On the other hand, spending playtime together can do more to renew a feeling of closeness between you than you might realize.

"Hot Tub Time"

Several years ago, Mayer and I moved from a house that did not have a hot tub to one that did. Right away, we developed the habit of taking a leisurely soak almost every evening before bed. It was delicious to climb into the hot water and relax. But what we loved even more was the kind of time it gave us to be together. We would start talking in a way that we never would have deliberately initiated elsewhere. We'd evaluate how things were going in general, or start planning our next vacation, or ask each other questions we'd forgotten to ask earlier, such as, "Did you like that painting they had over their couch?" We began to realize how valuable this "hot tub time" was, but how easy it might be to go day after day without it.

We call it "Hot Tub Time," but a more generic title would be "No-Agenda Time," and of course the hot tub itself is unnecessary. The only requirements are that it last a minimum of thirty minutes (a couple of hours or a whole day is much better), and that there be no way you can be doing anything else besides relaxing with each other. Plan no specific topic of conversation ahead of time; let whatever is going to happen between you simply emerge. Often, it's nothing very momentous. Sometimes you may become affectionate and lovey-dovey. But what is significant is that these are the times when topics of discussion — or even isolated comments — come up *that might never otherwise get a chance to surface.* You could quite easily go along for years without ever discussing some things, but given un-structured time when you are "forced" together in some way, these topics arise, and your relationship is much the richer for them.

On one occasion Mayer and I were idly talking about our son, and we began exploring the idea of sending him to an art school, an idea that neither of us had considered before. (He actually did attend art school, by the way.) We often get to talking about Mayer's work or mine, and we become sounding boards and sources of ideas for each other. The time has been extremely valuable, but neither of us would ever have said, "Let's take an hour and talk about how you could change your business."

There are many ways to get good No-Agenda Time. Before Mayer and I had a hot tub, we used to cover the overflow outlet in our regular tub (plastic wrap works well), and squeeze in there together. We'd light the bathroom with a single candle and add hot water whenever the water got too cool. We could idle away hours in there, getting silly, or talking, or just being together. I highly recommend this activity. You can do it on a moment's notice. It's free, it's relaxing, and it gives you luxurious time together.

Cocktail hour (with or without real cocktails) can be a nice time of day to unwind and talk casually, especially if there is no particular agenda for the rest of the evening.

Driving is one of the best ways to get No-Agenda Time, because you really are trapped with nothing else to do. One couple I know (who work together and have their office at home, so they have no regular commute) get in the car some weekends and drive. They find beautiful back country roads and enjoy the scenery and each other.

Eating out can be good No-Agenda Time. Renee and Jay look for-ward to Sunday morning brunch at one of several spots around town. They read the paper before they go, and when they get to the restau-rant they just have what they called "leisurely conversation." (I rec-ognized it as No-Agenda Time!)

"Getaway Time"

Couples who thrive create special times just for themselves — every-thing from informal, spontaneous trips out for frozen yogurt to eve-nings at the theater and weekends away. These are times away from the distractions of home, work, and children when the main agenda is to relax and enjoy each other and whatever activity is at hand. The subject of getting away to relax together on a regular basis came up spontaneously and with a certain amount of urgency in most of the conversations I had. Tim and Sarah have a blended family and two demanding careers. She is a journalist, he's a contractor.

> TIM: We absolutely insist on one weekend a month totally for us. Really. We have our B&B reservations made for the next twelve months. Because we found out that if we don't save the weekend specifically, something always comes up and we never get away. But it is really important for us. We look forward to these weekends so much. Once a month is pretty often, you know. It comes up again before you know it. Sometimes we're so behind, we think about just staying home and catching up on laundry and phone calls and shopping, but after we get away, we are always so glad we did. I mean we have had some absolutely fabulous times. And those weekends kind of linger with us throughout the month. The feelings of peace and quiet stay around in the background. And the feelings of togetherness. You can never get too distant when you spend that much time together.

> MARGARET: We'll go for months without getting away anywhere. Partly it's because we like our life. We enjoy our work and our routines and our kids. But then when we finally take a break and get away, just the two of us together, it feels so wonderful. We can't believe we don't do it more often.

Relationship Development Time

Most of the happy couples I interviewed talk about their relationship itself with some regularity. With few exceptions, they weren't surprised by anything I asked them, for they had already talked about it themselves. Quite the opposite of taking their relationship for granted, they paid attention to it. They took its pulse fairly often, casually and naturally.

In addition, just as many of us regularly seek to upgrade our professional skills, thriving couples actively seek ways to nurture and strengthen their relationship. Quite a number of them had taken advantage of one or more weekend workshops designed specifically to enrich marriage. I heard about Tantric Yoga weekends, Gestalt groups, communications skills seminars, intimacy workshops, parenting classes, marriage enrichment weekends, and Marriage Encounters.* One couple enjoyed Intimacy Marathons suggested by psychologist and writer Nathaniel Branden. They simply spend at least twelve hours together in a room with no books, television, telephones, or other distractions of any kind.

In my own Thriving Marriage Workshops, couples gather for the weekend in a hotel. We meet together for lectures and group exercises. Then the couples are invited to return to the privacy of their hotel rooms to do certain exercises with each other. The weekends are designed to give couples the experience of communicating in new, very deep ways, and most couples find them extremely pleasurable. The instruction and light structure the weekends provide give participants the opportunity to experience heartfelt intimacy with each other. In addition, the couples gain new tools to help them sustain their closeness.

Happy couples are quick to look for help if they get bogged down in their relationship in any way. They are not afraid to go to marriage counselors, for they know themselves and each other well enough to know that there will be no huge surprises. They have a low tolerance for troubles in their relationship or for obstacles between them, and they are eager for new insights that might help them over their rough spots. If they can't figure out how to solve a problem, or they recognize that they are boxed into a communications corner, they will talk with a trusted friend or have a few sessions with a marriage counselor. Rather than assuming that their relationship will take care of itself, they recognize the usefulness of an objective point of view.

One of the reasons our relationships often get the short end of the stick is that "relationship tending" is not the sort of thing we put on our calendars. On the calendar go items like "faculty meeting," "pick up the kids," "bake a cake for the potluck." We usually don't write, "Pay attention to my marriage." But we should!

Most of us follow the natural urge to do first those things that we deem urgent, whether or not they are truly important. The problem with this system is that some activities that are truly important never get done — because they don't feel urgent. Nurturing, building, and experiencing the relationship with the person you love is probably the most important activity in your life, or at least one of the two or three most important. Does it receive its appropriate amount of time?

I spoke with a corporate lawyer who made a conscious choice early

*For information about Marriage Encounter Weekends, call (800) 828-3351.

on to limit his career so that his life would not be consumed by it — and his family left out of it.

> There are meetings I do not attend and dinners I forgo that would be good for bringing more business into the firm. I do my fair share of the work, but that's all. It is definitely a professional sacrifice for me not to be a more gung ho partner. Part of me worries that I could have achieved more faster. But I have made my choices consciously and over-all I can see that I am happy and fulfilled because I do.

It is common wisdom that people who are on their deathbeds never say, "I wish I had spent more time at the office." They say, "I wish I had spent more time with the people I love." Couples who are happy together realize this long before they die.

Real Time*

We live in a fast-paced society. Instead of letting timesaving devices, such as microwave ovens and computers, provide us with more leisure time, we have allowed them to raise our expectations about how much we can accomplish in an hour. So we rush about, trying to have it all and do it all, eating fast food, speed-reading book summaries, and communicating with each other via terse voice-mail messages. We operate on high-tech time.

The rhythm of the natural world is altogether different: think of the pace at which ocean waves roll in and out, the time it takes the sun to set or a bud to become a flower. The natural world is never in a hurry. It has its own tempo, and nothing is so urgent that it can't simply follow its own gentle, deliberate pace.

Real time, like natural time, isn't slow or fast; it's whatever pace it needs to be.

Lovers operate in real time. The usual day-to-day rush simply fades away for them, and they set their own rhythms. The world may be flying past them, but they can't be hurried.

Couples who thrive for many years together occasionally find themselves in little oases of real time. It may be on a weekend getaway or a long vacation. It might be triggered by a discussion or an emotional event, either happy or sad. The two of them are completely present with each other. They hold each other; they look at each

---

*I am indebted to Lee Glickstein for introducing me to his concept "real time."

other; maybe they talk or take a long, slow walk. They become un-aware of time. It has no control over them; everything happens naturally.

When I explained "real time" to Sherry and Tom, they gave each other a knowing look.

SHERRY: We won a trip to Las Vegas in a drawing. We aren't gambling types, but we went to the shows and fancy buffets and people-watched and just sort of took it all in. We happened to be in a really happy, mellow mood that weekend. I had recently gotten tenure, which is a long, tough battle, and it was a huge relief; our son had won his gymnastic competition; and we were starting an addition to our house, which was very exciting. It was just one of those really nice times when you feel good all over. Well, there was nothing to do in Las Vegas after a couple days. So we just started to mellow out and we got into this amazing space — it was really like when we were first in love. We just sat really close and talked for what seemed like hours, and then we made love, and then we talked some more.

After we came back, I wanted to hang on to that whole feeling, but I felt like Tom went back to the other world. I'd remind him, and try to entice him back into it. But we couldn't make it happen exactly that way again. But the feeling lingers on — for me at least. I just love knowing that I can have that sort of fantasy experience with the man I love.

TOM: It will happen again sometime. I'm not worried about it. I think you just have to let these things emerge. You can't plan them.

Experiment #8

List each of the following on a page of your notebook: daily exchanges, rituals, playtime, No-Agenda Time, getaway time, relationship development time, and real time. Now think up one activity in each of those categories and schedule all of them for sometime in the next four or five weeks.

When a relationship seems to be in trouble, it could be that all it really needs is a generous dose of time. The problem is often misdiagnosed. Couples will blame each other or some stressful event that has occurred. But the truth is, even the most thriving couple will get out of sync if they have no quality time together for several weeks. They become self-involved, and they stop feeling close.

Variety is important also. Couples who live the same routines week after week may feel they are becoming bored with each other, when the real problem is that they simply need variety in their schedules. Just as money experts plan diversity in their financial portfolios, thriving couples diversify their relationship schedules.

The thriving couples I spoke to all agreed that becoming wealthy with love and affection is of more value to them than becoming wealthy with money. The way they spend their time reflects this value; they all make certain they spend a variety of time with each other, and a lot of it.

Planning a full, diversified relationship schedule could be the most exciting thing you ever do. Start now, for the way you spend your days is the way you spend your life.

Chapter 4

TRAIT 3: CLEAR VALUES
Part B: Aliveness

COUPLES WHO THRIVE value life. They experience it as an adventure. They may experience fear, but they don't let fear stop them from getting what they want. If the two kinds of people in the world are those who would rather avoid pain than experience pleasure, and those who would rather experience pleasure even if it means experiencing some pain, thriving couples are the latter. They have the courage to live life fully.

When I asked my thriving couples about their feelings when they met, I heard many, many comments like these:

It didn't even take me five minutes to see an inner fire that I knew I wanted to see more of.

There was a quality about him that I couldn't put my finger on — a kind of *joie de vivre* — that just zapped me.

I could tell I had met a peer in some important way, someone who had the same excitement about life that I have.

I knew this was someone who wouldn't let life pass him by.

She was different. I didn't just want to share experiences with this woman. I wanted to share life with her.

She had passion. You couldn't miss it. I couldn't believe she was available. I kept waiting for her to say "we." I finally asked her, and when she said "No, there's just me," I know my heart stopped. I was already in love. So was she.

In addition, I noticed that other writers, in a variety of contexts, have also searched for ways to talk about this quality of aliveness, sometimes by trying to describe life without it:

> *To live in fear of being fully alive is the state of most people.*
> —Alexander Lowen

> *The biggest danger in life is missing out on the promise of life by avoiding the issues and retreating in fear.*
> —Ashley Montague

> *Never marry a person who is not a friend of your excitement.*
> —Nathaniel Branden

> *I have found, at times of heightened perception . . . that it is not hard to fall in love several times a day; that is, to keep finding myself deeply moved not only by the people [around me], but also by the landscape, the sounds of the forest, the moon at night, or the changing patterns of wind, light, clouds, and rain. Although this vividness of perception may seem special, it is also quite ordinary. If it be magic, it is ordinary magic, because it is only a keener awareness of what is already there. Though we cannot hold on to such moments, they leave us with a sense of what life could be like if we could live more often at this threshold of vivid presence.*
> —John Welwood

I saw this unmistakable quality in the couples I interviewed over and over, but I found it hard to describe. I kept erasing and renaming the file folder for my notes on this chapter. At various times, the folder had the names "Happiness," "Intensity," "Positive Attitude," "Consciousness," "Awareness," and "Exuberance." But each of these would turn out to be only part of what I was talking about. I began to realize that the quality I saw in virtually all these couples didn't have a name, and that I would have to invent one. "Aliveness," I wrote on my tattered file folder, and it stuck.

Aliveness is simply full — rather than partial — participation in life. It involves deep knowledge of oneself, genuine connection with other people and with one's environment, and a heightened awareness of the present moment. People who are fully alive have an expanded capacity for pleasure, a feeling that life is flowing and they are flowing with it. They recognize that happiness is a choice. They focus on what they like, not on what they don't like. They are willing to experience pain, for they know that if the body shuts down to close off painful feelings, then pleasurable feelings will be closed off as well, and they want, above all, to *experience* their life, not simply to live it by rote.

I'm reminded of the parable of the skylarks and the frog told by Theodore Roszak in *Making of a Counter-Culture*. The frogs lived in the bottom of a dark well. From time to time a skylark would fly down to visit them with tales of the gorgeous world outside the well. She told them about sunshine and green grass, flowers and trees, and burbling brooks. The frogs had never seen such things. They thought her stories were quaint, but became annoyed when she tried to coax them out of their well, for they needed to get on with the important business of life such as manufacturing lightbulbs. In the end, since the skylark represented a threat to their way of life, the frogs killed and stuffed her.

People who lack the quality of aliveness can't even imagine what it is like because they have never been there. They don't want to believe in anything better, because then they might have to do some kind of work to get there. So they have excuses, stories they tell themselves about why they can't change. "I'm a born pessimist." "I'm shy." "It runs in the family." They seem unable or unwilling to accept the idea that they could choose to experience more in life, that they could be not necessarily happier but more in touch with their own experiences, connected to others at a more heartfelt, mysterious level.

Of course the world is not neatly divided into two discrete types, the alive and the numb. Most of us have some of each of these qualities and may fluctuate back and forth between them. But couples who have truly wonderful relationships seem most often to consist of two individuals who exhibit a great deal of aliveness.

Aliveness and Achievement

One of the most obvious and yet best-kept secrets of happy marriage is that couples who thrive value aliveness as much as they value achievement, even though this attitude goes against the grain of our culture. No matter how great their accomplishments or how involved they are with their work, their relationships come first. Rick put it this way:

> For me the whole point of doing anything is to share it with Marne. Just recently, I got a journal article published that is the culmination of four years of work. It was really exciting; I got interviewed by several newspapers and received letters from colleagues all around the world. It just feels to me that achieving that without Marne to help with the excitement would have been empty, useless. I mean, I can't imagine it. Long after the newspapers forget about it, Marne's appreciation will still be here. It is all part of the history we are building together.
>
> To me, relationships are not merely one more aspect of life, like job, money, sex, house. Relationships *are* life. Everything else is just there to contribute to relationships, and relationships support everything else. Name any valuable work anyone does. Why is it valuable? Because it enhances human relationships.

In many relationships that don't thrive, one of the problems is that either one or both of the partners view their relationship as one department in their lives, kind of a nice addition. And for many of these couples, their work, their achievements, are more important to them than their love for each other.

Several years ago a friend of mine decided to give up her psychotherapy practice in Berkeley to take a job teaching at a large university in an eastern city. When she returned for a visit after six months, she told me,

> What I like is that I'm getting ahead in my field. I'm quite well respected by the other faculty members, and it feels great. But you know, I've lost something. I feel like part of me has died. I work all the time. When I was in Berkeley, I felt like I took delight in every day. I cared about things more. I don't mean I was necessarily happier all the time — because I had some hard times here. But I was more involved in life. I was more wide awake. I paid more attention to what I was feeling, whatever that was. I've turned that whole part of myself off now. I'm just a work machine — a good one. You know, I think there are two things in life: achievement and aliveness. And believe me, achievement is overrated!

Let's assume for the sake of discussion that each of us has two basic needs: the need to achieve and the need to experience "aliveness" or vitality. Roughly speaking, this is the dichotomy between work and play; between power and pleasure; between worldly success and inner contentment; between the ego, which feeds on achievements, and the body, which craves pleasure.

Since our culture rewards achievement, work, and success, and ignores or, in some cases, actively discourages, the aliveness that comes with play, engagement with others, and creativity, many of us as individuals have a poor balance of these qualities in our own lives. We know a lot about achievement. Virtually all of our formal education prepares us for "success." But the importance of feeling fully alive is barely hinted at in school. We don't think much about it; we don't systematically acquire the skills to enhance it; and as a result, we trivialize it. If you fail to achieve something, everyone knows it, and you are supposed to feel bad about this. But who cares or even knows whether you are feeling pleasure and aliveness? You may become so accustomed to being closed down that even you aren't aware of it. The nineteenth-century theologian Søren Kierkegaard captured this irony, when he said, "The greatest danger, that of losing one's own self, can pass off as quietly as if it were nothing. Every other loss — that of an arm, a leg, a spouse, five dollars, etc. — is sure to be noticed."

MORE OF WHAT YOU NEVER WANTED IN THE FIRST PLACE WON'T SATISFY YOU

There is a more insidious problem, even, than our tendency to minimize our aliveness and pleasure, and it is this: We don't know how to distinguish between aliveness and achievement, and we often confuse the two. We assume that by striving for "success" we will reap the rewards of a fully lived life, but instead, the harder we work on achievement, the less alive we feel. It's a bit like the Aesop's Fable in which the sun and the wind entered into a contest to see who could make a man remove his coat first. The harder the wind blew, the more the man pulled his coat around him.

Many of us are engaged in a similarly futile endeavor. Though we are only dimly aware of it, we crave pleasure, aliveness, and meaning — yet all we know how to pursue is achievement. We can never achieve enough because, as it turns out, it is not "success" we seek, but aliveness. More of what we never wanted in the first place doesn't satisfy. We seek achievement because we don't know how to seek feelings of well-being and aliveness. We try to substitute success for true pleasure.

This folly reached its extreme form in the eighties, the decade of greed, of yuppies, and of the glorification of wealth and power. In his book, *The Passionate Life*, Sam Keen captures the confusion of seeking inner meaning in inappropriate ways:

> Men and women who become obsessed with power are driven by a repressed feeling of their own powerlessness and worthlessness. Power is sought to prove to some absent critical eye that we are worthy of the love and acceptance we did not receive. Armaments are a substitute for the arms that were meant to enfold us. Spiritual power is sought when grace is missing. Sexual power is sought when men have lost the conviction of their potency to move others except by the use of violence. Economic power is sought when we fall into the illusion that commodities can compensate us for the absence of the household and the community.

Couples who thrive understand instinctively the difference between achievement and aliveness, and they value aliveness more. Bruce and Jan, for example, both made decisions that would limit their worldly "success" so that they could enjoy their life and their relationship more.

Bruce decided to sell his retail business at the height of its success because it was running him ragged. His passion was to become a writer, so he sold the business and lived off the proceeds for several years while he launched his writing career.

Jan, meantime, is a therapist who worked for a hospital. Though all her colleagues were going into private practice where they could make more than twice the money she made, Jan had no intention of doing so, for she loved the hospital with its team approach, its regular hours, and its constant stream of clients.

Jan and Bruce are both engaged in their work and get enormous satisfaction from it, and they have plenty of time to spend with each other in a variety of ways. They have time to run together every day. They frequently entertain friends for dinner. Their life is relatively stress free, with an easy, relaxed pace. This is due to a deliberate choice on their part — because they value aliveness. They don't want to miss life. They don't want to wake up one morning and realize that they haven't spent any quality time with each other in months.

One year, Jan told me, she decided to take on an extra teaching job at a different hospital. It was a prestigious appointment, and the job itself was a pleasure for her. But the extra time it took and the stress it added to their lives made it clear to Jan that the job was not worth the price she was paying. After one year she resigned.

Our failure to separate our need for achievement from our need for aliveness in our lives — and to give attention to our requirement for aliveness and pleasure — really does create more stress and less enjoyment of life. As Stephen Covey says, we "work harder and harder at climbing the ladder of success only to discover it is leaning against the wrong wall." But much of the time, we don't realize what the real source of our pain is.

Several years ago I counseled a couple who had achieved substantial wealth in quite a short period of time. Jessica was a lawyer, and Todd was an unusually successful real estate agent. They were way ahead of schedule in achieving the dreams they had for themselves when they got married. At ages thirty-two and thirty-five, not only were they already in their dream home, but Todd had received several prestigious awards, and Jessica had been enticed by an executive recruiter to take a job that almost doubled her salary. But they were very unhappy and they could not understand why.

As we discovered over time, their problem was that the satisfaction their egos were receiving from their achievements could not give them the feelings of pleasure and vibrancy they sought in their relationship with each other. They were confusing their need for achievement with their need for aliveness. Both workaholics, they simply never considered that happiness came from anything but fulfillment of career goals.

We may long for closeness, for pleasant surges of emotion, for the ability to open up, to act spontaneously. (One man told me, "I have a fantasy of someone dropping me off a tall building to crack me open like Humpty-Dumpty. I think that's what it will take to get through my shell.") We may be starved for pleasure, for aliveness. But if we try to alleviate these longings by getting a promotion, buying a car, dating the boss, making an even bigger sale, or getting people to laugh at our jokes, we will be addressing our ego needs rather than finding ways to experience the pleasure and aliveness that would satisfy our longings. The route to more pleasure and aliveness leads inward, into the self, not outward into the world. It has to do with enhancing the quality of each moment. Experiences in the world may trigger pleasure, but only a vital, open self can *experience* the pleasure.

Even activities that are actually designed to provide pleasure are often used in the service of the ego. I knew a woman who had season tickets to the opera because that is what people who have money do. She bought a new gown for each opera, and all she ever talked about was whom she saw there. I never had the feeling from her reports that she went there to let her body relax and let the music sweep over her. I'm not sure she even heard the music.

Even physical fitness, which might seem to be a pleasure-oriented experience, sometimes isn't. Dieting, exercising, skin care, running, and competitive athletics can be used to serve the ego's need for achievement rather than the body's need for vibrancy and sensuality.

ALIVENESS AND INTIMACY

If achievement and aliveness are life's major goals, where does love fit into the picture? Love takes place entirely in the realm of aliveness. There is no reason to be in a loving relationship except to enhance your own aliveness and your own capacity to experience life fully, and to increase the pleasure in your life. Relationships have nothing to do with achievement. If you are extremely achievement-oriented and ego-dominated and you have a diminished capacity for aliveness, you will automatically have a diminished capacity for love — and for a thriving relationship. If you are numb to feelings of pleasure and aliveness, you may experience the trappings of a love relationship, but the experiences of free-flowing goodwill, unconditional love, total acceptance, and spontaneous generosity will elude you.

Aliveness and pleasure are not the same thing. Your aliveness is your capacity to experience anything fully, whether it's pleasure or pain, joy or sadness, ecstasy or grief.

Aliveness has a lot to do with living in the present, with accepting that all we have in life is the journey, with all its mountains and valleys, all its bumpy roads and flat, boring stretches. If you aren't enjoying getting to the success you seek, chances are you won't enjoy the success when you get there. Any destination, any goal you seek serves only to enhance the quality of your effort to reach it.

But since pleasure is one of the aspects of aliveness that we diminish and suppress in our culture, and because couples who thrive do experience a great deal of pleasure with each other, let us examine pleasure in a bit more detail.

PLEASURE

The experience of pleasure can occur in any ordinary circumstance of life. In fact, it may appear in unexpected places and elude elaborate attempts to create it. You can derive pleasure from many sources, including the following:

- becoming so intensely involved in something that you lose yourself in it
- allowing yourself a full range of completely spontaneous self-expression
- experiencing a free flow of feelings throughout your entire body
- tasting, touching, hearing, seeing, and smelling sensuous things

In his book *Rediscovering Love*, Psychologist Willard Gaylin identifies some types of experience that often lead to pleasure: sexual and sensory experiences, play (especially when not corrupted by competition), transcendental or spiritual events, the joy of discovery, the thrill of mastery, and simply the relief of some anxiety or stress.

Love, of course, is one of life's most pleasurable experiences. A loving, intimate bond can add a backdrop of pleasure and happiness to every other experience of life. Thoughts about the loved one, memories, anticipation, shared experiences, and sexual and nonsexual touching all produce pleasurable sensations.

Most of us could experience more joy and pleasure in our lives than we do. We spend a good deal of energy censoring positive emotions and cutting ourselves off from pleasurable experiences, because in our childhoods, many kinds of pleasure were negatively reinforced, and we have come to associate pleasure with deprivation or anxiety. For example, if our parents were too busy to give us all the cuddling we craved, we will associate the pleasure of being touched with fear of deprivation or abandonment. Or if our parents or church taught us that sex is naughty, we may have trouble enjoying sex.

As adults, we behave as though too much pleasure will destroy us. We cling to the belief that genuine ecstasy is rare and that we should not expect it to occur with any regularity.

Pain, however, we accept as normal. Life is a series of problems and stresses. True enough. But why shouldn't we expect exactly the same measure — or more — of ecstasy and pleasure? Why shouldn't we expect deep joy and a heightened sense of aliveness to be woven into our daily lives, just the way stress is?

Couples who thrive believe in pleasure, and they allow themselves to experience it — often.

THE BODY/EGO SPLIT

The achievement/aliveness split manifests itself in our lives as a struggle between the ego and the body. The ego always craves achievement, and the body always craves pleasure and aliveness.

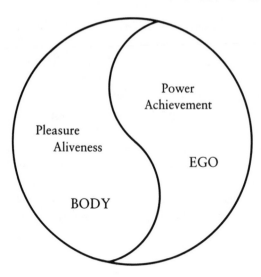

Aliveness is experienced in the body, not the mind. A thought or an external experience may produce a pleasurable sensation, but the pleasurable sensation occurs in the body.

While we spend years formally educating our minds and developing our capacities to think, we spend no organized time formally educating our bodies by developing our capacities to sense (taste, touch, see, hear, smell), breathe, move, feel, or express ourselves. We pay little attention to our bodies except as tools to feed (or traps to deflate) our egos.

With his television series and book *Healing and the Mind*, Bill Moyers revealed to Westerners what Eastern religions and indigenous peoples have known forever: the mind, spirit, and body are not separate; they are one.

Non-Western religions involve the body in the celebration of life. Native Americans and Africans engage in vigorous dancing to honor the gods, thereby exploiting the body's ability to move, to breathe, and to express emotion. Yoga emphasizes the integration of body, mind, and spirit through rigorous body disciplines including deep and subtle breathing. Buddhists practice special postures and breathing in connection with meditation. The Chinese meditation known as Tai Chi Chuan also teaches the body to breathe fully and to expand its capacity to move.

Christianity, on the other hand, influenced by Hellenistic philosophy that split mind and body apart, has tended to belittle the body. Judaism and Christianity are largely intellectual religions. Worshipers are invited to sit, stand, or kneel — activities that do little to put us in touch with the unexplored potentials of our bodies to move, breathe deeply, or express emotion.

Most people are capable of moving much more than they ever actually do. When is the last time you said, "I haven't danced in months, and all that moving felt so good." And unless you are engaged in a specific practice of some kind, such as yoga or meditation, you have probably barely tapped your body's capacity to breathe. It is movement and breathing that free our bodies up to feel emotions and to express creativity. According to psychologist Alexander Lowen, "Most Americans are living their lives on a limited budget of energy and feeling."

The only way we can increase our capacity to experience pleasure — and therefore intimacy — is to begin to pay attention to aliveness needs as well as to achievement needs. If you decide to give your pleasurable experiences gradually more of your time and attention, don't count on getting any approval for it, except from within. Imagine this conversation:

Joe: Hi, Sam. What have you been up to lately?
Sam: Oh, I just signed two big new contracts for the company, and I came in second at the club golf tournament this weekend. How about you?
Joe: Oh, I've been doing a lot of deep breathing and stretching lately. My wife and I make love a lot and take walks in the woods near our house. I'm getting a massage once a week now, and I'm taking a yoga class.

Such a conversation is unlikely, for achievement is still far more respectable than aliveness. Indeed, most people still equate the two.

Paying attention to your body and to what you are experiencing more of the time is a way to start letting more aliveness into your life. But inattention to pleasure is so well established a habit in most of us that we require help in breaking it.

Here is an exercise to help you begin to notice and to change your patterns of awareness and to begin to "tune in" to your body. You will find it useful whether you are a "beginner" at the awareness game, a veteran, or somewhere in between.

Experiment #9

1. You may want to have a friend sit with you for this exercise, just to be there and listen. But if you are alone, speak to yourself softly, out loud. Do the exercise the first few times with your eyes closed. Later, be sure to try it with your eyes open.

   Sit or lie down and get comfortable. If you are sitting, sit up straight.

   Begin saying to yourself, "I am aware of ———." Keep saying it over and over, filling in the blank with whatever is appropriate at the moment. For example, "I am aware of the car going by. I am aware of my toes being cold. I am aware of my leg muscle being tense. I am aware of the rice simmering on the stove. I am aware of my nose itching. I am aware of feeling silly. I am aware of my back resting on this chair. I am aware of the quiet in this room. I am aware I just moved my feet."

   Keep going for a while, say five or even ten minutes.

   Repeat this exercise once a day or twice a week — whatever fits for you. But do it at least fifteen times. See what happens.

2. See if you can deliberately pay attention to what you are experiencing in your body several times a day.

   Stop for a second and say, "I am feeling ——— in my ———." For the first blank, substitute a feeling and for the second blank, a part of your body. For example, "I am feeling tension in my jaw," or "I am feeling hungry in my stomach," or "I am feeling warmth in my chest."

Most of us know couples who have balanced the pleasure/power needs in their lives who can serve as models for the rest of us. Generally, they are people who have found ways to reduce the stress in their lives. They have found work that fulfills them or that they enjoy but that does not consume them entirely. They may be striving to achieve certain goals, but not with the sense that their lives depend on it. And they are enjoying the process. They understand that life is a journey, not a destination. We are drawn to these couples precisely because they seem to be "alive," to have a zest for life.

In order to develop a thriving intimate relationship in your life, you must learn to distinguish between power and pleasure. When you feel empty or inadequate, consider whether more power or more pleasure is going to fill the void. We all need a balance in our lives. For most of us, this means that we need to expand our interest in and capacity for pleasure. We must learn that a continual striving for additional achievement will never satisfy our longing for aliveness; instead it will increase that longing. Remember that what my friend said, "achievement is overrated," is probably true and begin to make choices designed to increase your own capacity for aliveness. Practice pleasure.

In a book called *If I Had My Life to Live Over*, eighty-five-year-old Nadine Stair gave us all some wisdom born of experience when she wrote,

> If I had my life to live over, I'd dare to make more mistakes next time. I'd relax. I would limber up. I would be sillier than I have been this trip. I would take fewer things seriously. I would take more chances. I would take more trips. I would climb more mountains and swim more rivers. I would eat more ice cream and less beans. I would perhaps have more actual troubles, but I'd have fewer imaginary ones.
>
> You see, I'm one of those people who live sensible and sanely hour after hour, day after day. Oh, I've had my moments and if I had it to do over again, I'd have more of them. In fact, I'd try to have nothing else. Just moments, one after another, instead of living so many years ahead of each day. I've been one of those persons who never goes anywhere without a thermometer, a hot water bottle, a raincoat, and a parachute. If I had it to do again, I would travel lighter than I have.
>
> If I had my life to live over, I would start barefoot earlier in the spring and stay that way later in the fall. I would go to more dances. I would ride more merry-go-rounds. I would pick more daisies.

When I was discussing pleasure at one of my workshops, one participant asked whether I was advocating hedonism, and a lively discussion ensued. Increasing your feeling of aliveness, your ability to experience life fully, has nothing to do with hedonism. Hedonism is the doctrine that pleasure is the highest good, and that one should devote oneself totally to pleasure at the expense of everything and everyone else. I submit only that pleasure is one of life's good things, and that to avoid it as many people do is an unnecessary tragedy. We have been forced to bury our capacity for pleasure in order to tolerate the life we have set up for ourselves. In the process, intimate relationships have suffered. Consider these words of wisdom from Thomas Jefferson: "The happiest moments of my life have been the few which I have passed at home in the bosom of my family. Public employment contributes neither to advantage nor happiness. It is but honorable exile from one's family and affairs."

Experiment #10

1. List all your activities for a typical day or week.
2. Go back over the list and put a big AL next to the ones you believe contribute to aliveness for you, and a big AC next to the ones that have to do more with achievement. You may find a third category to be useful: M for basic maintenance tasks. Some activities may receive more than one designation.
3. Do you feel good about the balance you see? Can you find a way to spend more time contributing to your own overall feeling of aliveness?
4. If money were not an issue and you had complete freedom to spend your week exactly as you would like, what would you do with your time? Can you find a way to incorporate any of the things you would like to be doing into your real-life schedule?

Thriving couples are alive and vibrant because they start out with the attitude that life is exciting. They look for excitement, and they find it. They have interesting work, but they don't let their career goals take over their life. They value achievement and creativity *and* aliveness and love.

To be alive in mind and spirit is to have a bright, positive outlook. To be alive in your body is to breathe, to move freely and gracefully, and to feel and express whatever emotions arise. None of this is complicated. To start feeling more alive right now, take a deep breath, stretch, move your shoulders around, think about how much you love your spouse, smile.

Chapter 5

TRAIT 4: BOUNDARIES

WHEN ROBERT FROST observed long ago that "good fences make good neighbors," he was tapping into one of the fundamental ironies of human existence. Each of us longs for love, for intimate connection, for closeness and a feeling of belonging, for bonding and even merging with others whom we love and who love us. Yet each of us has an equally strong yearning to be independent, to control our own lives, to make our own decisions, to be free of the demands of others. These two needs exist in continuous tension, and each of us dances between the two polarities. As soon as we give in to one need, the other screams for attention. If I am feeling alone, I long for closeness; if I am feeling too close, I crave autonomy. In the end, it is our ability to build good fences, carefully crafted personal boundaries, that allows us to give ourselves fully to closeness and even intimacy with others.

Thriving couples move back and forth easily between separation and togetherness because they know how to establish boundaries. Their ease with autonomy lets them experience themselves as a unit, as close and together. One couple told me, "We are not 'married singles'; we are two people, but we have one life, and we consider each other in everything we do."

It is easy to observe the movement between connection and autonomy in children. The infant begins by depending entirely on her caregivers. But as soon as she is capable of it, she begins to assert her

independence from them. The two-year-old fiercely refuses everything
her parents suggest, but then gets upset if they aren't there to tuck her
in at night. Although the balancing act may be more obvious in children, it is something adults never perfectly resolve. Like the constant
tiny adjustments made by the tightrope walker, our back and forth
between autonomy and connection is a continuing endeavor. It is the
central task that every intimate couple faces: I want to be a part of this
relationship, and I must remain an individual. Come closer/leave me
alone. When do I take care of my own needs at my partner's expense,
and when do I take care of my partner's needs at my expense? What
is my business, what is my partner's business, and what is our business? What should I keep private, and what should I share?

Frost had the answer: Those who can build the best fences can be
the best neighbors. Fences are not hostile barricades, but rather,
clearly defined limits that allow people to operate more freely, confi-
dent that they will not be encroaching upon each other's territory.

The hardest part of fence-building for married couples is not actually building the fence, but determining where to build it. Neighbors
have deeds and surveyors who determine preset boundaries. But couples have no handy maps or charts. Every couple starts from scratch,
and every couple must work out the answers over time to these critical
questions: What is your territory? What is mine? What is ours? The
clearer the boundaries and structures are to begin with, the easier and
freer the relationship can be. If no clear boundaries are set, the individuals in the relationship cannot be free, for they must always give
part of their attention to watchdogging their territory.

If you have clear predetermined boundaries, you don't have to keep
establishing distance between you. Couples spend years negotiating
various boundaries with each other. This is one reason, incidentally,
why good relationships become more wonderful the longer they go
on: after years of being together, couples know and honor each other's
boundaries. They don't have to spend time and energy negotiating,
and they can be freer to be close.

Every couple must establish boundaries in a variety of areas: What
time is yours, mine, and ours? What *space* is yours, mine, and ours?
What *household tasks* are yours, mine, and ours? What *money* is
yours, mine, and ours? What *secrets* are yours, mine, and ours? What
emotional responsibilities are yours, mine, and ours?

Time, space, household tasks, and money are the easiest territorial
issues to see and often the first to emerge in a relationship. Secrets,

emotional responsibilities, and psychological tasks are subtler. They may be harder to negotiate because although couples may be willing in spirit to negotiate these matters, they may not be able to achieve change as easily in these areas. Let's look at the simpler (though not necessarily easier) issues first.

Time

When I got married after six years of being single, the hardest adjustment I had to make was that I suddenly had far less time to spend with my women friends. Before I met Mayer, most of my life happened out in the community, not in my apartment. I was always out and about, usually meeting friends for one thing or another — often a different friend each night of the week. Suddenly, after we married, most of my life began happening at home. Mayer just assumed that I would be home most evenings, and that in any case we would plan our evenings together. Of course I wanted to spend time with him too, but I wasn't willing simply to abandon my friends! They were putting pressure on me too, pulling at me from the other direction, asking, "Susan, when can *I* see you?"

I felt torn. When I did take an evening out, Mayer always wanted to know when I planned to be home. I would give him a time, say 10:30, and then find myself calling him at 10:30 to say I would be later. I felt foolish doing that, yet saw that he had a right to know what to expect.

Neither of us was happy about this situation. Whenever I planned an evening out, I felt guilty — and resentful that I felt guilty. Mayer could see that I was trying to cut back and leave time for him, but he felt all the control was in my hands. Our first solution was to negotiate each separate event, but that didn't work. Again, I felt resentful about not being able to plan the slightest thing without checking with him first. And these negotiations became a nuisance for both of us.

We were each trying frantically to balance our own needs against the other's. Our spirit of goodwill was obvious; we each saw and honored the other's need. But neither of us could "give in" to the other without feeling a big loss. Finally, out of my own need to establish a boundary that would work for me, I developed a plan whereby Wednesday night would be my night for myself — every week. Mayer would know I was never available on Wednesdays, and I would know when I could plan my get-togethers with friends. After we put the plan into effect, sometimes I had Wednesdays booked five or six weeks in advance, but at least we both knew where we stood. My plan helped everyone feel good, not only Mayer and me, but my friends, too. We all had control within the plan, and we all had our needs met. The Wednesday-night plan has lasted for twelve years as I write, and continues to work beautifully.

Space

Nancy and George resisted moving in together for a long time, because they feared the negotiations they would have to make over space issues. Their tastes were different: She liked a spare, Japanese feeling; he liked a more "lived-in" look. She had cats; he was allergic to cats. She favored a small, efficient place; he wanted a large, rambling one. They felt they were doing fine living separately. Then Nancy lost her lease, and this nudged them into looking for a place together.

They made it work, because they had enormous goodwill toward each other, and they were both good at setting limits. George said there would have to be common areas where the cats were not allowed to go. Nancy said she would have to have one room that she could keep spare and tidy. They kept looking for a place until they found one that could accommodate both of their needs.

Couples who thrive honor and respect each other's needs. Because they have goodwill toward each other, they easily establish a balance between *guarding* to be sure their own needs get met, and *giving* to be sure their partner's needs get met as well. Since both parts of the balance are there, thriving couples rarely become adversarial in situations like the one George and Nancy faced. They can work together in harmony because they each watch over their own needs. No one is in danger of being swallowed up by the other in their togetherness.

Household Tasks

I encountered very little conflict about household tasks among the thriving couples I interviewed. It was one area where the goodwill between these partners became obvious. Their spirit of fair play led them to divide up tasks in a way that both found equitable. These were not traditional households in which women bear the giant share of household and parenting responsibilities. Husbands shared or took total responsibility for shopping, cooking, cleaning, hiring baby-sit-ters, helping kids with homework, and paying bills. I also found wives who did yard work, household repairs, and car maintenance. Mostly, the chores divided along more traditional lines, but no one felt unduly burdened. In some cases, one partner or another didn't love the chores they had to do, but they agreed that the division of labor was fair.

A man who has goodwill toward his wife cannot fail to see the injustice of her doing most of the housework, especially if she works full-time. Yet, as we know, in many, many households, the woman works full-time and then comes home to a "second shift" of work, while her husband relaxes in front of the TV.

Because the division of household tasks does remain a source of conflict for many couples, and because it so easily highlights the presence or absence of goodwill, let's stop here to do a little experiment.

Experiment #11

---

1. List all the household, family maintenance, and parenting tasks you can think of. Leave three columns to the right of the list.
2. Now, to the right of each item, in the first column, put the initial of the person who does it. In the second, put the amount of time the task takes each week. In the third column, give the task a "pleasantness" rating with 1 being downright distasteful and 5 being extremely enjoyable in the opinion of the person who does the task.
3. Using this data, see whether you think you each carry a fair share of the load. If you are doing this exercise together, do this step by yourselves and then compare answers.
4. If you agree that one of you is doing an unfair share of the work, look at your list again, and find one or two tasks that the person who is doing too much can transfer to the other partner. Consider this an experiment, and reevaluate it after several weeks. If it isn't working, try a slightly different division of labor and experiment with it. It may take some time and effort to switch old patterns. Someone might have to learn how to cook, for example, or how to clean bathrooms or shop for children's clothes, but you will both feel better if your mutual work is evenly divided, and you have years to benefit from the changes.

Money

Jenny and Will had been married for eight years when I spoke to them.

JENNY: Early in our relationship, money emerged as the "biggie." Will was worried about it, and didn't feel comfortable living quite as close to the edge as we were at that time. We had a long-range financial plan in place that looked quite good, so I wasn't too worried, and I didn't feel we had to deprive ourselves excessively until we got to a better place. In the beginning, we were so eager to please each other that we gave in a lot. I would agree not to buy something and feel pretty much okay, and Will would spend some money I wanted to spend and be able to see that it didn't mean our financial ruin.

But then we came to a tough one. I wanted to fly back to Los Angeles for my high-school reunion. Will couldn't see why it was so important, was adamant we couldn't afford it, and tried very hard to talk me out of it. I considered not going, but became certain very soon that this issue was not negotiable for me. I had been a class officer, I had lots of friends in the class, and I wasn't going to miss this reunion. I remember the night it became clear to me; I acknowledged Will's anxiety but told him I simply could not give this up. I told him I did not agree that saving this fairly trivial amount of money was worth my having to miss my high-school reunion. He accepted it. He still didn't like it, but he understood that I had reached a limit and that he had no choice but to accept it. His role switched totally. Now his job was not to work as hard as he could to persuade me of his point of view, but to work at being comfortable with my choice. This was a very different task, and a far less anxiety-producing one as it turned out. I made an important realization because of this incident. I used to think that I always had to negotiate, but now I saw that when something was simply nonnegotiable, my decisiveness actually reduced his anxiety.

Jenny and Will's story reminded me of some of my early conflicts with Mayer about money. Mayer used to say, "We can't afford that." I always pointed out to him that this was his opinion only, not an objective fact. I asked him if he would be willing to say instead, "That's not something *I* feel we should spend money on." It soon got to be a joke between us, because he would say it so often, but it really worked. This sentence put the issue where it belonged — out on the table between us — rather than on his side where he could make a unilateral decision about it.

Couples who thrive do have to negotiate about money sometimes, but their negotiations are made easier because they can trust each other to maintain their own boundaries. If I know I can always persuade you to do things my way, I won't be able to trust the negotiation process. I will have to worry about watching over your needs as well as my own. The ability to maintain your own boundaries is a favor to your spouse as well as to yourself. Thriving couples understand this fundamental principle.

Secrets

Generally speaking, couples who thrive don't keep secrets from each other. A big part of the reason they are so close — and that they value their love so much — is precisely that they can be totally and fully themselves with each other. They have each had the experience of sharing their darkest side — even parts of themselves or their history that they could not accept themselves — with their loved one and still feeling accepted. Sharing of deep secrets is a big part of what constitutes intimacy, and what makes love so valuable.

For many people, deep secrets are not easy to share. I spoke with a man, Kyle, who was engaged to be married to a woman named Ginger. It was to be his third marriage. Kyle was a thoughtful, bright man, concerned about the quality of his relationship, and eager to do whatever he could to make this one work. He told me at some length about the qualities he and his fiancée shared that he felt would make this marriage wonderful. They both loved to garden, dance, and read. They had been delighted to discover early on that they had already read many of the same books. They were comfortable together; she laughed at his corny jokes.

Then he told me, "Ginger doesn't know this is really more like my fifth marriage, if you count the two women I lived with for three years each. I feel she just doesn't need to know all that. I think it might threaten her, and I want to start our life together with a clean slate. I've learned my lessons. I don't think she needs to hear all the sordid details."

Whom was Kyle trying to protect by keeping big, significant parts of his past secret from the woman he loved? If Ginger would really be threatened by the truth, was he doing her a favor by deceiving her into marrying a man whose real past would upset her? Or was he in fact protecting himself from having to reveal parts of his past that shame and humiliate him?

Kyle's secrets were serving no one. If he can love himself only by burying and denying the truth, then his self-love is like the thinnest sheet of ice over a frigid lake. The slightest step in the wrong direction will plunge him into icy waters. Worse, he knows that Ginger's love is based only on the parts of him that she can see. His constant companion is the fear that if she knew the real truth, she would abandon him.

I asked Kyle to imagine what it would be like for him and Ginger to take a weekend retreat together so they would have plenty of time for him to tell her everything. He could tell her not only the parts of the story that he felt ashamed and embarrassed about, but the lessons he feels he has learned now, and the mistakes he knows he will never repeat. If she could accept the real him, their love would be based on trust and forgiveness, and would be deep rather than superficial. The pleasure of sharing pain and humiliation with one who can love unconditionally is greater than the pleasure of dancing or gardening together when the dancers or gardeners are shells of their real selves.

On the other hand, if she couldn't accept the real Kyle, if she was in fact threatened by something in his past, then was this really the woman he wanted to live with for the rest of his life? The marriage would institutionalize Kyle's fears and regrets about his past, and his opportunity to heal his pain would be gone forever. Other people in the world would know Kyle better than his own wife knew him. With his own wife he would have to maintain a facade.

Kyle didn't like my idea, and didn't feel inclined to risk any such weekend retreat. Instead, he gave me a lecture about the importance of privacy in a relationship. "Two people can't merge totally when they marry. There have to be areas they share and areas they keep to themselves. If they feel they have no private territory and that their space could be invaded at any time, they would resent each other. And some people have to be more private than others."

There is definitely some truth in Kyle's statement. But couples who thrive have a different concept of privacy. Their shadow side, the inner self that they have spent years honing and developing, is precisely what couples who thrive want to share with each other. The most valuable, most precious love in the world is the love someone gives you when you can't love yourself. Couples who thrive have shared their most painful secrets with each other and can support each other when the deep secrets rear their ugly heads, as they inevitably will.

Yet there are some areas that the closest of couples do keep private. I had the opportunity to talk separately with several of the thriving couples with whom I worked so that I could ask them each whether there were any secrets they kept from each other. Lou and Cory were one such couple, and Cory was quick to respond, laughing:

> I never tell Lou when I get a parking ticket — if I can help it. He thinks there's no excuse for it, but I'm just a bit more careless than he is. I figure, why upset him? And why embarrass myself? . . . We each have private checking accounts and money that is just ours. I couldn't possibly check with him about every dollar I spend. That's not exactly a secret, but it's private territory. Sometimes, if I want to charge a purchase, especially clothes, I'll pay part of it with cash so the bill looks more reasonable when he sees it. I'm not going to not buy a suit I see in the department store just because he thinks I should do all my shopping at discount places. I don't have to adopt his style, but I figure, why not spare him the pain? That's not a secret; that's setting my boundaries without causing him any anxiety about it. I see it as a little gift to him.
>
> Apart from things like that, there's nothing we need to keep secret from each other — and nothing we'd want to. I mean, for example, if I get a crush on some guy, Lou's the first to know. Not that this happens a lot, but we do both get flirtatious feelings about other people. We'd be dead if we didn't. We both know we're never going to do anything about these feelings — except enjoy them. It's not heavy; it's more like a joke between us. We are so affectionate and loving and communicative with each other, I mean our lives are so enmeshed, nobody else could ever possibly be a threat to what we have with each other. It seems to me, people would have to keep secrets if they didn't trust each other — and then the secrets would erode the trust. I mean if you have secrets, you have a reason not to trust each other. . . . When I say I trust Lou, I don't mean I trust him not to keep secrets from me; I mean I trust that there is nothing in his life that he would need to keep secret from me.

Many of the couples I interviewed echoed Cory's sentiments. They did have private territories in their lives. Many had separate hobbies, separate friends. They claimed private times around the house to read or putter alone. Some had their own private space at home. But they valued their ability to share tough, difficult things with each other. As one man put it, "When we look each other in the eyes, there can't be anything secret between us. It would make a mockery of the experience. To me the whole point of being married is not having to fake anything with each other."

Experiment #12

Write down — or if you don't want to commit it to paper, just think about — any secrets you are keeping from your spouse, any feelings or information you are withholding from him or her. Then write several paragraphs about why you are keeping these secrets. This can be a very revealing exercise.

The only way to learn the pleasure of the closeness that results from not keeping secrets is to experiment slowly with sharing what feels too dangerous to share. Choose one small secret, perhaps something you feel ashamed of, or something you fear your partner will not like. Begin with a secret that is fairly minor in intensity. Find a time when you both feel relaxed and have no schedule to keep. Start by telling your spouse your feelings about this thing: "I feel very ashamed of this," or "I'm afraid this is going to make you angry, but I believe it is interfering with our intimacy for me to keep it to myself. I want to be completely honest with you."

If you feel too much fear to try this experiment, you may want to ask a couples counselor to assist you in doing it, for if you never share what you know are secrets, you are limiting your potential to be truly close — and to thrive.

Emotional Responsibilities

Thriving couples understand the difference between emotional *support* and emotional *ownership*. If you have a problem, I can support you more effectively if I am careful not to take on the problem as my own. If I become emotionally invested in what was originally your problem, there will then be two people with problems and no one left to be a support person. I want to stay close to you, but I also need to maintain some emotional distance from the problem. This is not always easy, but the thriving couples I interviewed had learned — sometimes painfully — how to do it.

When I was asking them about secrets, Mary and Wes told me this story: Wes had dented another car in a parking lot and had decided not to leave a note on the windshield. It would have been his second incident with his insurance company and he was afraid they would raise his rates. He felt quite guilty about it. He told me he was tempted not to tell Mary because he was so embarrassed, but he really wanted her comfort. He wanted to know she could love him, even when he didn't feel good about himself. So he told her.

Mary was angry, but as they talked she made the realization that she did not have to take on his moral transgression herself. It was not she who had made this decision. She disengaged from the guilt herself. Then she was able to be a friend to Wes, and simply to support him in his struggle. They ended up having a good talk about moral dilemmas in general.

The key to the successful resolution of this potential fight was Mary's recognition that she was not responsible for Wes's decision. She was angry initially because she felt implicated. She had to see that she was a separate person from Wes, and that she was not implicated.

Couples who thrive have learned to take an appropriate amount of responsibility in their relationship — not too little, and not too much. They have each learned to disengage emotionally from problems or tasks that belong solely to the other person. For example:

Janet had bouts of depression. At first, Carl couldn't separate himself from her. He worried that there was something wrong with him that made her unhappy. He "took on" her depression, made it his problem, his fault. Worse, he took it upon himself to "fix" her depression. He tried to convince her to go to therapy. He suggested solutions, like having friends over or going to a movie. He began to feel depressed himself, especially when nothing seemed to work. By trying to help, he was actually complicating the problem enormously. Now, on top of feeling depressed, Janet felt guilty. And where there was only one depressed person before, now there were two.

Carl was trying to do for Janet something that only Janet could do for herself. Janet's depression was her problem, her task. Carl had to disengage himself from her depression. He had to realize that he was not responsible for it, and that he could not fix it. By trying to help, he was actually perpetuating and even exacerbating the problem.

Disengaging emotionally from Janet's depression did not mean that Carl had to be indifferent to it. He could still be comforting and supportive to Janet. It simply meant that he would stop taking responsibility for causing or for curing her depression. He could stand by supportively while Janet did — or did not do, if she chose not to —

this work. The matter was out of Carl's hands. What a relief to both of them. Their clear boundaries allowed them to be close, affectionate, and genuinely helpful to each other once again.

In fact, when Carl asked Janet what she felt would be most supportive for her at times when she felt depressed, she asked him to be especially affectionate and loving at those times, but to stop trying to "help" her. She wanted to know that Carl loved her, even when she could not love herself; but it did not help Janet for Carl to become entwined in her emotional problems. His task was to stay clear of the depression himself, so that he could be a strong, loving support for Janet. Carl commented:

> Even after I knew what I was supposed to do, it wasn't always easy because Janet's mood affects me. I didn't blame her for her low moods, but I missed her sunny disposition. I felt bad for her. But it was a great relief to know I didn't have to do anything to help her. Showing my love and support for her was easy.

The emotional challenges and responsibilities that you face are unique to you. Even if you and your partner face the same difficulty, such as a financial setback or a problem with your child, each of you feels the emotion in your own unique way. No one can feel your disappointment or your guilt or your grief for you, and no one can take it away. If a decision is yours to make, no one can make it for you. Thriving couples understand this. They know that support means listening, doing extra favors, hugging, holding, and loving. It does not mean doing another person's emotional work.

Karen and Earl faced a difficult challenge. Their story is an illustration of a struggle being made easier because they cleanly separated their emotional tasks and took responsibility only for their own.

When they married, Karen and Earl had planned to have children. They waited twelve years, until they were thirty-eight, and then found that Karen could not get pregnant. They supported each other through all their attempts at medical intervention, each keeping the other's spirits up, but when they finally agreed to stop trying to conceive, Karen's anguish was almost unbearable. She wanted to adopt a baby, but Earl began to drag his feet. He felt some relief at the idea of not having a baby at all. By now they were over forty. Without Earl's enthusiastic support, Karen felt reluctant to go ahead. The fact was, she felt a great deal of ambivalence herself. Earl never said he wouldn't adopt a baby if Karen had her heart set on it, but if it was going to happen, Karen would have to be the moving force behind it. Gradually, they began to give up the idea. Karen agreed it was the best decision, but she was heartbroken. She was in grief.

This stage would have been complicated if Karen and Earl had not been able to separate their emotional tasks. Although Karen at times felt resentful toward Earl, she did not blame him for her pain. She knew she could have made the adoption happen if she had been highly enough motivated. And Earl did not begrudge Karen her pain. He did not take responsibility for it, and he did not try to make it better. He just held her and let her grieve. Because Karen was able to feel her grief and to experience it fully, in due course she was able to move through it. Although she never could have imagined beforehand that she could be comfortable with a decision to remain childless, she did, after all, make this adjustment.

Karen and Earl's story illustrates the importance of keeping your emotional tasks to yourself. They had a difficult struggle, but it was clean. They both stayed true to what they most wanted, remained willing to be flexible, and did not try to do the other person's work.

Anger is often the hardest area in which to separate emotional tasks. Julie and Michael, who participated in one of my ongoing couples groups, present us with an illustration of how muddy this area can become if boundaries are not maintained.

JULIE: Michael has a temper. One thing that sets him off is my lack of organization — when he can't find things in my office, for example. Or when the kitchen counter gets piled high with junk mail. The problem is, I don't really like being disorganized either. For years, I've tried to get a handle on it. So when Michael would get angry with me, I'd blame myself, and I'd just feel awful. I'd feel like the bad guy, and promise to improve. Then I'd feel guilty when I didn't improve. I felt like I was ruining the relationship by not being able to be better organized.

It was the couples group that changed all this. They pointed out what we couldn't see: that it was not my responsibility that Michael lost his temper. And that I did not have to become organized — which was a futile endeavor anyway — to please him or to keep him from getting angry. If Michael wanted to get angry, that was his problem, not mine. I'm disorganized. I don't like it, but it's a fact. If Michael didn't like that, *he* needed to figure out what to do about his feelings. I couldn't be someone I wasn't for him. You can't imagine how freeing it was to make this realization! It was good for both of us. I couldn't make Michael not be angry. But that's what I was trying to do.

ME: You had to disengage from Michael's anger.

JULIE: Precisely. When Michael got angry, I just went about my business. I would sympathize. Like, "I'm sorry you feel angry." But I knew it wasn't my fault.

MICHAEL: This was hard for me, I have to tell you. I could see the logic of it, but emotionally, it still seemed to me that Julie was the one who screwed up. I couldn't just make myself not be angry. But the fighting stopped. Now it wasn't a fight. It was just that I was angry. So it really did become my problem. I saw that I had a choice: I could get angry or not. Period. It started taking me less and less time to get over my temper tantrums. The real shift came when we started making fun of the anger — not when I was angry, but at other times. I deal with it differently now. I see that it is my problem.

Michael was not accepting Julie for who she was. She was a creative genius, but not especially well organized. His inability to accept her was his problem, not hers. She felt good about who she was until Michael attacked her. She had to work at not letting his attacks undermine her otherwise intact self-esteem.

Many couples told me stories about having to learn to separate their emotional tasks. Jean and Betsy, a lesbian couple, told me that Jean had started out by taking responsibility for Betsy's career. Betsy wasn't sure what she wanted to do and kept experimenting. Jean felt that, to be supportive, she should offer suggestions and then make sure Betsy followed through on them. When Betsy didn't, they both felt they had failed. Betsy felt she had let Jean down, and Jean worried that Betsy would never find meaningful work.

Jean smiled and waved her hand as though to indicate that those times were way behind them. "Now I just tell her, if I can be helpful, let me know."

As we have learned from the field of family therapy, every family is a self-contained system with its own structure. Everyone in the system plays a role in keeping it functioning — or dysfunctioning. As a general principle, *if you find yourself blaming someone else in the family for something, you have to search hard for your own role in keeping the problem afloat.*

For example, it was Wes who dented the car in the parking lot. Mary was angry, and of course, this whole fight seemed like Wes's fault. Mary hadn't dented the car and not left a note. But when Mary searched hard for her role in the fight, she saw that she was angry because she was taking on Wes's morality. If she had been Wes, she would have behaved differently. But she wasn't Wes. She needed to let Wes be Wes, and she needed to be Mary.

Similarly, it seemed as though Carl and Janet's problem was Janet's depression. But a problem between two people never belongs to just one of them. What was Carl's role? His problem was that he was trying to "fix" Janet. When he stopped doing that, their problem ended. Or take Julie and Michael: when Michael couldn't find something in their office, Michael had a right to be angry, right? The problem was Julie's fault. She had misplaced the item. But Michael's role in perpetuating the problem was that he expected Julie to be someone she wasn't.

It is important to understand that disengaging emotionally from your partner's problem does not mean disengaging emotionally from your partner. Quite the contrary: if you can successfully separate yourself from the problem, you can engage with your partner much more effectively. Your partner needs your emotional support — but not your advice, and not your own need to have the problem solved.

Boundary issues continue to emerge throughout a relationship. The more practice a couple gets in identifying their respective territories, the easier this becomes in subsequent negotiations, but the need for vigilance never ceases. You can support your partner in an appropriate, effective way only when you are able to maintain your own boundaries. And when you are good at supporting your partner, supporting becomes a pleasure, an opportunity for both the giver and the receiver to feel and enjoy their love for each other.

When Fences Become Fortresses

So far we have discussed problems that arise when couples have insufficient boundaries or when their boundaries are unclear. But some couples err in the other direction: their fences are too high, too rigid, and too numerous. Most of us know people who are overly self-involved, who build fortresses around themselves to keep other people out altogether, and who would rather forgo intimacy than allow anyone to depend on them for anything.

How did we become so preoccupied with self-sufficiency?

Since the sixties, virtually all the "movements" that have had a major impact on our culture have emphasized autonomy, independence, and self-sufficiency: the Human Potential Movement (Fritz Perls: "I am not in this world to meet your needs."); the Feminist Movement (Gloria Steinem: "A woman without a man is like a fish without a bicycle."); the Recovery Movement (Melodie Beattie: "We are not here to mind other people's business."). All these movements were vital correctives for a generation that grew up being expected to fill predetermined roles, and that had never asked itself, "Who am I, apart from all my roles? What are my very own real needs?" We were reacting against too much dependency and conformity.

The seventies was the "Me Decade," and its impact was to make both men and women more self-sufficient and less dependent on each other, though men and women played this out quite differently. Women recognized that their economic and emotional dependence on men was limiting their potential as human beings and diminishing their self-esteem. They declared their independence from men and launched the contemporary feminist movement. For a time, some women were caught in a dilemma: while they renounced dependence on men in general, at the same time, they craved it with individual men. Magazines were filled with articles about women who couldn't decide whether they wanted to become intimate with a man, or prove that they could live their lives without one.

Men experienced a similar aversion to dependence. In the old system, they ran the world but were dependent on women when they came home. They couldn't wash dishes, change diapers, run the vacuum, or talk about feelings. When women declared their unwillingness to continue managing these responsibilities alone, men did not immediately take over these roles or begin to share them; rather, they began to do without them. The "flight from commitment" became widespread. Fortified by the playboy philosophy, men declared their independence from women and holed up in bachelor flats, freed from emotional or domestic commitments, entirely independent and self-sufficient.

The seventies seems a long time ago, yet for too many of us the pendulum has not yet swung back to center. Many people are still preoccupied with their own independence and self-sufficiency. Their fences are creating not good neighbors, but solitude and self-sufficiency, an unwillingness to become interdependent. And now the recovery movement, for all the healing it has brought about, also makes us cautious about "codependency." So careful are we to avoid becoming codependent that we eschew any dependency at all.

Perhaps the worst lingering fallout from our obsession with independence is the license it has given us to be uncaring. From a government that supported the wealthy and hoped that the poor would take care of themselves, to couples who have lost the art of doing favors for each other, to "commitmentphobes," who choose not to risk expanding their self-sufficient worlds to include the welfare of another person, our culture is filled with overly independent people, people who have forgotten the pleasures of giving, who have lost a spirit of generosity.

The balance between being too dependent and being too self-sufficient is *interdependence*. Interdependent people are those who are independent enough that they do not find it threatening to depend on others or to let others depend on them. Interdependent people recognize the all-important difference between healthy dependency and unhealthy dependency.

Couples who thrive know that healthy dependency is a critical part of every thriving relationship. A person who cannot become dependent on someone else is just as deficient as a person who becomes too dependent. These days, more than "God helps those who help themselves," we need to hear that "God helps those who let themselves be helped."

In thriving relationships, both partners are dependent upon each other, and they are comfortable enough with themselves that they are not threatened by this dependence.

I depend on Mayer to provide me with companionship; to respond to my sexual desires; to be there when I need him; to broaden my circle of friends by including me in his business and social life; to do his share of our family and household maintenance; to parent actively and consistently; to meet his share of our financial agreements, and so on. Before I met him, I did without some of these things or met my needs by myself. Now, I love having him fill many of my needs. I have become quite dependent on him — and vulnerable to him. If he were to leave me or to stop doing some of the things I care about, I would hurt. A long-term intimate connection is simply not possible without a willingness to become dependent — and therefore vulnerable.

Yet I am not aware on a daily basis of my vulnerability to Mayer, because our mutual commitment and our trust level is so obvious to us both. I am, however, aware of how much I depend on him. It is part of the pleasure I feel every day being with him. It is entirely healthy dependency.

What does *un*healthy dependency look like?

You are dependent in an unhealthy way if you depend on someone else to do for you anything that you should be doing for yourself. If you depend on someone else to make you feel good about yourself, you will be in trouble, because no one else can provide you with self-esteem. If you compromise your own standards and acquiesce to your partner's desires in a way that erodes your own integrity, then you have become too dependent, too lazy. If you feel incapable of being self-sufficient and fear that you could not survive on your own, this fear will be a debilitating pressure on your relationship.

Only a strong, independent person can enter into a relationship of interdependence. The more secure you are, the more you can risk. Self-sufficiency and intimacy are not opposites, as many people fear; rather, they complement each other, they complete each other. Self-sufficiency and intimacy — or independence and dependence — form a complete whole. Couples who thrive are not afraid of losing their independence, and they are not afraid of sharing themselves fully. They can do both because they can do each. They are interdependent.

Couples who thrive build fences, not fortresses. They balance their independence with dependence. They divide up their time, their space, their work, their money, their secrets, and their emotional responsibilities carefully between "mine" and "ours." And because they have taken care to do this thoughtfully, they are free to depend and rely on each other, to let go fully into their intimate connection, without fear that they will lose themselves.

Experiment #13

---

1. Assuming you err, at least a little bit, in one direction or the other, are your own boundaries too weak or too strong? Do you have a tendency to give in, to acquiesce to your partner's needs, or to be stubborn and extremely protective of your own needs?

2. Watch for the next situation that confronts you with the basic question, "Should I meet my own needs at my partner's expense, or should I meet my partner's needs at my expense?" Whatever you identified to be your tendency in step #1, deliberately choose the opposite behavior this time. This will be difficult, but give it a try, and see what you find out — about yourself and about your partner.

Experiment #14

Set aside an hour with your partner. (You may end up needing longer, but an hour will get you started.) Take a look at your relationship with regard to the issues of time, space, household tasks, money, secrets, and emotional responsibilities. See if you can identify any obvious boundaries either of you has established. If you discover any areas that continue to create conflicts for you, see if you can establish some mutually acceptable boundaries or guidelines that might resolve the conflict.

Experiment #15

Draw a boundaries map of your relationship by drawing two interlocking circles. The portions of the circles that overlap are your areas of interdependence; the portions of the circles that do not overlap are your areas of independence. In the appropriate portion of the map, list aspects of your life. Vary the size of your circles appropriately. I have provided some sample boundary maps below.

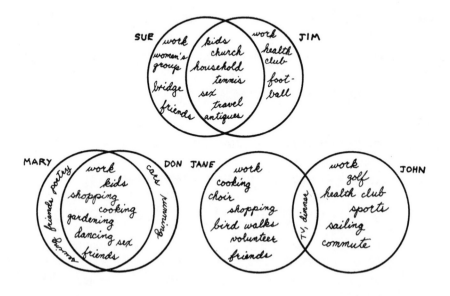

From couples who are not thriving, we often hear about the "power struggles" in their relationship. This widely used phrase implies that there is a limited amount of power, or control, in a relationship, and that a couple must "struggle" to see who is going to end up with how much of it.

Couples who are able to establish and honor their personal boundaries don't have power struggles. In my thirty-two lengthy interviews with thriving couples, I never heard the words "power struggle." More often the unspoken feeling with these couples goes something like this: "I am in control of my own life. I have an unlimited amount of personal power, all that I need to operate happily and effectively in the world. My partner does not limit my personal power, but greatly enhances it. *And* we are together in this life. We are not two separate individuals, but a team. We function as one unit with moving parts. The stronger each moving part is, the stronger the unit. As we strive, never to limit, but to empower each other, we empower our unit."

Clear personal boundaries are the bases for personal power, which is the essential foundation for unlimited couple power.

*   *   *

We have now examined four of the eight essential traits of couples who thrive. Before proceeding to the last four critical traits, let us pause to reflect on the progress you have already made in your own relationship.

Write your answers to these questions in your notebook, or discuss them with your spouse or a friend.

Since you began reading this book,

1. List your favorite ideas from the first four traits.
2. Have your feelings or your attitude about your marriage shifted in any way? How?
3. Has your marriage itself changed in any way? How?
4. Think of several specific incidents between you and your spouse that might have happened differently before you read the first four traits.
5. What specific ideas, little or big, have you thought about using in your own marriage?
6. What specific ideas, little or big, have you actually applied in any way? What are the results?

7. At the beginning of chapter 1, you chose a number indicating how happy you would like your marriage to be. Would you choose the same number now? Why or why not?

8. Are there concepts you find appealing in general but that you feel don't apply to your own marriage? Explain.

9. What have you read that you are skeptical about or disagree with?

10. What questions are lurking in your mind about a thriving marriage? What would you ask me if I were with you right now?

11. Now, tap into your own inner wisdom, and answer the questions you asked in #10 yourself.

12. What is the next step you want to take in your marriage?

$\mathcal{C}hapter\ 6$

TRAIT 5: PERSPECTIVE

E ACH RELATIONSHIP HAS a rhythm of its own. Couples who thrive have learned to identify their rhythms — and to accept them. When adversities or stresses arise, or when the couple is in a period of more distance from each other than usual, they don't panic; instead they trust that they will move through the difficult times and return to the pleasant times.

Over the years of a relationship, there will be ups and downs. The down times may not be very pleasant, but in a relationship of goodwill and commitment, they are not a reason for worry. In fact, just as the rising tension of a musical phrase makes its resolution all the sweeter, so the hard times in a relationship strengthen and enrich the good times.

When I met Rebecca and Jonesy, they were about to celebrate their thirtieth wedding anniversary. Their two sons were planning a party for them. They knew the date, but everything else was to be a surprise. They were extremely relaxed and happy together, joking and giggling about this party, almost as though they were teenagers. But during the course of their interview, I learned that things had not always been so.

After they had been married for five years, they decided to start their own business, manufacturing and selling a distinctive type of jewelry. The business allowed them each to use their talents and to work together, and they were quite excited about it. Rebecca kept her corporate job for a while, but after everything seemed to be going well, she joyfully gave it up. But the business suffered a series of bizarre, unpredictable setbacks. A combination of bad luck and inexperience led their incipient business into a rapid decline. They were both terribly disappointed. They were anxious about their finances, and couldn't agree on what to do next.

REBECCA: It was an awful time. We were so happy and secure when we got married. We thought we had a guardian angel who had brought us together and made everything happen magically. We found an incredible house; I got pregnant the first month we tried. We had this incredible woman for day care right across the street. When everything started to shatter so fast, we weren't prepared. By far the biggest problem was not the business failing, but the tension and distance between us. It was so heartbreaking. Somehow we blamed each other, and we just couldn't recapture our magic.

JONESY: You know, neither of us talked about this at the time, but we both admitted later that we were afraid the other was going to leave.

REBECCA: We didn't have enough experience to know that the problem wasn't us and our relationship; it was the stress we were under. It was too soon in the relationship. It was just too much all at once. . . . Thank heaven, our guardian angel appeared again: Jonesy got a good job offer, just in the nick of time — just before we put our house on the market in desperation.

JONESY: And I'll tell you, it was amazing. Almost the day I got the job, it all shifted. It was as though the dark cloud just vanished. One night — this has now become a famous story — we stayed up until four-thirty. (I had to go to work, too.) We just talked it all through. We saw what we couldn't see when we were in the thick of it. And we just clung to each other. The thought of losing what we had terrified us, but we also knew we would never let this happen to us again. I mean, it just wouldn't happen again. Because now we knew.

REBECCA: We've had plenty of tough times since then, but now we always say, "I think we better stay up 'til four-thirty tonight!," and that's about all it takes. I mean, we can always get things in perspective now.

Jonesy and Rebecca made talking until 4:30 in the morning a little in-joke. Although their ordeal — and their breakthrough — felt very serious to them at the time, they are able to make light of it now that they have some distance from it. Their ability to laugh at themselves is an indication of their capacity to keep their difficulties in perspective. I saw this same sense of humor in most of the other thriving couples I spoke with.

Among the couples I have worked with, I have seen a great deal of misunderstanding about humor. People virtually always put "sense of humor" on their lists of qualities they enjoy in their mate. Yet when these same couples get into conflicts with each other, they don't have much of a sense of humor about it at all. For having a sense of humor does not mean being a clown or a comedian or laughing at someone else's jokes. People with very little sense of humor can do those things. Having a sense of humor means having the ability to see the humor in situations that are not so obviously funny. It means having flexibility in your personality. Above all, it means being able to laugh at yourself, at your shortcomings and imperfections, to place your own situation in the grand scheme of the cosmos, rather than making your situation the cosmos. For example, it is important to maintain high hopes, to cherish lofty ideals. But it is equally important to be able to laugh at the gap between these fond goals and your real, human self. To have a sense of humor is to avoid taking things more seriously than is appropriate, to keep them in perspective.

Couples who thrive have the ability to maintain their perspective about themselves, each other, and their relationship. They would love their world to be perfect, but when it inevitably falls short, they are able to laugh — or at least smile — and move on.

All the couples I interviewed talked of ups and downs in their relationships, and always without anxiety or anguish. They were unflappable. It was the untroubled quality with which they related even the most painful of circumstances that caught my attention. The air of serenity and security about them was unmistakable.

Perspective about good times and bad in a relationship comes from living through some of each, and then drawing back to look at and remember the big picture. It is the ability to hold on to the distant remembrance of good times during difficult times, and it means having the wisdom to know that the good times will return — as they have before. As one woman put it to me, "When we're feeling discouraged or depressed, part of the feeling is the sense that we have always been depressed and that we will always be depressed. But in my head, I know this isn't true, and it is that *thought* that gives me comfort and keeps me going."

Perspective is one of the great prizes that couples who endure get to enjoy and that short-term couples don't know they could ever have.

But even couples who endure can develop perspective only if they cultivate their capacity to keep the big picture of their relationship in mind. Even if for only fleeting moments at a time, they must be able to observe their marriage and the difficulties they may be going through almost as an outsider would, detached from the emotion involved. If a couple can at times become observers of their own marriage, then their history — all the challenges and rich, delicious times they experience together — creates their perspective. They know that between the periods of growth, uncertainty, and transition, they will enjoy periods of calm, when they will be able to savor what they have learned and feel secure and pleased with themselves. And then — *boom!* Another challenge will present itself. But every new challenge is easier now because the couple already has a storehouse of wonderful times, and they can draw on an inner confidence that their good feelings will return again.

Anxiety and Intimacy

One lesson that the thriving couples I interviewed had to learn on their way to developing a perspective about their relationship is that anxiety and intimacy are incompatible.

Couples who thrive expect that they are going to be able to help each other through tough times. Several couples mentioned the shock and fear they experienced the first time they faced a hard time, and, instead of being able to rely on each other for support, found that they were emotionally distant, or that they had a hard time connecting at all.

When one or both partners are anxious or depressed or completely preoccupied with work or a family matter, the quality of closeness and connectedness between the two partners is adversely affected. If I am close to someone, it means I have my attention on that person. I am able to be attentive toward him, to be aware of how he is affecting me. I am able to listen fully, to engage in an interaction. When a large part of my energy is given over to dealing with some anxiety in my life, I will not be able to give that kind of attention to my partner. Not just in an intense, passionate interaction, but even on a normal evening or a Sunday excursion or a day of puttering around the house, the general ease, the flow, the ability to enjoy each other's presence just isn't there if one or both people are anxious or under stress. And it is hard to give yourself fully to making love if you are worried or preoccupied.

If a couple doesn't realize that it is the anxiety or stress that is causing their diminished intimacy, they may exacerbate an already strained situation by blaming each other, and by doubting their whole relationship. When you are feeling distant or cool toward your partner, it is difficult to remember what it felt like to feel close. You may not even be able to imagine that you will ever feel close again.

Couples who have perspective have learned to have confidence, even though it is hard to feel close when they are stressed out. They know that when the anxiety-producing situation is resolved, they will feel close again.

Learning this lesson can be very scary, as it was for Jonesy and Rebecca. Another woman I know, Ellen, went to law school when her two children were six and ten. Her generous and good-natured husband fully supported her, and helped her by taking over her share of housework. But she had a long commute and endless hours of study, and it all began taking its toll on the relationship. A year after law school was over and Ellen had passed her bar exam, she told me,

> Our relationship was really in bad shape, especially during the last year of law school. We were fighting all the time. The house was filled with tension. We were both upset and sad — and we just didn't get it. We didn't realize that the problem was not us — it was law school. As soon as law school was over, the problems evaporated. We were back to our old selves. It was an enormous relief.

Many (although not all, as we shall see in a moment) of the happy couples I interviewed had lives that were more or less free of long-term, chronic stress. And I began to ask myself: Are they happy because they are stress-free? Or are they stress-free because they are happy?

For the most part I believe the same qualities that keep couples thriving also keep them relatively free of long-term, chronic stress as individuals. These are people who want to be happy, who want to feel good, who want to enjoy their lives and their relationships. They believe that this is possible, and they are committed to making it happen. They don't leave these matters up to fate; they take control over them. For the most part, they have work that they enjoy and that they feel makes good use of their talents. Many of them have children, and many are two-career couples, so they don't have simple lives, but they are unwilling to live with long-term stress, and they have found ways to manage it. Whenever they find themselves in unavoidable stressful circumstances, they know that their problem is the stress and not the relationship. They are well aware that this is a passing episode, and they either deliberately take care of the relationship in the meantime, or simply get out of each other's way until the episode is over.

I heard several examples of generally stress-free couples managing stress quite systematically when it did occur. We heard earlier about John and Carla's challenge. John had a difficult six-month stretch when he was developing three new courses. Since he and Carla were not getting the time together that they were used to, they noticed that they began to fight and bicker.

"We knew we were fighting because we just weren't getting the time together that we needed," Carla said. "But we also knew that the semester would be over, and that this wasn't a permanent situation. In fact, it was a big step forward, because John was getting to teach the courses he really wanted to teach. So we basically just waited it out." John's semester was just ending when I spoke with them, and they were already laughing about the triviality of some of their fights.

In another example of a couple's managing episodic stress, Wendell was a physician with a part-time practice, and Elizabeth was a corporate lawyer. When the recession caused a major slump in the law firm's business, Elizabeth was asked to cut back her hours, and then eventually to leave the firm. It was an emotional and financial setback for them. Elizabeth was unprepared for such a turnaround and felt stunned and anxious about her future. Wendell, meanwhile, was greatly enjoying working part-time. He could take on major household responsibilities, spend a lot of time with their children, and have time to pursue his other passion, tennis. The law firm's setback meant he had to raise his medical practice to full-time, a big change for him.

WENDELL: It is stressful, but I don't feel bad about it. I just see it as a contribution I have to make. What is harder is Elizabeth's decision about what to do next. We are working very hard to view the whole thing as an opportunity.

ELIZABETH: I never thought I would work for the law firm forever. I sort of welcome the chance to be forced to look at other alternatives. But it is also scary. It won't be that easy to just pop over to something else.

ME: What kind of impact is all this having on your relationship?

ELIZABETH: Our relationship is the only thing that is going well right now!

Mayer and I learned about the effects of stress on relationships first-hand the year he bought and renovated a house with the idea of selling it — and then couldn't sell it. As the months went by and we were carrying both the mortgage and the renovation loan, our anxiety escalated. We worked very hard at supporting each other, but anxiety is such a personal experience — no one can feel it for you, and no one can make it go away. We each retreated into ourselves. We could feel the difference, and we would comment on it: we just weren't "there" for each other. Our lovemaking became sort of plain vanilla. We felt as though we were treading water.

As we look back on that year, we realize it was important that, even though we didn't feel like it, we took several weekend retreats for ourselves. They gave us the impetus to slow down and reconnect, to forget our worries as much as we could for a time, and to focus on each other in a way we found hard to do at home.

When we finally decided to give up on selling the house and move into it, we were like a new couple again. The relief, the fun of the new house, and, above all, our renewed closeness, turned everything around almost overnight. The experience added immeasurably to our perspective, to our long-range view of our marriage.

Something else we noticed during that experience and that other couples echoed was that we had a tendency to balance each other's moods. We functioned as an organism, and, without giving conscious attention to it, compensated for each other. When Mayer was especially down, I would find the chipper part of myself and carry us along. Then just as I became exhausted and felt like giving up, Mayer would find new energy and would buoy us along for a time. I found other thriving couples relied on this natural rhythm also; they learned to sense the intensity of each other's moods and give attention to the person with the greatest need at the moment. As one man put it, "She's my sun on a cloudy day, and I'm her port in a storm."

Long-Term Stress

All the happy couples I interviewed told me about stressful episodes in their lives that they survived and that contributed to the perspective they had about the way relationships ebb and flow.

But what about couples who are under stress, not just occasionally, but all the time? Unprecedented sources of anxiety plague couples today. The recession has created terrible financial stress for countless families. Pressures on those who are still working is greater than ever and workaholism is rampant. The corporate world thrives on stress. Two-career couples with children can sometimes barely ever see each other, let alone be close.

It is easy for couples in these circumstances to lose their sparkle and settle into ho-hum relationships just because stress has become a way of life for them, and they don't realize the toll it is taking on their relationship. Instead of blaming their financial woes or the demands of parenting or their exhausting schedules or her intolerable boss or his health problem, they blame each other, or assume this is the way life is and simply lower their expectations about marriage. Unwittingly, they let their comfortable distance become their life. They let stress defeat them.

Some couples under these circumstances may maintain the trappings of a close relationship. They may make love regularly and be pleasant to each other, but inside, they worry that they don't feel enough passion. Other couples may become more openly tense with each other, bickering and arguing. But in neither case do they realize that long-term, ongoing stress is the culprit, and that it is virtually impossible to be stressed out and close at the same time.

Some of the happy couples I interviewed also lived with stress that was more enduring in nature and not given to simple remedies. Most of the chronic stress I heard about was related to having small children or financial worries, or both. But for these couples perspective (the ability to place their day-to-day hassles in a larger picture, and the ability to laugh at themselves) was most important.

One two-career couple with a new baby — also a doctor/lawyer combination — have a policy they call "mood, schmood." It means they make love no matter how exhausted or "not in the mood" they are.

"It really works," Adrienne told me. "It's amazing how you can get in the mood if you just get started." They laughed. Both Adrienne and her husband, Clen, are athletic, and they miss their hikes and weekend trips to the mountains. But they view this as a temporary loss and plan to resume their outings as soon as their daughter is old enough. Clen told me,

> Children are a certain amount of work. As far as I can tell, you have only two alternatives: You can either pay someone to do some of it, or you have to cut something else out of your life, and do it yourself. It's really only a few years that children are small, and I can't imagine anything more important than spending lots of time with them during

those years. But other stuff just has to go. It's a choice. If you don't want to give up those other things, don't have children.

Jeff and Gail started their own consulting business and their family at the same time. When I spoke to them, they were three years into their business and had a four-year-old and an infant. As Jeff put it to me, "It's intense." They were definitely under a great deal of stress all the time. But no one could miss their buoyant attitude and their ardent love for each other. They didn't like the stress, which they described to me at length, but they still considered themselves very lucky and happy. What made everything work for them was that their relationship with each other remained their top priority.

Theresa and Peter were perhaps the most stressed couple I observed. They had both been aching for a relationship when they met and fell madly in love. She was forty-two, so they wanted to start a family right away and were four months into the pregnancy when they got married. They were ecstatic. But the recession hit during their first year together, and Peter's small retail importing business slowed way down. Theresa was an account executive for a computer services firm, a job she tolerated. She took a four-month leave when the baby was born, but then she simply had to go back to work. They needed her income more than they ever dreamed they would. Her commute and long work hours meant she was exhausted all the time, and felt terrible that she rarely had quality time with her daughter. They tried to find solutions. Peter couldn't simply abandon his business. Theresa's firm wouldn't let her job-share or work part-time, and no other jobs she looked at offered any better conditions.

In the end, they formulated a two-fold plan: First, they resolved to make the time they could get together as high-quality as possible. They made certain they talked about what was going on between them, and they basically had a "mood, schmood" policy too, although they didn't call it that. And second, they formulated a long-range plan and put it into place as quickly as they could. Peter began closing down his business and taking steps to look for a teaching job. It would probably mean a move to a different city, but they were quite prepared to do that and hoped to find a town with a much lower cost of living than the large city where they lived.

In one way or another, every thriving couple I spoke with used some variation of the same two strategies Theresa and Peter developed as a way of managing stress, whether the stress was episodic or long-term:

1. They recognized that anxiety and free-flowing intimacy are basically incompatible, and that a concerted effort to nurture and sustain at least a minimal level of closeness must be made during times of stress.

2. They identified the source of their stress, and began executing an explicit plan to eliminate it.

As I was isolating these two strategies, I became curious to see whether they were also used by couples whose relationships were not thriving. As I had suspected, I found that in my small sample, the strategies were conspicuously missing. These couples, instead of making a concerted effort to manage stress, were actually creating it. Instead of working to be sure they did get some quality time together, they were using stress as a way to maintain distance. And they did not have a plan for somehow changing their lives so they could eliminate their stress; they had simply become resigned to it.

A relationship that is in a period of stress can be compared to fallow land (land that is not being cultivated for a season or more). It just lies there, quietly nourishing itself and waiting. The soil is still rich and fertile, but no one has planted anything new.

Relationships go through seasons like this, whether they are undergoing stress or not; its just the natural rhythm of life. But couples who thrive do not get attached to these low-energy times in their relationship. They have confidence that the fallow periods will be followed by rich harvest, perhaps even richer because of the period of rest. The off-season may not be just fallow; it is sometimes violently stormy. Couples who thrive don't enjoy the storms, but they don't worry about them; because they have the perspective of years together, they know that the storms or dry seasons will pass, and that periods of abundance will always follow.

Experiment #16

---

1. Make a list of the sources of stress or anxiety in your relationship right now. Are they temporary or long-term?
2. Are you in a period of closeness and excitement in your relationship right now, or are you in a "fallow" phase? How long has this phase been going on? Write a short paragraph saying why you think you are in the phase you are in now and how long you think it might last.

3. If you have long-term, chronic stress in your life, work on the two guidelines thriving couples use in this circumstance:

    a) Set up some ways to nurture and sustain at least a minimal level of closeness. For example, plan ten or twenty minutes every day when you focus only on each other and talk only about positive topics. Plan some playtime with each other every week. Plan a thirty-minute conversation about the topic that is troubling you in which you talk about how you feel for the first half and then try to think of solutions during the second half. Make a special effort to spend time together every day.

    b) Identify the source of your stress and develop a long-range plan to eliminate it. This may require quite a bit of discussion and strategizing. When you arrive at a plan, write down the preliminary steps you will need to go through along with the dates by which you hope to accomplish your intermediate goals.

Viewing Problems as Opportunities

Conflicts and disharmony within a relationship are painful, and, because pain is unpleasant, most couples naturally do everything they can to avoid it. They tend to think of problems as a sign that their relationship is less than ideal and to believe that if they were more compatible, their lives would be smoother.

Couples who thrive have a fundamentally different view of problems. They understand that difficulties in their relationship represent an opportunity for them to learn and to grow. One of the biggest secrets of great relationships is that the partners understand that pain caused by their relationship can be generative. Of course it isn't pleasant or easy, but it is nevertheless welcome because it allows their relationship to move forward. Couples who thrive are not threatened by problems because, whatever the difficulty is, it is taking place within the context of their mutual goodwill, love, and commitment. If they are willing to learn from their pain rather than resist it or run from it, they will gain insight about themselves as individuals and as a couple.

If you have been lifting heavy objects all day and you experience pain in your back, you pay attention because your body is giving you a signal. You will probably alter your behavior the next day and find out what you need to do to strengthen your back to avoid future problems.

Problems in a relationship are a signal in the same way. *A conflict with your spouse is an opportunity for you to find and then heal your own inner wounds.* For example, when you reach an impasse with your spouse, what may be going on inside you underneath the superficial fight is something like this: "I know you are going to hurt me as my parents did, so I can't open my heart to you. I need to keep focusing on the negative parts of our relationship so I can justify keeping my heart closed."

Couples who are locked into negative patterns like this one have to move slowly to learn how to trust. They start by realizing at a conscious level, "This person is not my parent and is not malicious. This person has goodwill toward me. This behavior may seem like my parents', but this person is different." Each time couples risk trusting a little more, the trust between them builds.

Couples who don't recognize the conflicts in their relationships as opportunities, or who don't have a feeling of goodwill toward each other, treat a difficulty as something to be disposed of rather than something to be learned from. The difference is immense.

It takes persistence to stay with a conflict long enough to learn from it rather than cleaning it up on the surface and sweeping it under the rug. What gives couples that kind of persistence? One thing: They *believe* that if they persist through the difficult parts, they will learn, and they will emerge stronger as individuals and closer as a couple. That belief in challenge as a great teacher is one of the most significant traits that distinguishes couples who thrive from couples who don't.

A desire for personal growth and a belief that challenges can lead to spiritual and psychological breakthroughs place every marital conflict, from the smallest argument to the largest battle, in a distinctive light. I saw this quite clearly in my own family during the first several years I was married. As I mentioned earlier, my husband's son, Gabe, was eleven and living with my husband full-time when Mayer and I met. I was eager to be the loving mother Gabe had never had and threw myself enthusiastically into that effort. Too enthusiastically from Gabe's point of view. He saw me as unwelcome competition for his dad's attention, and he had plenty to sort out for himself before he was ready to take on a relationship of the sort I hoped for.

I had to struggle hard every day to avoid taking his rejection personally. And his antagonism toward me made me furious at times. I felt rage I never knew I had inside me. My husband felt torn between the two of us and often wasn't sure what to do.

We were acquainted with another couple at the time who seemed very much in love but who had been unwilling to work through the stresses of blending their two families and had given up and gone their separate ways. Also, we had access to an alternative living situation for Gabe that would have left us free to be with each other. If we had been operating on the most common model of avoiding problems and pain, we almost certainly would have taken one of those two options because the stress became unbearable at times. But because we both valued our own (and Gabe's) personal and spiritual growth and believed we could learn from this unexpectedly painful situation, we persisted with it. Excerpts from my journal at the time are revealing:

> This is really, really hard. But there is a part of me inside that knows that I'm going to be a wiser, more mature person if we can ever get through this. I have gone beyond limits in my own behavior I never thought I'd come up against let alone cross. But it's clear, at the same time I'm angry or hurting I still have a feeling underneath somewhere that I'm glad I'm having this experience. I wouldn't want to miss it. It is just what my life is right now, and if anyone can handle it, I can. I am learning so much. I'm getting a lot of practice in setting boundaries. I see clearly my tendency to be too lenient with Gabe so he'll like me. I do that elsewhere in my life, too, and this is a good laboratory to work on setting limits. I'm grateful for this whole experience. It is a challenge. I know that Mayer and I are building respect for each other and getting to experience what "support" is all about. And I fully trust that some day, I'll have a really good relationship with Gabe. This is what life is about. We could have Gabe live [elsewhere], but we'll never do it.
>
> I always thought I needed to be "happy." But now I understand that what I want is to feel good about myself. Well, this whole thing with Gabe gives me the chance to see myself in action in situations that require some skill, some judgment, some restraint, and trying a whole new behavior, and when I do well, I get to feel really good about myself. (And when I screw up, I get to practice not putting myself down for it.) A relationship is not about having no problems or challenges. It's about learning to handle the problems and challenges well. A lot of times this isn't pleasant, but I do feel that it is very, very good. I'm glad to be here. I'm doing what I need to do right now. The main thing is not to fight it and wish it were otherwise, but just to accept what is, welcome each day, and do the best I can.
>
> People don't have children to make their lives easier — but to make their lives richer. Well, "richer" comes in some strange packages.

I recently saw an exhibition of photographs of old people. They were beautiful portraits of people with deeply creased faces and bright, dark eyes. Several times I heard the viewers make comments like this: "How wise this person looks. How I wish I could hear all she has learned in her many years. Her face has such beauty and character and depth." These people acquired their wisdom by living rich lives, full of challenges. They earned their faces. I think I sensed when I wrote my journal entry that I was in one of those situations in which I could learn deep lessons that could be learned in no other way.

I learned day by day when I was in the middle of this situation. But after some time passed, I found I was able to see even more clearly what some of the important lessons for me were. In the words of nineteenth-century Swiss philosopher Henri Frédéric Amiel,

> To understand things, we must have once been in them, and then to have come out of them; so that first there must have been captivity and then deliverance, illusion followed by disillusion, enthusiasm by disappointment. The person who is still under the spell, and the person who has never felt the spell, are equally incompetent.
>
> We only know well what we have first believed, and then judged. To understand we must be free, yet not have been always free. The same truth holds whether it is a question of love, of art, of religion, or of patriotism.

Only if you graciously accept the struggles, adversities, and conflicts with which your partnership — and your life — present you, and recognize them as opportunities for wisdom and strength will you gain the understanding Amiel talks about, or the richness I wrote about in my journal.

Intimacy Causes Pain

Intimate relationships cause pain. If you have gotten into a relationship as a way to end the struggles in your life, you may have been better off staying single, because love naturally creates tensions and clashes. The attitude with which you approach a marital altercation helps determine its outcome. If you regard it as a defeat, a sign of your weakness as a couple, or an indication that you have married the wrong person, then the quarrel will be all the more painful, and you are not likely to learn from it. If, on the other hand, you are able to see the fighting itself as a learning opportunity, the problem will be easier to solve, and you will be more likely to grow from the conflict because you will be looking for the learning in the situation.

Since it is important to expect conflict as a part of a close relationship in order to make the most of it, we should understand exactly how intimacy itself actually causes pain.

Intimacy is the process of stripping away your outer, more public ways of being, and sharing your inner life with another person. Some of the parts of that inner life will be painful, humiliating feelings of low self-esteem, guilt, or regret. Part of becoming close with someone is feeling and sharing those deep, old wounds.

Another reason a healthy intimate relationship is likely to cause you pain is simply that, for most of us, love has never been a pure, uncomplicated experience. When you fall in love, you experience the pleasure of loving and being loved by another person in the present moment. But at the same time, you experience the pain that has been associated with love for you in the past. Love is exciting, but it also feels like the pain of the last person who rejected your love, the wounds from people who have loved and then abandoned you, the ache of trust that has been betrayed. At the same time that you are drawn toward the pleasure of love, you will want to distance yourself from all this hurt. You will feel conflict and confusion, approach and avoidance. This is hard, but the positive side of it is that this love offers you the opportunity to heal these old wounds, to love and be loved in a different way this time. This is how intimacy causes pain, and this is why it is critical to view the struggles within a relationship as an opportunity for spiritual and psychological growth.

Consider the alternative: If you resist sharing your vulnerable inner self, if you keep your self-doubts and your painful old stories hidden, then you are in essence closing your heart. You won't have to look at the pain, but you won't be available to love or to receive love either. It is not easy, but this willingness to be open to the pain of love as well as the pleasure is the only path to a thriving love relationship.

If you seek only the pleasure of love and you hope to avoid the pain, then, in the words of poet Kahlil Gibran,

> *It is better for you that you cover your nakedness and pass out of love's threshing floor,*
> *Into the seasonless world where you shall laugh, but not all of your laughter, and weep, but not all of your tears.*

Intimacy, in all its pain and pleasure, is a great teacher. And it will allow you to experience parts of yourself that you can never experience alone. Alone, you can never find out how other people view you. You can never find out how well you endure in a long-term relationship, how generous or self-serving you are, how able you are to resolve conflicts, to offer support, to receive support. Intimacy will force you to face most of the fundamental issues of life: your family history, your personality idiosyncrasies, your goals in life, how you communicate, how you manage your feelings, whether and how you become committed, how you love, and how you receive love. Marriage is a rich learning environment — if you are willing to let obstacles teach you rather than defeat you.

Viewing problems as opportunities for growth is also one of the best insurance policies against boredom in a relationship, for there is always something else to learn about yourselves and each other. And the pleasure you get from observing changes in each other and from sharing little victories along the way is one of the great treasures of a long-term relationship. Virtually every couple I interviewed who had been married for more than eight or ten years reported major changes they had worked for and achieved over their years together.

Like all couples, couples who thrive have fears. But happy couples ask themselves not, "Am I afraid?," but "Am I going to let fear keep me from getting the closeness and love that I want in my relationship?" As writer John Welwood reminds us, while some would say that love is letting go of fear, it is probably more accurate to say that love is making friends with fear.

Couples who thrive have met their demons and made friends with them. They don't have to live with the fear that old wounds, painful regrets, or deep insecurities will rise up and destroy them, for they know these demons. They have shared their own with each other, and have thus divested them of much of their power. They understand that courage is not the absence of fear, but the ability to act in the presence of fear.

Experiment #17

Recall a challenge or a major hurdle that you have had to overcome in your relationship together. Together, discuss what you learned from it.

Do you think that you, as a couple, have a tendency to shy away from challenges, to paper over difficulties and try to ignore them? Or do you face challenges directly with the belief that, in the end, overcoming them will make you stronger, better people?

Happiness and pure joy are not the only yardsticks for measuring flourishing relationships. An equally important one is how well you weather the struggles and hardships that every relationship presents. Working through problems together makes you more secure with each other. You begin to realize, "If we got through that, we can tackle anything." You gain respect and gratitude for your partner and for yourself. And above all, you gain the valuable perspective that can carry you through future challenges more easily.

Chapter 7

TRAIT 6: RELATIONSHIP-ENHANCING

COMMUNICATION

THE QUALITY OF communication in a relationship is a decisive factor in whether it is able to thrive. A few simple principles, thoroughly understood and regularly practiced, can turn failing relationships around, and send already thriving relationships into the stratosphere. They are essential skills for friendship, for intimacy, for parenting, for any business or service that wants to offer customer satisfaction, for supervision and management, and for negotiating, whether it be an agreement between two people or a treaty between two nations. Virtually every relationship can be improved by the use of these simple principles and will be weaker without them.

Yet there is still widespread resistance to learning and using them.

The happy couples I interviewed almost universally reported that their communication is good; in fact, they usually mentioned their "good communication" early and with pride and pleasure. But as I questioned them in more depth, I discovered that, in many cases, they didn't think about or even necessarily know communication "rules." What they meant when they said they had good communication was one or more of the following: They had relatively few communication impasses; they were able to talk easily about difficult subjects; they felt they understood each other; they withheld very little from each other; and they could rely on their ability to resolve conflicts.

Those are the goals couples want to achieve when they learn communication "rules." Couples who have an abundance of goodwill may not be aware of the rules or skills they use in order to achieve good communication; they may simply be using them naturally. But I also spoke with many thriving couples who had learned specific communication skills from books, workshops, marriage counselors, or even magazine articles, and who had used them to great advantage.

All the important communication tools can be reduced to five basic skills. They are free, non-fattening, and legal. They can provide you with immense personal satisfaction. Your skills can be a generous gift to others. If you learn and use them, you will be able to give more to the people you love. You will achieve more of what you want in life, and you will be capable of achieving great riches in your human relationships.

They are:

1. Make "I" statements, not "You" statements
2. Listen
3. Understand and accept the differences between men and women
4. Ask for what you want
5. Affirm others

You can learn these skills simply by reading this chapter. Then, you'll need to practice them by using them in real-life situations that call for them, and the more you practice, the better you'll become.

1. Make "I" Statements, Not "You" Statements

When you are angry with someone or you feel very hurt by that person, your natural tendency is to say something like what Beth says in this hypothetical scene:

> BETH: You never pay any attention to me, and then you spent all that time with Sarah at the party. How do you think that made me feel? You just don't think about what you do. You're so thoughtless sometimes. Do you love me or not?

These are "you" statements. They blame, accuse, and criticize the person you are angry with. Beth's partner has virtually no alternative but to feel blamed, accused, and criticized. It is extremely unlikely that he will agree that he is thoughtless and never pays any attention to Beth. His natural reaction will be to defend himself:

ROBERT: What do you mean? That conversation with Sarah was nothing. I spend lots of time with you.

Then he is also quite likely to make some of his own "you" statements.

You are so sensitive. You're ridiculous. You react to the tiniest thing.

This scene would be completely different if Beth had used "I" statements. An "I" statement is a report about how you feel or how you experienced something. It says nothing about the other person.

BETH: Robert, I'd like to talk with you about something. I feel hurt — and a little bit scared — about the amount of time you spent with Sarah at the party. I know it may be irrational, but I've been feeling kind of distant from you anyway lately. It just seems like we haven't had that much time together.

Now Beth has given Robert some information about herself. Her statement is much more likely to elicit concern and caring from Robert than defensiveness — especially if this is a relationship where there is goodwill — because Beth is talking about a problem *she* is having.

ROBERT: Gee, Sweetheart. I had no idea you were feeling that way. I'm so sorry. Let's talk about it.

This simple device, making an "I" statement when you are upset, can make a staggering difference in a relationship. It can actually transform what might otherwise be a fight into a constructive and even very close, warm conversation. Most people use "you" statements spontaneously when they are emotionally charged. But as soon as you catch yourself doing it, stop. Shift gears, and make an accurate "I" statement. Simply let the other person know how you feel.

Listen to the difference:

You spend too much money on clothes! You aren't thinking about the big picture!

vs.

I feel very anxious when you spend that much money on clothes. I feel like there is a big iron vise in my stomach.

You always interrupt me!

vs.

I feel like I don't get to finish what I want to say.

You forgot to bring home milk *again*?

vs.

I'm feeling really annoyed right now.

Using "I" statements, together with the second skill we will discuss, listening and reflecting back what you heard, a couple should be able to work through virtually any anger, hurt, or difficult feelings they have without fighting.

Experiment #18

To get some practice making "I" statements, so you can begin to develop the habit, think of something that is bothering you right now, and make some "I" statements about it — either to yourself or to the person who is annoying you.

---

2. Listen

When we hear about the need for "good communication skills," we usually think about talking — expressing ourselves more clearly, saying things in the right way, getting our message across. In fact, however, 98 percent of good communication is listening.

Effective listening is probably the most widely taught communication skill, and also the most widely ignored and abused.

The reason is simply that in situations where effective listening is most important, the listener is usually more focused on his or her own needs than on those of the person who needs to be listened to.

Listening means putting yourself in the other person's shoes. It means trying to understand a different point of view before you try to make yourself understood. It means empathizing — that is, identifying with or vicariously experiencing — the feelings, thoughts, or attitudes of another person. That's all. It couldn't be simpler.

Contrary to the belief of some, listening is not a highly refined skill that is reserved for deep, intimate conversations or delicate negotiations. Rather, it is a simple habit, that, unless you are living alone on a desert island, you will have numerous opportunities to use every day.

Let's look first at some extremely common situations in which listening is called for. First we will hear a typical *nonlistening* response. Later, we will see what an effective listening response would be.

Store clerk: Gee, we seem to be out of that.

Customer: No, you can't be! I called this morning, and I just drove twenty-five miles to come pick one up! I need it tonight.

Store clerk: I've been here all day, and no one told me you called. We missed a delivery last week, so we are out of a few other items too. We'll be getting more in next week.

The clerk immediately becomes defensive. She tries to get the customer to understand her point of view by explaining what happened. She sees only her own position. She is seeking not to understand but to be understood. Her message is, "It's not *my* fault, don't bother *me*, this isn't *my* problem."

If the store clerk had been listening, and had put herself in the customer's shoes and empathized, she would have said, "Oh, how frustrating for you! You need it tonight? I am so sorry we are out! I don't blame you for being upset." Then, of course, she could see whether she might actually help the customer by calling another store or looking in the warehouse or suggesting a close substitute. But first, she would be conveying that she understood the woman's frustration, and she would be validating it. Her understanding and validation would probably allow the woman to stop venting her fury and move on to finding a solution.

Parent: Johnny, you have to wear your raincoat!

Johnny: No, Mom. I don't want to!

Parent: Don't argue with me. Just put it on!

The parent is thinking of herself. She doesn't want to be argued with; she wants the raincoat on. If she had been listening and seeking to understand, she would have said, "You really don't want to wear that raincoat, do you? It's really got you unhappy." Then she could ask him why he doesn't want to wear it or enlist his help in solving the problem of staying dry in some other way. But first, she would be conveying that she understood his feelings and desires, and validating them.

> *Wife* (to husband who had just arrived home with the news that the bakery was out of the fruit tart she had specifically ordered — and a carrot cake): I'm so angry. That tart is my dad's favorite, and I really wanted to surprise him with it. I just can't believe this. I ordered it three days ago and was very specific.
>
> *Husband:* Oh, Honey, this carrot cake is good. Nobody will know you had planned the tart. Really, it doesn't matter. Carrot cake is fine.

He was trying to be helpful, but he didn't listen. He stayed in his own shoes. It didn't matter to *him*. Carrot cake was fine with *him*.

I actually witnessed this scene. What happened next was predictable. The wife felt all the more irritated by her husband's remarks. "But my dad loves that tart and I was counting on surprising him. How could that bakery do this!"

The husband saw that he wasn't going to convince his wife of his point of view, so he turned and took the carrot cake out to the kitchen. No connection. No good feelings. No chance for warmth and kindness to pass between the two.

The man could have made any number of remarks that would have made his wife feel heard and understood. He could have said, "I knew you'd be disappointed," or "I'm so sorry, Honey, it *is* infuriating."

As we can see from these examples, there are always two steps to listening. The first is to hear what the other person is saying, experiencing, and feeling. The second is to convey to the person that you have heard and that you understand.

Perhaps the most important and at the same time the most difficult time to listen is when someone else is upset with you, especially someone who has *not* learned effective communication. The natural human tendency is to become defensive in this situation. Let's see what happens when the upset person has *not* learned to make "I" statements:

"You are always late!"
"I am not!"

"How can you back out on me? You promised!"
"How could I know the boss would need me this weekend?"

"This is the third weekend you haven't fixed the broken window!"
"I've had too much else to do!"

How different these simple interactions would have been if the accused had empathized first — had first heard and then conveyed back to the accuser, in effect, "I understand your feelings."

"You're always late!"
"I know it upsets you when I'm late. I'm sure it must be exasperating."

"How can you back out on me? You promised!"
"I know you're disappointed. I'm sorry. I don't blame you for being angry with me."

"This is the third weekend you haven't fixed the broken window!"
"I'm sorry. I'd be annoyed too if I were in your shoes."

One of the common excuses people give for resisting the use of listening skills is that reflecting back what a person has said sounds fake and feels silly. But as is apparent from these examples, it is entirely possible to convey that you have understood someone without using formulas or simply repeating the same sentence back to the person. It is important to reflect back what you have heard, not by rote, but with your heart. If you are listening deeply, and if you truly care, then what you reflect back to the person who is speaking will not be mechanical. Like any new skill, listening may feel awkward at first, but when you begin to experience the difference that listening makes in your life and the lives of those around you, the awkward feeling will abate quickly. Remember, you must always use both steps when you listen: First listen carefully and then say what you heard and validate it.

When listening is at its best, the listener reflects back, not just what the speaker said, but what he or she was trying to say:

"This room is a mess!"
"You're feeling upset with me, I can tell."

When you sense that someone wants to talk, the simple sentence, "Tell me about it," or "Tell me more," works wonders.

Another objection people frequently give when they are being introduced to listening skills is that they do have a different point of view, and they want to be able to express it.

Listening to someone doesn't mean you can't also talk. It simply means that you listen *first* — and convey to the other person that you have heard and understood and taken in what he or she said. Then you can give your side of the story. And of course, if you have listened well, your remarks are much more likely to be on target.

If you want a relationship that truly thrives, there is no more important skill for you to master than listening. Listening is the foundation of affirmation and verbal intimacy, of conflict resolution, of negotiating, and of being happy together day in and day out.

IS IT TRUE THAT HAPPY COUPLES NEVER FIGHT?

Most of the happy couples I interviewed rarely fight. Many of them told me about major blowups they have had, but fighting is not a way of life for these people. For the most part, they resolve their conflicts and differences without fighting, making each other "wrong," hurting each other, putting each other down, or "winning" over the other.

People argue when they feel they are not being heard.

When two parties in a conflict are willing and able to listen to each other and to understand each other's point of view, they can negotiate peacefully. If they are angry or hurt, they may need to express their emotions for a few minutes in a way that is not rational or reasonable. But unless they are simply mean-spirited, they will soon regain a spirit of goodwill and make an effort to resolve the conflict.

Here are some simple, effective guidelines for peaceful conflict resolution.

1. Don't let yourself respond defensively. If you feel defensive, simply say, "I feel defensive, and I don't want to respond when I feel this way." Then wait. Talk a little more, or let your partner talk. See if the defensive feelings subside.

If you feel you have put your partner on the defensive because of something you have said, say, "I'm sorry I put you on the defensive."

2. If your partner wants to talk about something that is disturbing for either of you, curb your desire to respond. Sit quietly and listen. If your partner pauses, say, "Tell me more." Let him or her know that you are there and that you are truly listening.

3. When you do respond, state your partner's position as clearly as you can. If you don't understand, or you don't agree, or you can't imagine why your partner holds this position, ask why. Search for the reasons behind what your partner wants. Try to understand fully before you respond with your own point of view.

4. Take turns talking and listening.

Perhaps the single most important guideline for resolving conflicts without fighting is this one: Remember that your goal is to find a resolution that works for both of you, not to "win."

Often people who do fight and argue a great deal place a lot of importance on being right. They may not be aware of this, but deep inside, they believe that in order to feel good about themselves, or in order for other people to feel good about them, they have to be right and prove to others that they are right. These people would rather be right than have friends; they would rather be right than be happy; they would rather be right than be respected or liked. Couples who thrive and who have little conflict in their lives can let go of being right. They can move away from a position if they see it is getting them negative results. They can give in without feeling humiliated.

Remember, there is a very big difference between disagreeing with a person and judging a person. "I disagree with you" is a very different statement from "You are wrong" (implying you are a bad person for having that point of view).

A man I know was dating a woman who liked to dress lavishly and wear makeup and expensive jewelry. He was more of a down-home fellow himself, and he felt her wardrobe was pretentious. The two enjoyed each other, but this aspect of her troubled him. "Why can't she see how superficial all that fashion stuff is and how conformist?" he said to me.

"You can disagree with her, and dislike what she does, but still not make her wrong for what she does," I told him. "You are entitled to your opinions, but you don't have to judge her. Obviously, she doesn't think it is superficial and conformist, or she wouldn't do it."

When my friend was able to make this distinction, it lifted a great weight off his shoulders. He did not have to change his friend or convince her to modify her behavior. Reasonable people could differ on this issue. They simply had different tastes. No one was wrong. He didn't like her clothes, but he didn't have to convince her he was right. What a relief!

A second important principle in peaceful conflict resolution is to avoid blame. When you find yourself blaming the other person for anything, ask yourself, what is my role in this conflict?

One couple I interviewed said their main ongoing problem was that he felt she bought too many books. He thought people should use libraries and that owning books was stupid. They take up space, collect dust, and usually get read only once — if that. But she loved books and loved to write in the margins, lend them to friends, and keep them around for reference. They couldn't get any resolution until he realized that he was blaming her, and that he might have to look to himself to resolve the conflict. When he began to look at his own role, he saw that pestering her about her books was just as offensive to her as owning books was offensive to him. *He* was the source of the conflict, not she. She was just being herself. If he could change and simply relax and let go of his criticism, there would be no conflict. He did make the change, and it was an enormous relief to them both. He resolved this conflict by giving up his blame and looking at his own role in the conflict.

The real secret to avoiding fights is to learn to listen, to put yourself in the other person's shoes, to understand the other's point of view and convey that you have understood it. Remember, people fight only when they feel they are not being heard.

Experiment #19

Hold a practice listening session with your partner:

Choose a real or hypothetical situation in which Partner A is angry about something. Let Partner A vent and express the anger.

Partner B should first respond in a way that is *not* good listening. Either become defensive or offer solutions to the problem or talk about your own feelings. Deliberately stay in your own shoes. See only your own point of view. After you complete the role play, each of you say how the interaction made you feel.

Now Partner A, repeat the angry scene. This time Partner B, be as empathetic as you can. Climb into your partner's shoes. Try to understand and convey that you understand what your partner is feeling. Again, after the role play, discuss how it made you each feel.

Now switch roles.

---

3. Understand and Accept the Differences Between Men and Women

For a decade or so around the seventies, we were excited about our newfound freedom from strict gender roles. Men and women aren't all that different; women can be professionals, men can change diapers. Unisex fashions were the rage. We were intent upon eliminating gender distinctions. But we soon realized that while our roles can be interchanged, our psyches cannot. Men and women are very different.

Joe Tanenbaum, Anne Wilson Schaef, Lillian Rubin, Deborah Tannen, John Gray, and others have shed much light on male/female differences. Their work is a great gift. We now recognize that men and women belong to different subcultures, and that, even though the other sex's behavior is different from ours, it is not wrong. If we judge it as "bad," we are simply being myopic — and old-fashioned. Because we can now anticipate how the other sex will behave and recognize it as normal behavior, we can give up railing against it and instead accept each other and change our expectations.

We have at last realized that there are valid historical and psychological reasons for most of the dramatic differences between men and women. If we understand our differences, we can get along. We can honor and celebrate our separate subcultures and still continue to work for social, political, and economic equality. And we can even broaden our own range of behaviors by learning from each other. Different is good, not bad. Our only problem was expecting that we would be exactly like each other. Now that we know we are different, we can give up that expectation, and focus on learning how to get along with a different subculture. We can stop impugning each other's motives and recognize that we are both trying to achieve the same goals. We simply use different language and different behavior to get there.

This monumental shift in consciousness from "equal means identical" to "*vive la différence!*" is as significant an advance in our culture as the Sexual Revolution was in the sixties. Let's look here at its implications for communication.

THE F/PS RULE

From Deborah Tannen's important work we have learned that men often use conversation to solve problems and make decisions, while women often use conversation to work ideas through, to express feelings, to feel their connection with each other, and to establish rapport and intimacy. Conversationally speaking, women are feelings sharers (F), and men are problem solvers (PS).

If a man and woman don't know each other's styles, their conversation can be terribly frustrating. For example:

> *She:* I am so tired of that stupid job. Just listen to what a customer did to me today!
>
> *He:* Honey, I keep telling you to ask for a transfer.

Before we had this magic key — women-are-rapport-builders-and-feeling-sharers; men-are-problem-solvers — the above exchange could have sent this couple to a counselor in despair:

> *She:* He won't listen to me. He just cuts me off. He knows I can't ask for another transfer so soon. He doesn't care about me or how I feel. He never wants to talk about anything. I just wanted to tell someone about this stupid customer to get it off my chest, but instead, he just puts me down. And he always thinks he knows more than I do. He makes me so mad. I just don't feel close any more.
>
> *He:* I don't know what she wants! I do care about her. I was trying to be helpful. I don't see any reason why she can't ask for a transfer. I don't understand why she gets so angry. She's hysterical. She'll go on and on about one scene at the store. She won't listen to me.

The impasse in this scenario is caused by the couple's ignorance of the F/PS Rule. They both had goodwill and were both doing what they did best. She was doing a fine job of sharing her feelings and of trying to connect with him. He was doing a great job of trying to help her by solving her problem. Because they didn't have the simple key of the F/PS Rule, they even misjudged each other's motives. They couldn't see through their disparate approaches to their goodwill.

So how can knowledge of the F/PS Rule help? What might they have done — and what can you do — to make use of the F/PS Rule in your daily life?

The answer is so simple it can be applied instantly, and with very little practice: Simply label the type of conversation you want to have, and ask the other person to join you. For just because men have a tendency to solve problems and women have a tendency to share feelings doesn't mean that each isn't capable of the other mode. Here's how the above conversation could have proceeded. Assume that this couple have already discussed the F/PS Rule and understand both types of conversations.

She: I am so tired of that stupid job. Just listen to what a customer did to me today!

He: I keep telling you to ask for a transfer.

She: You know Honey, I'd like to have a feelings conversation right now, okay? I just need to get this thing off my chest. Could I tell you about it?

He: Of course. Thanks for the clue. Why don't you tell me about it.

(She relates the incident. He empathizes. When she seems finished, he continues.)

He: That was an awful situation. But it seems to me you handled it really well. Would you be willing to have a little problem-solving conversation now? Because I do feel some frustration that these situations continue to come up. I'd like to talk about some ways you might be able to change the situation.

She: Sure. I appreciate your concern. I think I could talk about some ideas now. *or*

She: Truthfully, I'm too exhausted to do that right now. I promise I'll talk about it some time in the next several days. How about Sunday morning. Would that be okay?

Labeling a conversation "feelings-oriented" or "problem solving" — as soon as you realize the two of you may be in different modes — is a magic tool. Of course I'm assuming that there is goodwill present on both sides. No one is suggesting that men are wrong to be solution-oriented or that women are wrong to be feelings-oriented, or that one of these modes is better than the other. You are honoring the validity and importance of both styles but agreeing to use one or the other of them for the time being.

I have noticed other differences in conversational styles between men and women as well. In my workshops, both men and women have found it very useful to anticipate these strong tendencies:

Women give — and want to hear — lots of details; men give broad outlines and get straight to the point.

Women talk about people, about feelings, and about personal issues; men talk about "topics" like politics, sports, work, movies, and so on.

Women want to be liked and included by others; men want to be respected and admired by others.

Men are subliminally aware of their "status" in a conversation, and try to engineer things so that they can be "one-up" rather than "one-down." Women, on the other hand, are more tuned in to whether or not they are being "liked," and are quite willing to sacrifice status if they feel they are being well received.

Of course, couples have been aware of these differences at some level for a very long time. What has shifted recently is that we have stopped putting each other down for them and have begun to accept them instead. We are now willing to recognize the validity of both styles and to try each other's modes. The problem has not been so much that women can't problem-solve and men can't connect, but that, until now, women didn't value problem solving and men didn't value connecting.

Awareness is the key. By recognizing what our respective subcultures have taught us to want, we can make choices for ourselves, and we can evaluate the other sex's behavior in an entirely different light.

For example, imagine this scene at a cocktail party. A man and woman strike up a conversation. They get to talking about politics. She offers an opinion. He agrees and goes on to elaborate at some length. She eggs him on by asking a couple of questions. He is delighted at this and explains himself at even greater length. They end warmly, smiling and saying how nice it is to find kindred spirits.

Later, she says to a friend, "He's very bright, but he's too impressed with his own importance." Meantime, he says to a friend, "She's really nice, but she's not too knowledgeable."

He was interested in getting her to respect him. He succeeded. But being not well liked by her was an unsought side effect.

She was interested in being liked by him. She succeeded. But losing his respect was an unsought side effect for her.

But look at how an awareness of these patterns can alter them. If both of these people take the trouble to think back on their conversation in the light of their knowledge about the usual habits of men and women, she may realize, "I need to speak up more. I had a lot to say too, but I just let him go on. That was silly. I was doing my passive woman number." He may realize, "I should have asked her what she thinks. After all, she brought up the subject. I didn't have to impress her. Why did I dominate the conversation so?"

MEN need to be aware that women like to share and talk things through in a non–solution-oriented way. Actually, this is their way of getting to a solution sometimes. But their main reason for talking this way is to build a connection with you. Relax. Listen. Ask questions. Acknowledge her feelings. Focus on experiencing the connection between you. Respect your partner for her ability to build this connection. And remember that by listening and refraining from solving her problem, you are giving her exactly the kind of closeness she craves with you. But also, don't feel you have to adjust your identity to communicate satisfactorily. When you have reached your limits for this sort of interacting, let her know — in a completely nonjudgmental way. She is not asking that you become an expert at this kind of talking. She is only asking that you shift to her mode for a while and refrain from problem solving.

When the woman you love is troubled, depressed, or upset about something, what she needs most from you is not a solution to her immediate problem. Rather, she needs to know you love her even when she can't love herself. Hold her. Let her talk, complain, or cry. Tell her that you love her, and that you understand. And when she's excited about something, let her tell you about it. Be interested. Pay attention. Tell her how happy you are for her.

Also, men, you need to know that you may have a natural tendency to try to impress others and win their admiration. But a woman cares more about liking you than admiring you. Admiration creates distance between the admirer and the admired, yet what she wants more than anything is closeness. If you want her to feel good about you, and if you want to please her, get in the habit of asking her questions. Show that you are interested in her. She will love you for this, and loving you is what she wants to do. Ironically, of course, she will respect you more, too.

Learn to ask your wife questions — about her work, her friends, her opinions. This is a gift to her, and it will do wonders for your relationship.

WOMEN need to be aware that men like to help and proffer support by making suggestions, giving advice, and offering solutions. They do this to help and support you. They have no intention of cutting you off or putting you down. Be grateful and appreciative of their help. If you want to talk more open-mindedly for a while, ask for this, out loud and nonjudgmentally, but be willing to shift to the problem-solving mode also. Let yourself be assisted in this way. Feel the support they are offering. Contribute your own solutions and suggestions.

Shift into the problem-solving mode yourself for a while, and work to make the conversation as useful to yourself as possible.

When you have established that the two of you are having a feelings discussion, and you are talking about your feelings but he is not talking about his, try simply asking, "How do you feel about such and such?" It could be that it just didn't occur to your partner to think about or mention how he feels.

Also, women, you need to be aware that you have a natural tendency to try to please others and win their affection. A man wants to like you, but even more, he wants to respect you. Don't play down your expertise, talents, and skills in order to let a man show his off. Always strive for equality in a conversation. Just because a man doesn't ask for your opinion or your stories, don't assume he isn't interested. Take responsibility for equalizing conversations with men. Show that you have a head on your shoulders. He will respect you for this, and respecting you is what he wants to do. Ironically, of course, he will like you more, too.

BOTH SEXES must be aware of the difference between problem-solving conversations and feeling/rapport-building conversations. Label the type of conversation you want to have, and get the agreement of the other party before proceeding. In all your conversation, work for a balance between talking and listening. Show you are interested in the other party by asking questions.

Experiment #20

With your partner, choose a topic that is controversial for the two of you. Now, for twenty minutes, have a feelings-only, rapport-building conversation about it. Then, for the next twenty minutes, have a problem-solving or solution-oriented discussion about it. You may need to do this only once to get the two different styles clear in your minds so that in the future you can ask for the type of conversation you want.

The last three basic communication skills are equally important for both men and women. One gender may be more naturally inclined toward one or the other, but in the end, both men and women need to master them all.

4. Ask for What You Want

Even couples who thrive have trouble sometimes asking for what they want in their relationship. From happy couples I heard as many anecdotes about problems in this area as in any other. Most of these stories were about times when the couples had eventually overcome their obstacles and had been able to ask for what they wanted. Couples who are not thriving often go for years without ever telling each other what they want.

Why is it so difficult?

Basically, because we are afraid that asking for what we want will cause conflict or discomfort of one kind or another. "The other person won't want to give what I want and will get mad," we tell ourselves. "I don't know what will happen if I ask." "My mate will feel criticized." "I'll never get what I want anyway." "What I want is probably stupid; I should just learn to live without it." "I've asked before and it doesn't do any good." "It just never seems like the right moment to ask." "My mate should know what I want and need. I shouldn't have to ask." "It spoils it to have to ask; what I want is for my mate to see what I want and give it spontaneously." "I'll just be nice and not bother my mate with my wish."

If you hear yourself saying or thinking one of these excuses for not asking for what you want, then tell yourself, "This is not a good enough excuse. If my partner is not giving me something I want, this is my responsibility. My partner cannot read my mind. I might even have to ask more than once. That's okay. If I want my needs satisfied, I must find a way to ask!"

Asking for what you want in your relationship is crucial for several reasons. First, if you don't ask, the consequences can be terrible. Anything you want and are not requesting becomes a secret, because now one person knows something the other person isn't privy to. It becomes a little wall between you. Worse, the person who is withholding will inevitably begin to resent not getting what he or she wants. Then the resentment becomes an additional wall, an additional distancing device. As one man told me, "She was resenting me, and I had not the least clue what she was resenting."

On the other hand, if you can bring yourself to ask for what you want, something in your relationship will shift. It is true that you do not exactly know what will happen when you ask. But you can be sure that whatever happens will move the two of you forward. Even if your asking creates a conflict, it is almost certainly something that needed to come out in the open and that can now be resolved. As long as you withhold, nothing can happen.

Kathryn and Max had been going together for more than a year when the events she relates occurred.

> We were having dinner at quite a nice restaurant. At the end, I offered to pay, but Max, as usual, brushed off my offer and swept up the bill.
>
> This time, I stopped him. I said, "Would you just ask me why I want to pay for my own dinner?" The question startled him a bit, and he slowed down. He sensed I was trying to get his serious attention. He asked me. Then I thanked him, and I told him what I had been longing to say for some time, that I believed so fervently in equality that I felt like a hypocrite letting him pay, that even though I knew he was paying for me in a spirit of generosity, it made me feel like he didn't respect me as an equal. I explained, I just liked the *feel* of paying my own way. It was a pleasure for me. It made me feel professional and independent, and it was an important symbol for me of my feminism. He was stunned to hear all this. He had no idea how I felt. But he understood right away, and he had no problem switching. He thanked me for telling him, and couldn't understand why I hadn't told him sooner. After his sweet reaction, I couldn't understand either! It had seemed so difficult to me. Actually, I know why it seemed difficult. It's because when I tried to pay with other men in the past, they didn't listen. They called my ideas silly, or put me down as a huffy feminist or whatever. In my head, I knew Max wouldn't do that. He is a feminist himself. But it was still very hard emotionally to ask.
>
> I don't know how I got the idea to ask him to ask me why I wanted to pay. It just came to me in that second. But it worked. It gave me the opening I needed to ask finally for what I wanted.

Hannah and Marty are a very happy couple in their mid-forties. They are both professionals, had been married for fourteen years when I met them, and have no children. Their affection and enjoyment of each other was a pleasure to see. When we were discussing secrets, Hannah was outspoken about the importance of complete openness, so I was rather surprised when she told me that she had only recently asked Marty for some of the specific things she likes during their lovemaking.

> It was really silly not to say anything all these years, but it was a combination of factors that just kept it from happening. First, our love-

making is absolutely wonderful. It's varied, it's really affectionate, we still turn each other on a lot. So it's not like I wasn't happy already. And second, once a long time ago, I asked Marty for something specific, and he got sort of defensive. He said, "Don't you like things the way they are?" So I sort of expected him to react that way again. Of course, I knew in my head that I could make it perfectly clear to him that I wasn't complaining, just making suggestions, and that I could be appreciative at the same time. Nevertheless, I think the memory of that one incident sort of deterred me. And another thing was, when we are making love, our talk is all lovey-dovey, which I love, and I don't feel like talking about it then. And when we aren't making love, I'm not thinking about it. It's sort of like you can't fix the leaky roof when it's raining because you'll get wet, but when it's not raining, the roof doesn't leak.

I mean, it was never a big deal for me, but a few months ago, we were curled up in bed reading, and for some unknown reason, I decided now was the time. I prefaced it by assuring him that I was not in any way dissatisfied or unhappy with our sex life, but that there were a few things I'd love to try. Of course he was delighted. And the next time we made love, I was so glad I finally asked.

Sometimes we fail to ask for what we want because it doesn't occur to us to get specific. Wendell and Elizabeth have been married for twenty-seven years, and only four years ago solved one of their thorniest problems.

ELIZABETH: We always seemed to fight about occasions — birthdays and the like. Wendell would forget them, and I'd feel awful about it. Once after an incident like this I was talking with a friend who said, "Have you ever told him exactly what you want?" So I went home and told him, "I need three presents a year — birthday, anniversary, and Christmas — and a card on Valentine's Day." Wendell loved it. He said, "That I can do!" It has been great ever since.

Patsy and Tyler are in their early fifties and have two teenage girls. In addition to working full-time as an editor, Patsy is extremely active in community work. When we settled in for our interview, Tyler started right in with these comments:

We just went through a transition that I could tell you about. It was getting so that Patsy was never home any more. Almost every night of the week, she had meetings. She's really involved with the girls' school, so it was hard to knock it, but our home life was going out the window. I was complaining about it a lot, and Patsy was just saying there was nothing she could do about it. She kept saying she didn't like being so busy either, but she also loved all the stuff she was doing and didn't want to give it up. Finally one night I got really angry, so the next morning — it was a Saturday — we went out to breakfast and we talked. I told her this just wasn't working, it wasn't fair, that I felt I was doing all the compromising and that she wasn't giving anything, and that I was really missing her and wanted her around more. And I said I just wanted us to look together at her schedule and see if there was anything she could alter. Her attitude was, she'd be willing to do it, but she thought it was hopeless. We talked for a long time, and by the end of the morning, she had agreed to turn the school newsletter over to someone else, and to drop the fund-raising committee of the P.T.A., two major commitments.

PATSY: I felt kind of sheepish and embarrassed — like I had to admit that Tyler was right. But I felt relief that very morning. And our life has been so much better since. I actually have leisurely evenings at home, and I'm not so frantic and anxious. I'm much happier.

TYLER: And so am I.

How do couples who thrive ask each other for what they want?

I interviewed two men, David and Peter, who have been in a wonderful relationship with each other for ten years. David had a well–thought out philosophy about asking for change:

As I see it, there are three levels of behavior. Level one is superficial, trivial behaviors, like closing the bathroom door or chewing with your mouth closed. They are behaviors that are easy to change, and that Peter and I happily and easily change for each other. All we have to do is ask each other — maybe even a couple times if the behavior is somewhat of a habit, and the other partner is happy to change. No big deal.

The second level is behaviors that might be somewhat of an effort for the other person to change, but they are changeable. For example, I tend to be quite absentminded. I can get immersed in work, and hours go by, and I forget to call Peter — who might have dinner waiting for me at home. I had to learn to call Peter and keep him posted. It had to happen only a couple times for me to see how upset Peter was not to hear from me. I changed. It is still an effort for me sometimes but I wouldn't consider not calling. I make an effort to remember, because

I can see how much it means to Peter. And I have no problem with his wanting this from me.

Then there is the third level of behavior: deeply ingrained patterns that are a part of your very personality, things that you can't be expected to change. I mean, I'm not ever going to be un-absentminded. Sometimes this may inconvenience Peter a bit, but he accepts it. I just can't change who I am. I think it is really important to distinguish among these three levels of behavior.

Common wisdom says that you should never expect your partner to change. But I have always felt that this is true in some circumstances but not others. It is inappropriate — to say nothing of futile — to ask your partner to change basic personality characteristics. But if your partner is capable of the change you want, and if it would make an enormous difference to you, ask! Even though you may be requesting something that will require great effort on the part of your spouse, you may be doing both of you a favor in the end.

Whether you are asking your partner to sweep the porch, to spend more quality intimate time with you, or to try to become a more thoughtful person, a few simple guidelines and principles will make success much more likely.

1. *Figure out exactly what you want to ask for.* Sometimes this is the hardest part. If you have only a vague sense that something isn't right, that you are unhappy or dissatisfied in some way, you can try one of several strategies for determining exactly what you want. Talk with a friend to see if you can clarify your thoughts. Or, talk with your partner. If you do this, set up the conversation to make it as nonthreatening for your partner as possible. You might say, "Would you be willing just to talk something over with me? I'm not asking for anything, I just want to see if I can become clearer about it."

The one rule that is critical is, If you feel emotional about something, talk about it. If something is gnawing away at you, if you feel angry or "charged up," bring it up and discuss it. Don't feel that you have to have your specific request all worked out in advance. You can't know ahead of time what will result from your discussion; that's all the more reason to discuss it. Unfortunately, the issues you feel strongest about are likely to be the hardest to bring up. They make you feel vulnerable, out of control. You fear the issue will cause a fight. When it comes time to talk about it, you may minimize it or even temporarily forget it.

Kathryn's strong feeling about not wanting Max to pay for her dinner is an example. She had held the feelings for several months. But she always talked herself out of saying anything. Kathryn told me,

> I never wanted to spoil our good times with each other. And I was afraid Max would be angry or hurt or insulted or feel criticized. I would convince myself that the whole thing was silly. I know what finally pushed it to the surface enough for me to bring it up: I talked with a friend about it. That just clarified the issue for me. It gave me a chance to see that I really did have feelings about it. But I was so reluctant to bring it up. I didn't know what would happen.

You can never work through a problem and get to a resolution if you don't have the courage to bring it up and discuss it. And you *will* work it through if you do have the courage to bring it up. Couples who thrive talk to each other about what is troubling them. If they feel emotionally charged up about something, they talk about it!

2. *Pave the way for your request.* Before you begin, tell your partner that you are not criticizing him or her, that you are simply stating a preference.

We all have a tendency to hear requests as criticisms. For example, one partner may say, "I'd really like to eat dinner at six rather than seven or seven-thirty. Would that be okay?" But the other partner may hear, "You are late with dinner. You can't get it together." Or one partner may say, "Let's go really slowly tonight," but the other may hear, "I don't like the way you've been making love lately. It hasn't been good for me." Most people get defensive rather easily. But on topics that are not especially sensitive ones, most people can soften or even give up their defensive feelings if they are given an opportunity to do so.

In the first example, the one partner could have paved the way by saying, "I have a request, but please understand, I'm not criticizing. It's just a request. Would you be willing from now on for us to eat at six instead of seven?"

In the second example, the way could have been paved by saying, "I have a request, but please understand, I'm not saying anything about how our lovemaking has been. It's been fabulous. But tonight, could we go really slowly?"

By recognizing defensiveness, we can often cut it off at the pass. This can happen at any time during a discussion, not only at the beginning. If something you say causes your partner to feel defensive, you can say, "Wait a second. I really didn't mean to make you feel defensive. I'm sorry I put it that way. Let's just talk about it." You are giving your partner a chance to shift. In the same way, if you notice yourself starting to feel defensive, the best thing in the world to say is, "I'm feeling defensive." This lets your partner know that something he or she has said felt critical to you. It stops any fighting or bickering before it begins. And it gives you a chance to shift off the defensive stance and to open yourself up to listening to your partner in a non-defensive way.

Paving the way by telling your partner that you have no intention of putting him or her on the defensive and admitting that you feel defensive are both effective methods of putting an end to negative communication and opening up positive interaction.

3. *Time your request appropriately.* Try not to ask for a favor when your mate is tired, stressed, or in a bad mood. If you are making a major request, set up a time when you won't be interrupted, and when you can have some time to talk it through.

4. *Be specific.* If you are annoyed that the dishwasher hasn't been emptied, don't say, "I wish you'd be more helpful around here." Say, "Would you be willing to empty the dishwasher sometime this morning?" Rather than, "I'd like you to be more affectionate," say, "I'd like us to have a big hug every morning when I leave for work."

In our examples above, Kathryn didn't ask to be respected more; she asked to be permitted to pay for her own dinner. Hannah didn't ask Marty to be more attentive during sex; she asked for specific behaviors. And Tyler was getting nowhere by asking Patsy to be less busy or to stay home more. He had to get very specific with her about what she could let go of. (Actually, Tyler went even further than he needed to by helping Patsy see her way to a solution. His request would have been specific enough if he had said, "I'd like you to agree to be home three nights every week.")

5. *Be brief.* Do not embellish your request with a list of reasons why you think it is a great request. This is extremely unappealing and ineffective: "Honey, I have to shop and pay bills this morning, and I was up so late last night. You don't have to be anywhere for another hour. I'd love to get some help, I mean, do you think maybe you could empty the dishwasher or something?"

6. *Ask in an open-ended, nondemanding way.* Understand that your mate has a right to say no. If you make a reasonable request and you get a negative response, it may be time for you to do some listening. Maybe for some reason your mate doesn't consider your request

to be as reasonable as you think it is. Before you argue back, find out.

The phrase "Would you be willing to . . ." is very useful. It subtly communicates that you understand that your mate may not be willing for some reason. It allows you to be specific in a nondemanding way. "Would you be willing to take the kids to school tomorrow morning?" "Would you be willing to pick up some milk on the way home?"

7. *If asking in one way doesn't work, try a new method.* There is a difference between asking for something, and actually communicating your request to your partner. Your partner's background experiences and frame of reference — and your partner's own needs — may be so different from yours that he or she may actually not fully realize what you are asking for.

If you feel frustrated that your request is not being responded to, try one of the "techniques" at the end of this chapter to communicate your request again. Or, try saying it in entirely different words. Explain why what you want is important to you. Be patient. Sometimes successful communication happens in stages.

*   *   *

When I asked the thriving couples I interviewed what they wanted from each other, either they couldn't think of a thing, or they mentioned standard old issues that were quite familiar to them both, such as "I'd like him be a little freer with money," or "I'd like her to be more tidy." For the most part, these couples keep current with asking what they want from each other. They genuinely want to please each other, so they have made it easy to ask for things.

But, as Elizabeth and Wendell told me, it wasn't always that way.

ELIZABETH: We both learned right along with the rest of our generation. We started out with a very traditional marriage. I was home with our babies for a few years. When I went back to law school, I had to ask Wendell for a lot of things. It took us both a little while to become enlightened about not having to play traditional roles. We had some rough times over all these changes. We feel very lucky that we changed together. Of course, we know couples who didn't make it through the seventies. . . . We've learned how to ask each other for what we want after years of practice.

Couples who thrive have also achieved a balance between asking for changes in their partner and accepting those qualities in their partner that will never change.

Experiment #21

---

1. Make a wish list of things you would like from your partner.
2. Choose one item on the list and, following the guidelines above, ask your partner for it.
3. Either by yourself or with your partner, evaluate the way you made the request. Is there something you will do differently next time?

---

5. Affirm Others

Couples who thrive pepper their conversation with affirming comments regularly and consistently. They take pleasure often in expressing their love and appreciation for each other. I frequently heard comments like these in my interviews:

> I don't think a day goes by that one of us doesn't say "I love you."

> We have a rule that when someone says, "I love you," the other person is not allowed to say, "I love you, too," back. You just have to take it in, usually silently. Then you can say it on your own some other time. But the "I love you" comes in all kinds of forms like, "You're really special," "I feel lucky to be with you." Stuff like that.

> We wink at each other. I just love it — at some unexpected moment, across the breakfast table, or at a dinner party, or in the grocery store. I look up and get this little wink and smile. After eleven years, it still lights me up all over.

Everyone needs to be affirmed, complimented, praised, thanked, and acknowledged. A study of couples reported in *Psychology Today* found clear evidence that "both men and women deem romance and passion far *less* important than affirmation and warm fuzzies."

If you find that you are an "underaffirmer," it is probably due to one of these common reasons:

1. You just forget. You become preoccupied with yourself and actually don't notice when your spouse looks especially good or does something unusually well. Because you aren't in the habit of giving strokes, it simply doesn't occur to you.

2. You are afraid your spouse will tire of hearing the same sentiments over and over.

3. You assume your spouse knows that you love and appreciate him or her: As Honeymooner Ralph Cramden said to Alice, "I told you I love you once ten years ago. Well, it still stands!"

4. You are afraid your praise or thanks is going to sound obsequious or is going to put you in a one-down position. "You're so well organized." (Implication: I wish I were that well organized.)

Virtually all the thriving couples I spoke with affirm each other in a variety of ways, regularly and consistently. The understanding between couples who thrive goes something like this: "This relationship is rare and valuable. It must be actively cared for. Like a beautiful plant, it will thrive if given water and sunshine and food, and it will wither and die if it is neglected." Couples who thrive feel extremely fortunate to be together, and their entire relationship takes place against a backdrop of their feeling of being blessed. Consistent compliments and affirmations are more the *result* of a flourishing relationship than the cause of one.

On the other hand, compliments can make an extraordinary difference in any relationship. Listen to Margaret's story:

> Ross and I were at a very low point in our relationship. He was having a big struggle with his business. He really wanted out but couldn't find a way to get out, and basically he had been depressed for three years. He just wasn't there for me. I remember saying to him at the end of a vacation, "I feel like I've been on this trip alone!" I was committed to him, but I was feeling pretty discouraged.
>
> One night we were hanging around the hot tub. He has a big scar on his leg, and I was thinking, Yuk, what an ugly scar. And suddenly it hit me. I'm looking at everything negative and nothing positive. I've got to turn this around! Right then, I said to him, "Ross, you are such a great father. I really love how much you do with the kids." He looked up at me and smiled, and I just realized, I was probably a drag to be around, too! I started complimenting him on all sorts of things, and every day I told him I loved him. Those words had fallen totally out of our vocabulary! I'll tell you, it was the beginning of a major turnaround. I felt better because I was remembering all the things I love about him, and he started paying a lot more attention to me. Within a month, he had figured out how to split up and sell the company. And we regained the old *joie de vivre* we had when we first met. It was a total turnaround.

Affirming others means more than remembering to toss a few kind words in their direction: in the same way that genuine listening means climbing into the other person's shoes for a moment, affirming another person means thinking about how that person feels, remembering what that person is concerned about, giving your attention fully to him or her. If you compliment a woman on her appearance, at some level you are acknowledging that she went to a lot of trouble to pick out those clothes, find matching earrings, skillfully apply her makeup, and so on. Suppose your friend just gave a speech to your Rotary Club. When you see her afterward, you are aware that she put a lot of effort into the speech and that she really hopes that you — and other members of the audience — liked it. So you tell her it was well organized, the jokes were really funny, her presentation style was smooth. And you relate comments you overheard from others: "I just heard a woman say, 'She could replace Joan Rivers!'" You empathize with how it must feel to prepare and give a speech, and your affirmations reflect that empathy.

Your spouse deserves this kind of attention every day.

If a person has dressed up for a fancy evening, or if she has just given a speech, it is fairly obvious that she would like to be affirmed. But people who are skilled affirmation-givers realize that others enjoy being affirmed in all kinds of simple, everyday situations. "You do such a nice job cleaning up the kitchen." "You were so helpful to Nancy when she lost her job." "I appreciate how well you keep up with family correspondence."

The most heartfelt compliments are genuine expressions of delight on the part of the giver. When you say, "You look really nice tonight," in the most heartfelt way, what you will be *feeling* is, "You are a pleasure *for me* to look at. I'm really lucky." If you are feeling good yourself about whatever you are commenting on, your partner will feel the most complimented. When Mayer looks at me and asks someone, "Isn't she wonderful?," I know he is enjoying me, and not just trying to be a good husband.

One of the reasons so many of us are stingy with affirmations of others, and have to be reminded how important they are and taught how to give them is that we have a tendency to be extremely self-involved. We get preoccupied with ourselves. When two people are in love, they become preoccupied with each other. One of the qualities that couples who thrive for many years together have is that they pay a lot of attention to each other.

Since affirming is actually about paying attention to another person, another important method of affirming is mentioning details. Rather than, "That was a great speech," say, "You seemed so relaxed.

The joke about the little boy was perfect. I absolutely loved your ending." Be specific.

One of the best affirmations you can give a person is to ask a question that indicates that you remember what is going on in that person's life. Sales people are trained to jot down notes about their customers or clients so that when they see the person a month later they can say, "How did your son do on his science fair project?" or "How did that conversation with your supervisor go?" It's even more important to do this with our friends and lovers. When you see your spouse at the end of the day, unless something noteworthy happened to you that you are bursting to relate, ask him or her a question about something specific you knew was going to occur that day. This simple thoughtfulness can be a wonderful gift.

Another magical way to affirm and support the person you love is to say why you love him or her.

I once asked a man I was going with why he liked me. The question took him somewhat aback, as though he had never before considered it. He didn't say much then, but a couple weeks later, I received some flowers along with a beautiful handmade card. Inside the card was a long list of sentences, each in a different colored pen: "I like you because you sparkle. I like you because you are kind. I like you because you laugh at my jokes. I like you because . . ." The list went on and on. It was one of the loveliest gifts I ever received.

I spoke recently with a woman who had been single for many years but who had recently reunited with an old boyfriend. They were having a wonderful time together, but she still had a certain amount of disbelief about it. "I can't imagine what he sees in me," she confided to me. Wouldn't it be beautiful for her if he would tell her?

Experiment #22

---

1. For the next two weeks give your partner one specific compliment every day. Then, when the two weeks are over, don't forget the habit you have developed.
2. Write a love letter to your partner like the one my friend wrote to me. List all the reasons you can think of why you love him or her.

Everyone thrives on strokes. But John Gray, author of *Men Are from Mars; Women Are from Venus*, points out a subtle difference between the types of strokes that women like and those that men like. Women, he says, like consistency. Every small affirmation counts in a big way for them. The simple spontaneous comment "You look lovely tonight" counts just as much for a woman as what seems to her husband to be a much more major affirmation, like bringing her flowers unexpectedly. While men count saying "I love you" as a 1 on the affirmation scale, and bringing home flowers as a 100, women score both as 100. Little spontaneous acts or words of thoughtfulness mean a great deal to women. According to Gray, women are more oriented toward connection; men, toward accomplishments, so women want to be affirmed for who they are, men, for what they do. This is important information, because it is best to give the kinds of affirmations you know the other person most wants, not the kind you would like to get yourself.

You can easily brighten a woman's life every day with a verbal expression of your love. But men misunderstand this quality in women. The critical point men often fail to see is this: Women like to hear compliments and adoring comments, not because they are afraid that you don't love them anymore, not because they are insecure about their appearance, not because they are worried about your feelings for them. Rather, they want to hear these affirmations because it is a source of pleasure for them. A woman wants, not only to have, but to experience her connection with you. A compliment gives her enormous pleasure. It lets her know, not only that you love her, but that you are aware of your love, that you are thinking about it, that it gives you pleasure to love her.

A man will perk up when you verbally appreciate him for who he is and for the things he does for you.

In the end, for everyone, being affirmed is so important that any compliment works wonders. Indeed, a person who is getting no attention at all may pick a fight just as a way to get noticed, because negative attention is better than none. Couples who thrive affirm each other in a variety of ways, spontaneously, and often.

Any couple — whether thriving or hoping to thrive — can make a staggering difference in their relationship if they learn to use the five basic communication skills we have just discussed:

1. Make "I" statements rather than "you" statements, especially when feeling emotionally charged up.

2. Differentiate between "feelings-oriented" and "solution-oriented" conversations.
3. Listen nondefensively and focus on understanding the other person's point of view.
4. Ask for what you want.
5. Affirm each other regularly and often.

If you use these skills enough, they will become habits. But it is important to recognize that in stressful situations, when the skills are most important of all, you will have a tendency to revert to old behavior. Communication skills always require special attention and deliberate thought. Even if you know better, it is easy to become self-involved and forget to affirm your partner; to suppress your true desires and acquiesce to your partner without standing up for what you want; or to become defensive.

For example, my husband was on the phone the other day telling a friend that he would be unable to go on a weekend antique-buying trip that they had planned. The friend was clearly quite disappointed. I heard Mayer defending himself: "I can't help it. These relatives gave us no notice that they were coming to town. I really like these people, and I never get a chance to see them. I really thought I'd be able to go when I suggested it." Mayer was forgetting to put himself in his friend's shoes. He was seeking to be understood, not to understand. I quickly scribbled him a little note: "Be empathetic." With this little reminder, Mayer remembered to let go of defending himself, and to get into his friend's shoes. He said, "I know this is a disappointment. I don't blame you for being upset. I know if I were in your shoes, I'd feel very let down too. I'm really sorry. I hope you can forgive me." I could tell the person on the other end accepted the situation and lightened up.

But even Mayer, who has been receiving coaching from me for twelve years now, had to be reminded when he was smack in the middle of a hard situation and was feeling defensive.

Good communication skills should not be reserved for special situations. They can be used all the time and in a wide variety of settings. In your normal, day-to-day routines, you can remember to toss your spouse a kiss, or when listening, to make a simple comment like, "That must have made you angry." Good skills are especially critical when you are trying to resolve a conflict. But they are important all the time. They are the day-to-day substance of a thriving relationship.

Communication Techniques for
Resolving Conflicts and Enhancing Intimacy

Now that we have learned basic communication skills, we can look at some specific *techniques*.

The difference between communication skills and communication techniques is that skills should, ideally, be in use virtually all the time. We talk and listen all day long, and we can do this in a skilled, effective, relationship-enhancing way — or in an unskilled, ineffective, relationship-destroying way. If we want happy, satisfying relationships, we have no choice but to learn and use good communication skills.

Techniques, on the other hand, are what a business might call "added value." These are special activities that most couples do not engage in routinely. Relationships can — indeed, most relationships do — survive and even thrive without these special communication activities. But what they can do for a relationship if a couple does use them periodically is immeasurable. Choosing to go through an entire lifetime without ever trying at least one of the special activities I will describe is like leaving a million dollars in a dresser drawer untouched.

Any of the following techniques could be used to great advantage under the following circumstances:

a) you are trying to get something across to your partner, and you feel the real message is not getting through;

b) the two of you disagree about something;

c) one of you feels the need to talk something over;

d) you are unhappy about something in the relationship and you want to discuss it with your spouse;

e) you are especially happy and in a good place with each other, and you want to experience and deepen your intimacy;

f) you are simply looking for a pleasant, novel way to spend some time together.

I. A FEELINGS FORUM

A Feelings Forum is the first technique I teach to any couple because a) it helps them develop a facility with the first three communication skills ("I" statements, the F/PS rule, and listening) and b) it builds intimacy. A Feelings Forum is a discussion about feelings *only*, usually feelings about one particular incident. I strongly encourage couples to hold a Feelings Forum every day for one month so that they become extremely comfortable with it and can rely on it when they really need it. A Feelings Forum is a lovely way to spend a few minutes together anytime, and it should be the first step in any conflict resolution. It can be done in ten minutes or may go on for thirty.

1. Begin by selecting an incident or an ongoing feeling to focus on.

2. For at least five minutes, longer if necessary, each of you write out your feelings about this topic. Write it in the form of a letter addressed to your spouse.

3. Now, sit close together. As you proceed, touch and look at each other. One of you, read your letter out loud to your spouse.

4. Whoever was the listener, put in your own words what you felt your spouse was trying to say in the letter. Then, the first person, say whether you feel your spouse understood your feelings fully and accurately. If not, express them again verbally. Then again, listener, say what you heard. Keep going until the person who wrote the letter feels fully understood.

5. Now, whoever was the listener, say how the letter made you feel.

The critical rule for the Feelings Forum is that it be an exchange of *feelings only*. There must be no problem solving or decision making of any kind. This is an opportunity for the two of you to share, understand, and respond to each other's feelings. Sometimes they may be appreciative and loving. (I felt deeply touched when you offered to drive the kids when it was my turn. I knew you could see how tired I was, and I felt very loved and taken care of.) Sometimes they may be feelings of hurt or neglect. (When you forgot to introduce me at your office party, I felt so embarrassed and so out of place. It hurt.)

You are encouraged to use similar situations to convey feelings that may be hard for your partner to understand. For example, "Remember how you felt when your boss forgot to mention you in his thank-yous even though you did all the work? Well, that's what this felt like to me." Or, "I felt like I was in high school and I found out I didn't get invited to a party."

When all the feelings surrounding this one episode or event have been expressed and understood by both parties, conclude with a kiss.

After you have completed your month of daily Feelings Forums, make it a weekly ritual, and feel free to ask your partner for a Feelings Forum any time. Occasionally you will find that a "quickie" will come in handy; you may even prefer to skip the writing portion sometimes.

The Feelings Forum is intended to give you an opportunity to talk about your feelings in a way that many couples never do. It is a most intimate activity. Couples who hold Feelings Forums regularly — or even just whenever they feel a need or desire to — report that it keeps them close in a way they never felt before they did this.

Don't skip this technique. Try it. Many couples have told me how important the Feelings Forum has become in their lives.

2. TELL ME MORE

When one partner wants to talk about something, usually something he or she is upset about, the other partner can offer the most loving and the most helpful response by responding simply, "Tell me more," over and over. The phrase conveys a lot. It says, "I'm totally here with you. I'm listening. I care. Right now I'm not going to offer you solutions or try to fix things. I just want you to have the chance to say everything that is in your heart." This is actually an easy formula for having a "rapport-building" or "feelings" conversation, as I described above.

3. PROBLEM-SOLVING AND DECISION-MAKING PROCESS

Whenever you have a major decision to make or a problem to solve, using this process will save you time, diminish your anguish, allow for an essentially positive emotional interaction even in stressful circumstances, and, perhaps most important, ensure that you will end up with the best possible result.

Mayer and I have used this process often with positive results. Sometimes it has highlighted factors we had overlooked. More than once, we applied the process even when we thought we already had a decision, and ended up changing our minds after this systematic review.

STEP 1. Together, write down the dilemma or conflict as a statement or question. Be sure both partners agree this is an accurate representation of the actual problem.

STEP 2. Together, list as many possible solutions or possible scenarios as you can. When you think you have listed all the possibilities, force yourselves to think up two more. Sometimes that is when your best creativity comes out.

STEP 3. Each of you, discuss your *feelings* about the whole thing, rational or not. Don't judge or appraise each other's emotions; just listen and reflect back each other's feelings until you both feel heard and understood.

STEP 4. Each of you separately, list on paper all the pros and cons you can think of for both sides of the dilemma, or for all possible solutions to the problem. Then compare lists. This is simply a thought-clarifying device, not a scorecard. One pro may be so significant that it outweighs ten cons. But this device will allow you to see what issues are at stake for each other.

STEP 5. If possible, wait at least twenty-four hours before proceeding.

STEP 6. Each of you state your desired outcome or discuss your ambivalence if you still have some. Then begin to discuss possible compromises and solutions until you are able to reach consensus. (Consensus means that all parties are willing to go along with whatever is decided even if it is not the outcome they would have chosen themselves.) You may want to return to any of the above steps at any time.

4. A DREAM BOARD

On a lazy Saturday, get out some old magazines and a big piece of cardboard or posterboard. Together, cut out words, phrases, and pictures and paste them onto the cardboard to make a collage that represents your dreams and goals for yourselves and your family. Virtually every motivational teacher demonstrates that people who write down their goals or picture them concretely achieve their goals sooner than people who do not have clear goals or who have them but do not express them clearly.

Experiment #23

Choose the communication technique described above that you find most enticing. Together with your partner schedule a time to try the technique together. Have a good time with it.

Once you begin to use relationship-enhancing communication skills, you will find them an enormous pleasure. In the same way that a properly placed coaching hint can transform your tennis game, good communication skills can revolutionize your relationship. You will achieve more of what you want in your marriage. You may even become closer, more loving friends than you ever realized you could be. The most direct route to becoming a thriving couple, if you aren't already one, is to begin to experience the pleasure of using effective, relationship-enhancing communication skills.

Chapter 8

TRAIT 7: INTIMACY

I ATTENDED AN an informal gathering at a friend's house recently. As one woman was crossing the room, she accidently ran into her husband. He grabbed her, wrapped her in his arms, held her close, and began showering her with kisses. The woman's father, who also happened to be at the party, said playfully, "Hey, that's my daughter!" Her husband replied, "Well, that's my wife! Don't worry, I'm taking good care of her!" Everyone was laughing and being just a bit silly — and the two of them were reveling in their loving, playful moment.

Toward the end of the evening, the couple and I found a private corner, and she spoke about a feeling that had come over her while she was nursing her son, a kind of overwhelming awareness of love and responsibility. She had tears in her eyes as she recalled the incident and talked about the gratitude it made her feel for her own parents.

Both of these moments were typical of the intimacy that couples who thrive experience every day. Their intimacy with each other is like a glow that surrounds them all the time. It is the backdrop on their stage of life. Intimacy pervades the lives of couples who thrive. It affects the quality of their whole life, and of everything else that they do.

In the last two or three decades, both the experience of intimacy and its place in our culture have changed dramatically. In this chapter, we will look first at what is new about our current style of intimacy. Then we will define intimacy and look at its close connection with self-love and self-disclosure. We will look at how thriving couples experience intimacy; at its "sacred" dimension; and at its relationship to one's personal freedom.

Our Style of Intimacy Is New

The notion of a lifelong connection with a "soulmate" is a brand-new marvel on the human scene.

For most of history, and still in many cultures, marriage was a family matter. If spouses weren't actually chosen for each other by family elders, at least the permission of elders had to be sought. The marriage itself then took place in the context of the extended family. People married primarily to raise children and to secure a place for themselves in society — not for intimacy.

Even with the rise of suburbia after the war when, in massive numbers, young couples began to move away from their parents, aunts and uncles, intimacy was not a matter of great concern to them.

A woman I interviewed showed me a remarkable letter. Before her divorce, some ten years earlier, which she had initiated because she wanted more intimacy than she felt she would ever have with her husband, she had received a letter from her then in-laws, who were very fond of her. They were imploring her to reconsider what seemed to them a trivial reason to break up a marriage. Their incredulity was probably quite typical of their generation:

> You are compatible and have many common interests. You get along well. Why is intimacy so important? We've had a wonderful marriage, and we never have been especially intimate. A marriage is a partnership — to live together. It doesn't have to be intimate to be successful. I'm not even sure what you mean by intimate. I know you are good friends. Isn't that intimate enough?

In just a few decades, that attitude about intimacy changed dramatically. After the Sexual Revolution, the Human Potential Movement, and the Women's Movement, quite suddenly given the history of human social evolution, we have emerged with a radically new concept of marriage. Now we want an equal partnership that is romantic, sexually passionate and deeply intimate, and we want it to last for a lifetime. We want to be lovers, friends, and partners — for years and years and years.

More than any other societal change, the contemporary feminist movement has made our new experience of intimacy possible, for genuine intimacy is possible only in a relationship between equals, and only since the radical changes wrought by feminism has an equal partnership between a man and a woman even been imaginable. Although on a societal level, equality between the sexes is still a dream, many couples have achieved it in their own relationships.

This is the first time in history that we have ever tried to combine intimacy with commitment.

No wonder a widespread aversion to commitment has emerged. No wonder single households doubled between 1980 and 1990. Committing oneself to a lifetime of sexual, psychic, and emotional closeness with one other person is a fairly radical act. It has its rewards, but it seems understandable that it may not be for everyone.

No wonder, also, that many marriages don't last. Socially speaking, this new kind of marriage is an experiment. We are innovators. As couple therapists explore this vast new territory, new theories emerge to help troubled couples find their way in a brand-new land.

We are carving out a new kind of marriage because we desire it. Now that we see they are possible, we crave full relationships that allow us to realize our potential as humans to relate mentally, emotionally, sexually, and spiritually and to explore these dimensions in depth over a lifetime with the same person. But it is important to recognize that such relationships are still in the exploratory stages and that the maps are still being drawn. The thriving couples of today are the Lewis and Clark of our times.

Another aspect of an intimate marriage that is novel in our times is that it is now optional. In previous times, marriage was an expected life choice; those who didn't choose it were deviant from the norm. Now, intimate marriage is only one of many options available as a potential lifestyle. Since community supports for marriage have fallen away and independent living is so widely accepted, the only reason for a person to marry is if he or she truly wants to.

Combining intimacy, sexual passion, and romance in an equal partnership, and committing to doing this for a lifetime, is — at least for some — an exciting idea. This fresh model for marriage holds enormous potential for us if we can get it right. It presents a major opportunity for personal and spiritual growth, and for great satisfaction and pleasure — but only for those who freely choose it.

The emergence of marriage as one lifestyle among many allows us to maintain loftier visions for what is possible between two people. If not everyone has to do it, those who choose to don't have to assume that marriage must conform to the lowest standard of norms in society. Couples who choose to can reach for the stars.

What Is Intimacy?

We all have our pictures of intimacy. Sex. A walk on the beach. A candlelight dinner. Reading in bed together. Finishing each other's sentences. Choosing the same dish pattern out of a whole store full. A foot massage after a stressful day.

When I ask couples to describe intimacy, they mention things like caring, sharing, complete comfort, touching, and being best friends.

All of these qualities emanate from an intimate bond, but the essence of intimacy, the component that makes all the other components possible, is self-disclosure. Intimacy is the process of stripping away your outer, more public ways of being and sharing your inner life with another.

If you are keeping significant secrets from someone, you might be able to have a pleasant sexual encounter or spend a cozy Sunday afternoon together, but you aren't being intimate. Conversely, the more deep, inner truths you share with another person, the more intimate you become.

Everyone has two selves: Your public self is the self you present to the general world. It is your personality, your appearance, the self that you use to interact with most people. Your public self has variations: the public self you present to your boss or an audience you may be addressing is quite different from the public self you present to your parents, and that self is different from the public self you present to your best friend or your lover.

Then there is your inner self. Underneath the surface lie very private realms. Secret feelings of pride and joy. Extremely private pleasures, fantasies, and dreams. And, deep in your private self lie the most unpleasant and difficult parts of your being as well: wounds from imperfect parenting and the traumas of growing up, painful regrets from the past, little pockets of low self-esteem, self-doubts, even self-hate, insecurities, and fears. Therapist Susan Christy calls this your "snake pit." Most of us do not visit this inner realm very often. We have enormous resistance to visiting it, understandably, because seeing what is there can be extremely frightening and painful.

But if you don't know all these parts of yourself, you can't love your whole self. Consequently, you can't give your whole self.

People who are self-loving are not self-loving simply because they are naturally wonderful people and therefore easy to love. Self-loving people have fears and self-hate just like the rest of us. They have become self-loving, self-confident people because they have been willing to become acquainted with their inner realms through repeated visits there. The visits are often terribly painful, but these people would rather face and overcome their demons than live forever at their mercy — because they have not had the courage to face them. Gradually, self-loving people come to see that what they find in their snake pit is not so horrible, and that they can forgive and accept even those things that seem so awful. It is easy to love the parts of yourself that you like. But genuinely self-loving people have worked hard and are able to accept and love even those parts of themselves that they at one time hated.

Again, if you don't know your whole self, you can't love your whole self. You can love only those parts of yourself that you let yourself see and know. So if you love your outer self — your personality, your accomplishments, your appearance, your performance — this is only partial self-love. And it means that you have to give some of your energy over to denial, to finding ways to cover up your snake pit, to pretend it isn't there, to run from it. And all that denial energy is energy that is not available for loving — yourself or anyone else.

And ultimately, if you don't love your whole self, you will never believe that someone else could love you, and you won't want to let anyone in close enough to see your whole self.

Paradoxically, at the same time self-love is a prerequisite for intimacy, intimacy is the primary method for achieving self-love — because it is intimacy that allows you to see the parts of yourself that give you trouble and that lower your self-esteem. So you must simply work on both at the same time. And you can work on them with different people. For example, I became intimate, that is, self-disclosing, with women friends, members of a therapy group, and a therapist on my way to becoming self-loving enough to let a man into my inner realms. And then his love helped me to accept even more of myself.

The only way to get acquainted with your snake pit so that you can begin to let go of hating it and learn to embrace and accept it is by — ever so gently and gradually — sharing it with another person.

Yes, it is hard. It may be the hardest thing you will ever do. It doesn't happen quickly. It takes time. It takes trust. But the rewards are commensurate with the challenge. There may be no greater pleasure in the universe than revealing your most humiliating secret to someone you love and trust, and having that person completely accept and love you in spite of it. That person's love can help you to overcome your shame, and to accept yourself, your real self, not the self you wish you were, not the self you pretend you are, not the self that you polish up and present to the world, but your real, whole self.

That's intimacy. It means being real with each other. Self-love and intimacy are inextricably linked: without an intimate connection, you can't know your whole self, so you are capable of only partial self-love. And as you become more self-loving, you become more eager to share your self with another person. As you have the courage to open up, you become more intimate *and* more self-loving — and then you naturally develop the courage to open up even more.

MEDITATION ON SELF-LOVE

No one is perfectly self-loving; I heard about many self-doubts and insecurities from the couples I spoke with. Yet the thriving couples with whom I shared this meditation responded enthusiastically to it as a statement of what they sometimes feel and always strive to achieve:

If I know myself thoroughly, and accept all that I know, then I don't have to be afraid of what you will find out when you get close to me. You will probably find some things you don't like. There are surely some things there that I don't like. But they don't scare me. I accept them. That's just who I am. Maybe with your help I can change some of them. But I'm not afraid of my weaknesses because I have learned to accept them. I invite you to accept them too. I know I am doing the best I can, and that is all I ever ask of myself.

If I know and love myself, then I won't try to change myself to please you. I want to be with someone who loves the real me.

If I have inner strength and I trust myself, then proving my worth to others will be unnecessary. I will not need to base my worth on outdoing or dominating others. If I know and love myself, I don't have to fear losing control. I trust that I will not betray myself, so I can relax. I can let myself be completely open. If I know and accept myself, then I love myself too much to give myself over to you completely. My self-respect won't allow it to happen. I can be devoted to you and still maintain my integrity. I can take care of myself.

If I know and accept myself, then my sense of power is not tied to success or approval bestowed by others. I have the power to make choices in my own life. My self-love gives me personal power.

SELF-DISCLOSURE

Intimacy, then, requires communication. And the most important part of intimate communication may be nonverbal. It may consist of tears, of holding, of eye contact, of sobbing or screaming, or of silence. But all this has to be brought about by some form of *verbal communication*, by conveying to another person what is in your heart — or in your snake pit.

Since the crux of intimacy is actually self-disclosure, we will spend some time focusing on self-disclosure to increase our awareness of how it functions in an intimate relationship. To be certain we cover all possible categories of self-disclosure and see how each functions to enhance intimacy, let's plot all the possibilities on a matrix. We can disclose events, ideas, and feelings about the past, the present, and the future, thus:

	Past	Present	Future
Ideas and Events	A	B	C
Feelings	D	E	F

Some couples spend a great deal of time talking about some categories of conversation but neglect others. Couples who thrive spend at least some time in all six categories. We will look at each category of conversation, or self-disclosure, in the approximate order of their importance for an intimate relationship.

E: Present Feelings. Perhaps the most difficult but certainly the most important category of self-disclosure between partners is present feelings. Far too frequently we fail to say what we are experiencing. For example, how often have you felt something like this, but failed to say anything about it?

Positive Feelings

I'm feeling very warm toward you tonight.

Your telling me that makes me feel proud of you.

I'm glad we could get together tonight. Driving home from work, I was aware of wanting to be with you a lot.

I have to tell you again: Your hair is beautiful. I like looking at it.

I take great pleasure that you are so competent in what you do.

Tentative Feelings

I'm annoyed at what happened at work today, but I want to forget it.

I'm afraid of getting close to you, but I don't want to back off either.

I've been feeling anxious and wrought up today, but I am not sure what about.

I must admit I am worried about how we are going to pay for that.

I sense I am going to like our new neighbor.

You seem to be angry. I feel uncomfortable with what you just said.

Negative Feelings

I feel miserable about this mistake I made.

What you just said makes me angry.

Honestly, I just can't get comfortable with your decision to go on that trip.

I'm feeling distant from you. I don't want to talk right now.

Total disclosure of present feelings makes possible the entire range of human emotions between two partners. If last night Judy told Mark how close she feels to him, then today it is much easier for her to tell him his behavior bothers her. On the other hand, withholding present feelings gives rise to the worst of barriers. If your partner is feeling guilty or angry with you, but is carrying on cheerful banter, then only that outer mask is available to you, and intimacy becomes impossible. Similarly, if your partner is feeling loving and vulnerable but can't let you know this, then you carry on a charade that bears little resemblance to intimacy.

Sharing present feelings is not easy. Even *knowing* what we are feeling at a given moment can be difficult. It requires paying attention to this aspect of ourselves, and it requires practice.

D: Past Feelings. Somewhat easier, and equally important, is disclosing past feelings.

> Last week when you went to that meeting, I felt left out and I was angry about it.

As soon as you realize what you were feeling, it's important to share it. A measure of your progress in learning how to share feelings is the length of time between the feeling itself and the point where you feel ready to talk about it. If eventually you can move from two months to two weeks, to two days, to two hours, and finally to two minutes, both your relationship and your own mental health will improve. If your partner sometimes brings up incidents or feelings from the past in order to discuss them or to get closure on them, be sure to listen fully. This is an opportunity for your intimacy to grow.

Past feelings also include feelings from the distant past. If intimates talk with each other about feelings associated with events in their childhood, their parents, their former relationships, their work situation, and their travels, they give themselves the opportunity to know and appreciate each other as real, whole people.

A and B: Past and Present Events. In sharing feelings, past or present, we are inevitably also sharing the events that gave rise to these feelings. It is, of course, quite possible to talk about events only, and to keep the feelings about the events hidden. Partial sharing of this sort is far better than nothing, but is limited in the context of intimacy. When your partner is relating to you the events of a day or a week spent apart, are you hearing about the feelings that went with the events — or only the events themselves?

C and F: Future Events and Feelings. Sharing future events and feelings is simply dreaming — and partners who want to know and love each other fully share — perhaps above all else — one another's dreams.

WHAT SELF-DISCLOSURE IS NOT

Self-disclosure does not imply compulsive honesty, the sharing of trivial details, or petty acts of confession for the sake of technical truths. If an omission or partial truth does not create a barrier of any sort, then it does not preclude intimacy. For example, a friend had some overdue library books. To her this is a completely trivial matter, but her husband finds it inexcusable and wasteful. She elects not to tell him, a wise decision. She is simply sparing them both unnecessary discomfort.

Solitude, emotional space, times of separation, and separate interests and activities are all very likely to be characteristics of a thriving, emotionally open relationship. People who are intimate are whole separate persons with their own private lives, which overlap in some ways and some times. Self-disclosure simply means they don't keep *significant* secrets from each other. They will tell each other about all the important events and feelings that occur in their private spheres.

People who are intimate will not be cruel to each other. When they must share events or feelings that may cause the other pain, they will time them carefully and be kind and compassionate.

In his discussion of truth, psychologist Scott Peck recognizes a few situations in which total self-disclosure is imprudent. He proposes six rules for withholding, which may serve as a guideline.

> First, never speak falsehoods. Second, bear in mind that the act of withholding the truth is always potentially a lie, and that in each instance in which the truth is withheld a significant moral decision is required. Third, the decision to withhold the truth should never be based on personal needs, such as a need for power, a need to be liked, or a need to protect one's [values] from challenge. Fourth, and conversely, the decision to withhold the truth must always be based entirely upon the needs of the person or people from whom the truth is being withheld. Fifth, the assessment of another's needs is an act of responsibility which is so complex that it can only be executed wisely when one operates with genuine love for the other. Sixth, the primary factor in the assessment of another's needs is the assessment of that person's capacity to utilize the truth for his or her own spiritual growth. Finally, in assessing the capacity of another to utilize the truth for personal . . . growth, it should be born in mind that our tendency is generally to underestimate rather than overestimate this capacity.

Self-disclosure is the starting point for genuine intimacy. The experience of sharing deeply and honestly with another person is exhilarating: when two people bare their souls to each other, they feel alive. They see their fears slipping away. They can breathe. They are two spirits whispering delicate secrets, psychic treasure maps that have been buried for centuries. Theirs is an indelible moment: they are connected.

Experiment #24

Many of us grew up in families that actively discouraged self-disclosure, that taught us to deny or bury our feelings and certainly not to share them with each other. Try the following exercise as an easy and safe way to begin experimenting with self-disclosure:

1. Facing your spouse, repeat one of the following sentence fragments over and over, giving it a different ending each time:
   When I was a child . . .
   I feel sad about . . .
   What I wish you understood about me is . . .
   What makes me happiest deep inside is . . .
2. Each evening at dinner for the next six days, choose a different box from the self-disclosure matrix (past, present, or future ideas, events, or feelings). Take turns telling each other things within that night's category. Children and teenagers may enjoy participating in this experiment, and an awareness of the categories will serve them for years to come.

Intimacy: The Experience

Now we come to a fine distinction. Intimacy is created by self-disclosure, by sharing one's inner life with another person. But the experience of intimacy itself is something far more than an exchange of information. Long-term intimacy is a quality as well as an event, a type of relationship, a range of feelings.

True intimacy is completely mutual. It is not possible to be intimate with someone who is not intimate in return. When two people meet and can tell right away that they are right for each other, often it is because they are equally available for intimacy. They are both "there." No one is holding back.

Couples who thrive are well matched in their ability to be intimate. They are not plagued with fear about getting close to each other. They can be fully there for each other — emotionally open and nondefensive, warm, attentive, and accepting. At the same time, they honor each other's need for "retreat time," and are not threatened by this because they have an abiding confidence in their overall closeness.

Intimates take enormous joy in each other's presence. They love being together. They love doing things together. They are best friends.

> REBECCA: After seventeen years, my heart still leaps when he comes into the room. I still can't wait to see him at the end of the day.

> MARTY: I can't sleep without her. I so love to have her body curled up next to mine, if she's gone for even one night, I miss her terribly.

> CORY: It is always such a pleasure to climb into bed with each other at night. Just the other day, I was near his office and we had lunch together, and Lou whispered in my ear, "I can't wait to snuggle up with you tonight." I love having this fun thing to look forward to at night. No matter how boring a day it has been, at least we have this little treat to anticipate all day long.

> ALICE: I used to hate to grocery shop. But now, if Brad comes along, which he usually does, I really enjoy it.

Intimates are deeply invested in each other's spiritual and personal growth. Virtually all of the couples I spoke with mentioned this, but perhaps Clen put it most beautifully:

> When you find in someone else the values that you yourself hold dear, you take responsibility for nurturing and supporting them in the other person. That's really what loving involves. It doesn't just mean giving flowers. In some religions they say, "The God in me greets the God in you." I greet God in Adrienne. I am constantly watching her grow. I'm always invoking that growth and urging it — rather than looking at her and wanting something. When I look at her, I see all the positive things that I know she has tried to be. Maybe they aren't completely there yet. But when I see her, I don't see that she hasn't succeeded yet; I see that she is trying.

An intimate bond connects two people at many levels. Clen continued,

> When I think of Adrienne, the images that come to mind are beautiful woman, skin, solid person, her maturity, her integrity, the earth, the

things that we share together, commitments to family, her intelligence, commitments to community — a lot of things that I really value. These fundamental things don't go away. When we are together, somehow I'm with the earth and I'm with my commitment to family and unity. I think you have to pay attention to the deeper processes that are going on in your relationship.

Intimacy is also a *process*. It is not a static condition that one strives for, suddenly achieves, and then forever possesses.

In a wedding preparation session, I asked a couple to spend some time writing down what they wanted to say to each other. In an emotional exchange, the man told his bride, "Don't expect too much from me too quickly — but don't give up on me either." He was well aware that intimacy is a process.

KAREN: I see our relationship as a long unfolding. We've both grown and changed so much. What did we know when we were twenty? I've found out how to find out more about myself — and about Earl. . . . You don't know what you don't know about each other early on. There is just no substitute for the years together, the shared experiences, the growing up together. I think you grow into closeness. We're closer now than we were when we got married, just because of all the time we've spent together.

It makes no difference when one decides to engage in the process of intimacy or how much one achieves. The decision to engage in the process is what can be life-changing. Such a decision can be made at any time, any age. It is not important to arrive; it is only important to be on the way. To share scary things, to reveal vulnerability, to become increasingly open, to work at letting go of defenses — this is intimacy. It's not something you have; it is something you do. That's why intimacy grows and changes: there's always something new to be honest about, some incident that evokes feelings. If a couple continue to share those feelings, their sense of adventure about life and their love for each other will grow.

Is Intimacy "Sacred?"

In virtually every culture, marriage is a religious sacrament, as it continues to be in ours. But in our high-tech age, when, even for those who are part of an organized religion, spirituality is not woven into the fabric of our collective lives (as it was for Native Americans, for example, and still is for tribal people around the earth), what does it mean to say that intimacy is sacred? If intimacy does have a sacred or spiritual component, does this quality actually have an impact on the day-to-day lives of couples who thrive?

In our deepest inner selves, we all long for wholeness, for all our wounds to be healed, for the purpose of life to be clear, and to see our role in that purpose. We want to be forgiven for our failures and loved for who we are. We long for a connection to the earth and the heavens, to feel a part of the natural cycle of life. We want to feel at peace with ourselves, and we want to feel unconditional love from some completely trustworthy source.

What opportunities does our asphalt, high-tech, achievement-oriented world give us to tap into these buried longings, to express them or to fulfill them?

Religion provides the opportunity in some cultures and perhaps once did in our own. But now, for most of us, one of the few experiences that taps into these larger religious questions is romantic love. In the first flush of new love we experience ecstasy. The purpose of life momentarily becomes clear. We feel healed, unconditionally loved, whole, and at peace.

Philosopher and writer Sam Keen points out that the original meaning of eros was not restricted to sexuality, but that it was "the impulse that made all things yearn and strive for fulfillment. The acorn was erotically moved by its destiny to become an oak, . . ." That deep craving for us to reach beyond what we are now and to become all that we can be is kept alive by love and the promise of love.

Romantic love awakens our spiritual aspirations because modern society provides few other arenas for them. The intensity and passion of an intimate connection with another person gives us a glimpse of nirvana, and it is one of the few experiences in modern life that can do this. The experience of the sacred is one of the great gifts of love.

But it can also be a trap. Romantic love can awaken our yearning for the sacred, but it can never fulfill it. No mortal human can be expected to make us feel whole, to give us meaning, and to keep life happy, purposeful, and intense. Insofar as we expect this from our love relationships, we will always be disappointed.

In thriving couples, there is a balance between the profound and the everyday dimensions of the relationship, and each aspect deepens the other. Feelings of awe and wholeness enrich the daily routines that make up the relationship, and the mundane details of life ground its deepest dimensions.

For example, couples who thrive touch each other with great frequency and variety. This physical intimacy is satisfying; it feels good. Yet it also recalls for the two of them their spiritual bond with each other. Their gentle touch, their enveloping themselves in each other physically, is a constant reminder of the vision with which they began their journey together and that continues to lead them. It is like saying, "I love you. I love that we are together. I honor you. Our relationship is a little miracle."

Thriving couples often support each other's individual spiritual growth. "I keep a dream journal," Wendell told me, "and have for more than twenty years. Elizabeth keeps one, too, and we often share our dreams with each other and talk about what they might mean." He went on,

> We do something called improvisational dance together every Friday night. It is free-form movement in which we create spontaneous choreography with one or more other dancers. It's fun and exhilarating — and it is a spiritual experience for us too. It feels like a celebration of our life together.

Other couples told me they worship together, share in a meditation practice, attend spiritual retreats together, read and discuss spiritual books, and generally nurture each other's personal and spiritual life.

Marriage, then, is sacred because it connects the individuals in the marriage to their higher selves and to the infinite and the divine.

But your full participation in your own marriage has an even greater sacred purpose for all of human kind — because the transformation of consciousness begins with tiny individual changes. There is a vast psychic rift between what psychologist Carl Jung calls the masculine and the feminine forces of the universe. Archaeologist Marija Gimbutas dates it from about seven thousand years ago when warlike and patriarchal Kurgan nomads invaded the Old European cultures that she describes as peaceful and art-loving, and whose deities were female. In expanding on the myth of *Tristan and Iseult*, Jungian scholar Robert Johnson claims that the figure of Blanchefleur "personifies the inner feminine soul of Western [humanity]." He says, "Her death records that sad day in our history when our patriarchal tality finally drove the feminine completely out of our culture and out of our individual lives."

Even though both the "masculine" forces of logic and power and the "feminine" forces of feeling and vulnerability abide within each of us, man and woman, still the masculine/feminine rift manifests itself today in the conflicts men and women are having with each other. And certainly culturally we remain dominated by masculine forces. Until we can achieve an equal partnership between masculine and feminine values in both our individual and our cultural life, we will remain antagonists working at cross purposes instead of allies complimenting each other.

So it *is* a sacred task for each of us to work at finding a healthy, vital blend of the masculine and feminine in ourselves and in our intimate relationships, for each of us contributes to the evolution of human consciousness and to the healing of this ancient schism in the human race.

Intimacy and Freedom

If an intimate relationship restricted the freedom of an individual, it could never work for a lifetime. A person who wants a full life would never agree to a relationship that was a prison of any kind. Yet a widespread view of intimacy is that it curtails one's freedom and autonomy.

People fear intimacy because they fear engulfment. They avoid intimacy because they fear it means a loss or diminishment of self. I hear this theme in my workshops all the time. One woman put it this way: "I'm afraid that giving myself fully to another person means giving myself *up* fully to that person."

In old models of marriage, there was validity to this fear. Women gave up entire careers to marry and have children. Men felt emotionally trapped. But those were marriages where there may have been commitment — but not intimacy. In marriages that combine intimacy with commitment, the individuals do not try to restrict one another's personal growth.

If we look at couples who thrive, we see anything but loss of personal freedom. These are individuals who, with the comforting, pleasurable, secure backdrop of their intimate relationship, are extremely independent and autonomous. For them, connecting does not mean merging. They are still two separate people with two discrete lives. In addition to their mutual goals for their lives, they have independent goals, and they support each other's. They find that their connection enhances their autonomy, and, conversely, that if they weren't independent individuals, their intimacy couldn't thrive.

Jonathan married Ellie when he was thirty-nine. He told me this:

> Before I married Ellie, I was afraid of the loss of freedom and independence. I'm sure that's what kept me single for so long. I was always asking, "How can you be both close and free?" I was obsessed with this question — I even wrote to Ann Landers about it! But my longing to be together with someone was beginning to overtake my fears, and when I met Ellie, my longings won. I'll tell you, it is nothing like what I feared. I would say, not only do I feel both close and free; I feel both closer and freer than I did when I was on my own but falling madly in love with every other woman. When I was single, I was free to run my own life, but I wasn't free, because so much of my energy went into obsessing about my relationships. And I was close to women periodically, but it was a kind of stand-in for the real thing — because it always had a temporary quality. . . . I haven't lost myself; I've gained a part of myself I never had before. Someone depends on me! I actually like it. . . . I have the answer to my question now. How can you be both close and free? You just do it.

Recently a friend called me to share his excitement about a new idea he and his wife had for expanding their small business. These two people *need* each other to make their whole adventure happen the way they want it to. They are pushing each other forward rather than holding each other back. Because they have each other, they are flourishing — separately and together.

Closing the Intimacy Gap: At Last, a Plan That Delivers

In chapter 7, we began to explore differences between men and women. All of these differences culminate in what I call the Intimacy Gap.

By now, the Intimacy Gap between men and women is well recognized. Still under the influence of a time when men had to be tough and fearless when they went out to hunt while women stayed by the hearth to nurture the children, women are more interested in and are generally better at feeling and expressing intimacy than are men.

But at last, to everyone's great relief, there has been a shift. We are at a moment in history when we have the motivation and knowledge we need to close the Intimacy Gap.

First, let's see exactly what the Intimacy Gap is.

THE CLASSIC INTIMACY GAP

An Intimacy Gap exists when one partner (usually, but not always, the woman) craves more intimacy than the other.

> DANA: I view my own husband, Ian, as a man who values feelings and expresses them to me. On one occasion, I had been feeling distant from him and out of touch. He seemed to be preoccupied with his work and not paying attention to his feelings for me. I decided to talk with him about it. My expectation was that he would say, "Oh, Dana, thank you for saying something. I have been spacing out and I don't feel good about it either. I don't like these times when I get out of touch with my feelings and out of touch with you." As my fantasy continued, he would take me in his arms and tell me all the things he hadn't been saying for a couple of weeks.
>
> I couldn't have been more wrong. Instead of thanking me, Ian got anxious and defensive. "Dana, I really don't know what you mean. You know I love you. I've got a lot on my mind now. Frankly, I don't know what else I could do. I think our relationship is wonderful. Could we just stop talking about this please? I feel like it's just one more thing for me to worry about and I can't take it on right now."
>
> I was genuinely surprised! I honestly thought my bringing the subject up would be supportive. I had assumed he was missing me as much as I was missing him.

Almost every couple has had some version of this conversation. The man feels pressured and criticized — and even inadequate, because he may feel he *can't* talk about his inner life as his wife would like him to. The woman feels disappointed, deprived and frustrated. Both feel that they are right and the other is wrong. Both feel misunderstood and, worst of all, they feel distant from each other — just the opposite of what each of them wants.

Most conflicts about the Intimacy Gap have the same general characteristics:

1. The woman asks for "more" from the man. Women all know what "more" is. They never need to explain it to each other. But they

have to explain what they mean to men. They mean more closeness, more *verbal* intimacy, more "attention," more focus, more feeling, more expressions of feeling, more heart, more evidence of love, more contact.

When a woman says to a man, "Let's talk," she feels excited, full of anticipation. But a man often winces when he hears this. He shrivels. He doesn't feel invited; he feels criticized and attacked. He feels unsafe.

2. They both tacitly agree that it is her responsibility to make him understand what she wants. She tries but she fails. He still feels criticized and inadequate.

3. She begins to feel that she is crazy. He's right. What she wants is not realistic.

4. He goes away feeling "right" and feeling that his worldview has been supported. She goes away feeling exasperated. As soon as she gets some distance, she knows she is not crazy, but knows he still thinks she is. She is caught in a classic double bind: If she asks for what she wants, he'll get defensive and create more distance. If she doesn't ask for what she wants, she will never get it, because he does not experience any problem. As one woman put it, "I'm willing to give him the space and alone time he wants. But if I give him space, will he give me closeness? Probably not."

> ANDREA: It's ironic. I think the reason my husband doesn't feel a problem in this area is that I'm so good at it. I often tell him how much I love him, and when I suggest I'd like to hear it from him, he says, "I tell you all the time." He never does. But he doesn't feel a need to affirm our relationship because I take care of it.

Women assume that if they ask for what they want clearly enough, men will get it, and that they will enjoy intimacy too. But psychologist and writer Lillian Rubin says,

> The problem lies not in what men don't say, but in what's not there — in what, quite simply, happens so far out of consciousness that it's not within their reach. For men have integrated all too well the lessons of their childhood — the experiences that taught them to repress and deny their inner thoughts, wishes, needs, and fears; indeed, not even to notice them. It's real, therefore, that the kind of inner thoughts and feelings that are readily accessible to a woman generally are unavailable to a man. When he says, "I don't know what I'm feeling," he

isn't necessarily being intransigent and withholding. More than likely, he speaks the truth.

THE CURRENT SHIFT IN THE INTIMACY GAP

The burgeoning Men's Movement is largely about the recovery of feelings among men. Together men have begun to discover how badly they have been betrayed and oppressed by the models of manhood that have been forced upon them. It was anger that first motivated women to throw off the burdens of patriarchal oppression; it is grief that is now beginning to agitate men. As they look inside, here is what they are unmasking:

Men are supposed to derive meaning and establish their identity through their work. But the world of work is set up so that it is genuinely fulfilling for very few people. Most workers are not using the full range of their talents and are not well rewarded for what they do accomplish. Slaves to their paycheck, most men suppress their true passions so they can conform to the definitions of success and manhood that they see all around them. When men are honest about what they feel, they feel unfulfilled, that they have failed to achieve meaning or to express their true identity. The fault is the way the workplace is set up, but men wrongly blame themselves. No wonder they shy away from expressing feelings, when what they feel is grief. As one man told me,

> The one thing that can bring tears to my eyes is when I hear that a man has left his corporate job to work with children or paint or garden full-time — or when a typist goes back to school nights to reach for her true dreams. When people are able to break free to live out some inner passion, that's what moves me. It is too rare.

Men long for close connections with their children, and no longer want to leave child-raising to women. They grieve for the relationships with their own fathers that they never had. They envy the deep, loving friendships women have with each other. And they resent the degree to which they are supposed to be identified by what they do.

Above all, men want to know how to love women, and they want women to love them. Increasingly, men want an emotional life — not because women want them to have one, but for themselves.

This is an exciting, unprecedented moment in history. How can we exploit it for the best possible results?

The first step is that both men and women must recognize the enormity of what men are confronting. Men need to be self-loving and patient with themselves, and women need to transform their anger and indignation toward men into empathy and compassion.

THE SIZE OF THE TASK MEN FACE

Only twenty-five years ago — a nanosecond in human history — we decided it would be a good thing for men to reverse thousands of years of conditioning and quickly change into something we like better. Norms that had been seen as a virtue were now, suddenly, seen as a curse. We must be aware that men are faced with a staggering undertaking.

It is not an accident that men are experts at burying emotions. This was a skill they needed in order to have the courage to hunt wild game and protect their families. It remained a useful ability in the industrial world where work was boring and was being done to fulfill someone else's goals. And today, in the corporate, bureaucratic, entrepreneurial, and athletic worlds where most men live their lives, they are expected to achieve, to win, and to succeed at all costs. Feelings get in the way of these goals.

For a very long time then, maintaining an "I'm great and everything's okay" facade has been adaptive behavior for men. The demand for them to change shocked the very foundation of their system.

Men are supposed to be strong. Asking them to become vulnerable is asking them to become the polar opposite of what they are used to being. They might value feelings intellectually, but they have little idea how to "feel" or what it will be like if they do. Are they supposed to give up being strong altogether? Can they be both? How can they feel like themselves or feel safe if they give up their familiar competent demeanor?

Men intuit that when they allow themselves to feel, one of the things they will feel is pain: grief over the feelings they have been missing out on, old childhood wounds, feelings of inadequacy, rejections, and fears. They may also realize that when they shut down feelings, they shut down *all* feelings, so unless they risk feeling this pain, they will never be able to feel the joy of intimacy. But letting all that pain come up is an enormous risk for any man to take, and we should not minimize it.

Also, men experience a double bind of their own. Women do still want strong, successful men. So men perceive, "If I don't express feelings, she'll reject me because I'm not vulnerable enough. But if I express my fears and insecurities, she'll reject me for being weak."

At this moment in history, men are in what we might call the "fertile void." It is in the nature of psychological and spiritual change that you have to give up an old way of being before you can embrace a new one. This period of time when you have released familiar, comfortable behaviors but are not yet fully engaged in the new ones is the fertile void. It feels terrifyingly empty when you are in it. You have had the courage to let go of something old that is no longer serving you, and your reward is to feel lost, unsafe, confused, and frightened. Only the faith that something better is about to fill this void will get you through it.

Men are in a void like this right now. The model for the new male doesn't exist yet. Men don't know what they are supposed to be headed for and they don't know how to find out. And to add to it all, they find it hard to express this confusion they are in.

We all believe that there is a better ideal for men than the one we have now: a man who is whole, who is not forced to mask any part of his real self, who is a perfect blend of his true masculine and feminine qualities. But how new this ideal is! We have only the most tentative models for it in society: Alan Alda? Robert Bly? How are men supposed to *learn* how to be? How are they to know what it will be like when they get there?

Men are already learning a great deal from each other. Just as women did in the early stages of their movement, men are bonding through their common experiences of absent fathers and inadequate male models.

But I believe that men will also need to turn to women. We are all in this struggle together. The two genders need to view each other as allies in the search for the new male. I saw this happening among the thriving couples I interviewed, and it is the approach that, I believe, will ultimately close the Intimacy Gap.

WOMEN AS EMOTIONAL MENTORS FOR MEN

I believe that the time has at last arrived for men and women to turn toward each other, and for women to offer to become "emotional mentors" for men.

The plan makes sense logically. Women have the skills, and men seek to acquire them. And both sexes stand to benefit, since women want men to become more emotional, too. However, for this very reason, the plan is fraught with risk. Because women have a vested interest in the outcome, they may make poor teachers.

Many women have already had the experience of attempting to

mentor a man in his effort to become a more feeling person, for this sort of thing happens informally in many relationships. Too often, it ends in disaster because either the woman feels she is giving more than she is getting back and becomes resentful, or the man feels he is being criticized and pressured, and he becomes resentful. So the question is, Can we find a way to avoid the hazards of an emotional mentoring relationship and to take advantage of the possibilities it offers?

In my last book, *If I'm So Wonderful, Why Am I Still Single?*, I discussed the tactics women unwittingly use in their frustration to try to get through to their men, tactics that are always doomed to failure: asking for what they want, *not* asking for what they want, playing "hard to get," using "emotional blackmail," lecturing, punishing, and denying their needs. So if these tactics don't work, what will?

GUIDELINES FOR EMOTIONAL MENTORING

1. The desire for an emotional mentoring relationship must be mutual. Both of you must believe you will benefit from it. Men, be sure you have your own reasons for wanting to change. If you are not highly motivated to become more intimate for your own sake, your wife's mentoring will become nagging and both of you will end up resenting it. You cannot be working on your intimacy skills to meet your partner's needs.

Women, let go of any feelings of anger, resentment, or superiority on this issue. Tap into your well of empathy and understanding. Remember what an enormous change your partner is trying to make. Think about the influence of his family in making him who he is. You can mentor and coach effectively only if you are patient and appreciative.

2. Learn the difference between a thought and a feeling, and practice using "feeling language."

One rule of thumb is, if a sentence begins, "I feel *that* . . . ," it will almost certainly be a thought, not a feeling. "I feel that you were being selfish last night," is a thought. (It is also a "you" statement rather than an "I" statement, which, as we learned earlier, is not good relationship-enhancing communication.) "I felt unseen last night," is a statement of feeling.

The simple formula, "I feel ———," will virtually always say everything you need to say when you are feeling emotional, whether it be warm and close or angry or sad. Since it is simple, it is a good way to begin practicing using feeling language.

Since men are not accustomed to talking about feelings, their feeling vocabularies are often limited. So I have provided a list of feeling words to give you ideas. I find it a helpful rule when discussing feelings to disallow the use of "good" and "bad." I force myself (and others) to be more specific. Here are a few synonyms for "good" and "bad."

Good

welcome	sweet	nice
inviting	engaging	captivating
seductive	enticing	ecstatic
elated	jubilant	overjoyed
thrilled	enthusiastic	excited
fantastic	happy	marvelous
pleased	satisfied	warm
receptive	pleasant	mellow
optimistic	glad	

Bad

ANGRY	DEPRESSED	AFRAID	HURT
agitated	blue	apprehensive	painful
annoyed	sad	embarrassed	disappointed
irritated	gloomy	insecure	offended
pissed off	discouraged	jittery	distressed
frustrated	lousy	nervous	upset
enraged	dejected	anxious	tearful
furious	awful	scared	stunned
	defeated	overwhelmed	self-pitying
	crushed	panicky	
	miserable		
	dreadful		
	desolate		
	despairing		

3. **Women:** The most important contribution you can make to your partner in coaching him to access and express his feelings is simply to ask him how he feels. This is a surprisingly easy, overlooked strategy.

In my first marriage, I used to spend a lot of time wishing my husband would tell me how he felt about certain things. It finally occurred to me to ask him. Whenever I did, the question would take him by surprise. But he would think about it and then usually come up with quite a detailed account of how he felt, or at least what he thought, which was far better for me than nothing at all.

Begin by asking your partner about positive emotions. Always model for him by stating your own feelings first. For example, "I felt so loved and taken care of when your folks treated us to dinner. I feel really blessed that you have such a great family and that I feel so much a part of it. How did you feel about that evening?"

Remember that, through no fault of his own, feelings may be like a foreign language for your partner. He may feel awkward and defensive — because he fears he might not be able to give you what you want.

Your job is to make this conversation feel *safe* for him. He has to know that, no matter what he says, he will not be attacked, belittled, or laughed at. Especially when you want to talk about feelings between the two of you, explain that you want to ask him for something but that this *does not mean that you are feeling critical* of what he already does.

Do not set yourself up as superior to your apprentice in any way. This is not like a professor/student or doctor/patient relationship, in which you have a body of knowledge and your pupil knows nothing. Think of yourself as a facilitator or coach, not an instructor. Your role is to help you both pay attention to feelings more often. Talk about your own feelings, ask him about his, and then *listen to him* with genuine understanding and empathy.

Remember that your help will be resented sometimes, no matter what your agreement is. When you ask a friend to help you stay on a diet, you still resent her when she says, "Do you really want to eat that?" It is the same with emotional mentoring. Don't get caught up in being resented. Let it slide off you. It will pass. Just back off and then bring up feelings again some other time.

Don't initiate a discussion about positive emotions when you are feeling the least bit angry with each other. If either of you has any lingering resentment toward the other, the conversation will not in fact be "safe," and you will do more to set back feelings conversations than to encourage them. For negative emotions toward each other, call a Feelings Forum as described in the last chapter, and participate as equals, not as mentor and mentored.

Women, here is your big caveat: Do not use the emotional mentoring idea to avoid accepting valid differences between men and women, between you and your partner. Remember that it is normal for men to want periods of time when they withdraw into themselves, space out, become absorbed in some activity, or go off on their own. This is not evidence of an intimacy gap as long as your partner becomes intimate with you at other times.

If men's task is to feel more, women's is to nag less. Most women have to work to accept their partner the way he is.

A friend told me recently that her new baby had created some unexpected tensions between her and her husband. "He had his hand on the highchair and was kind of stroking the baby, but he was absorbed in the newspaper. I gently told him I'd feel better if he interacted with her more. He got angry, yanked her out of her seat, and started to read to her."

This tension could have been avoided if my friend had trusted her husband to develop his relationship with his daughter as he wanted. There was nothing wrong with what he was doing. She needed to accept him, not try to reform him.

You will make your entire relationship safer for intimacy if you can learn not to take your partner's withdrawal times personally. When he seems distant and detached from you, he may be dealing with stress, solving a problem, or simply recharging his batteries. Support him by allowing him to retreat. Take this opportunity to get some good quiet time for yourself. Many women don't get enough time alone. Understand that your spouse's little retreat has nothing to do with you. This is often how men behave. It makes them self-sufficient and capable, qualities that you like very much in your man. The more freely you can allow him his retreat times, the happier and more eager he will be for connection with you.

4. **Men:** When your partner wants to talk with you about "the relationship," or when she asks you for more expressions of love, more feeling, understand that she is not criticizing you. Rather, she is reaching out to you; she wants to feel close. In the best way she knows how, she is doing what she does well: she is cultivating the emotional side of your relationship. If you feel yourself tighten up, if you feel attacked, if you start making defensive remarks like, "I *do* hug you enough; I *do* tell you I love you," relax. You might say to her, "I'm feeling defensive, and I don't want to feel this way." That alone will help the defensive feelings to abate.

Be open to what your partner is saying to you. Have the attitude,

"She's asking me for a favor, something she wants. I can try giving it to her. I welcome her efforts. I can learn from her." Listen to her very carefully. Don't worry about producing what she wants right away. Just listen. *Let her know that you have heard her by rephrasing what she has said.* That response will mean more to her than anything else you could possibly say. Then, try whatever she is asking for. If it helps, take a few minutes to go inside yourself and find out how you feel. Then express it in words as well as you can.

Most men misunderstand why verbal expressions of love are so important to women. As a man I counseled once many years ago said, "If my wife can't tell I love her by the way I make love to her, then she's got a problem, not me. I don't see what else she needs."

As we have pointed out before, a woman wants *verbal* expressions of love from her partner, not because she is insecure about his love, not because she is afraid he doesn't love her, but because verbal expressions of love are a pleasure for her. They allow her to feel his love, to experience it. The wife of the man I just quoted said to him, "What is the difference between love that never gets expressed and no love at all?"

Alexander Lowen, psychologist and author of *Depression and the Body,* says,

> Feeling is the inner life, expression is the outer life. Put in these simple terms, it is easy to see that a full life requires a rich inner life (rich in feeling) and a free outer life (freedom of expression). Neither alone can be fully satisfying. Take love, for example. The feeling of love is a rich feeling, but the expression of love in word or deed is a joy.

George Eliot, in a letter to a friend,* said,

> I like not only to be loved but also to be told that I am loved. I am not sure that you are of the same mind. But the realm of silence is large enough beyond the grave. This is the world of light and speech, and I shall take leave to tell you that you are very dear.

In addition to being a pleasure, talking about love can greatly expand your experience of it. You may actually realize things you never thought about before or never focused on. For example, when Mayer

---

*Letter to Mrs. Burne-Jones, May 11, 1875. *The George Eliot Letters*, vol. 7. Edited by S. Haight. New Haven: Yale University Press (1954–78).

and I first got together, I wanted to write some articles about his art work for an art magazine. For several mornings, we went out for breakfast and I interviewed him. I would ask him questions like, "What do you like about the ceramic medium? Why have you chosen to make bowls and teapots rather than something else? Where do your ideas come from? Do you see your pieces as expressive of under-lying themes?" The conversations were exciting, because, as Mayer rambled on with his answers, he uncovered insights about his work that had never surfaced in him before. Conversations about your re-lationship can be revealing in the same way.

> TYLER: Recently we took a walk and were talking, and Patsy told me she loves the way I take such an interest in my brother. She said she finds it really endearing. I like that, but we've been married sixteen years, and I never knew she paid any attention to this.

Most men have to make an active decision to talk about their feel-ings; it does not come naturally to them. With some loving, supportive mentoring from your partner, you can choose to open yourself up to a whole new dimension of your life.

5. There are two different kinds of learning experiences. The first is the method used in learning to play the piano: you repeat the same phrase or piece over and over, building ever so gradually on what you practiced yesterday and the day before. Improvement is incremental.

Experiences like learning to ride a bicycle are very different. You may try over and over without any apparent success. The tenth at-tempt may look even less successful than the first. Then all of a sud-den, one time, it all comes together and you have learned something you will never again be without. Even though all the first attempts appeared to be fruitless, the breakthrough would never have occurred without them. This type of learning requires perseverance in the face of apparent regression.

Personal growth is more like learning to ride a bicycle than learning to play the piano. You may work on something over and over and feel it is pointless. Then, suddenly in one moment, you feel as though you have known this thing all your life. Both mentor and learner must be aware of this phenomenon and must have patience and trust when it appears that no progress is being made.

6. Periodically evaluate your emotional mentoring experiment. The evaluation itself will be a feelings conversation. You must each evalu-ate yourselves, not each other. Women, your partner's progress must

not be measured by some absolute scale that you have established. You are not mentoring your partner to get your own needs met, but so that he can meet his own. Only he can judge whether he feels he is changing in ways that feel good to him.

*   *   *

Emotional mentoring is a mid-revolutionary strategy that will help us work together to forge a new kind of partnership between men and women — based on equality and a better balance between the masculine and feminine aspects of our psyches. The most important part of it is the recognition that men and women can be allies in their quest for more intimacy. Emotional mentoring won't replace women's political struggles for equality or men's own explorations of the male experience. But it will affect those movements by allowing us to have more compassion for each other's experiences.

Experiment #25

Women: For the next week, every time you catch yourself being critical or demanding of your partner in even the smallest way, write down what you were having a problem with. Keep pencil and paper with you, so you will be ready, and then transfer your items into your notebook.

At the end of two weeks, look over your list and ask yourself, "Is this something I could let go of and simply accept about my partner?" Now, for the next week, adopt an attitude of loving acceptance toward everything about your mate. Give him lots of verbal affirmation.

Men: During the next week, initiate a conversation with your partner about your feelings about each other. Take her out to dinner or for a walk or drive. Tell her various feelings you have about her and about your relationship.

Every day for one week, make a deliberate point of giving your mate one piece of *verbal* intimacy. Tell her how you feel about her. Practice self-disclosure about your *present feelings*.

---

*   *   *

Intimacy is the fruit of our deep longing for connection with each other.

We were not given the gift of life to remain isolated from each other. Yet amazingly, after several hundreds of thousands of years of human history, we are still exploring the frontiers of intimacy. We have gone to great lengths to explore outer space, which to our strange Western psyches, feels safer than probing the mysterious realms of our own and each other's inner space. But now, armed with new awareness and motivation, we have an unprecedented opportunity to probe the orbits that connect us. No huge national budget is required; we need only time, courage, and each other.

What are the frontiers of your own intimate experience? You may feel at times that you have already reached the outer limits: "How could we ever become closer than this?" But intimacy is many-faceted, and exploring its many dimensions takes a lifetime.

Bear in mind that the kind of intimacy we are exploring today is new, and that your own experiences contribute to its general evolution. Remember that intimacy is integrally connected with self love, and that to expand one is to expand the other. Open yourself to even the slightest opportunities for greater self-disclosure with your partner so that gradually you will close your own intimacy gap, fully enjoy your intimate experiences, feel the freedom that intimacy opens up in your life, and contribute to the sacred task of healing the age-old antagonism between masculine and feminine.

Your intimate relationship is an ever-unfolding adventure. Enjoy it.

Chapter 9

TRAIT 8: PLEASURE
Part A: Sex

WHEN MASTERS AND Johnson did their pioneering research about human sexuality, they reported that a stunning 50 percent of all married couples had sexual problems. To many, that sounded alarmingly high, and much press was devoted to this statistic. Bad news sells. But the obvious corollary to the bleak statistic is that fully half of all married couples have at least satisfactory or possibly quite wonderful sex lives. The press wasn't interested in their stories. No one found out what was making sex work for them. Until now.

It turns out we can learn a great deal from couples who thrive about what works for them sexually and why.

There was great variety among the thriving couples I spoke with, but they were all basically content or even very pleased with their sex lives. They agreed that sex is an important part of their relationship, and that their sexual attraction for each other has endured. But this was not because they have perfect sex every time, not because they were all perfectly sexually compatible, not because they had perfectly matched sexual desires, not because they both liked exactly the same activities during sex, and not because they devoted an extraordinary amount of attention to sex.

These couples enjoyed sex because *they accepted what they had together* — and they went with it. They both had a positive attitude about sex, they wanted to enjoy it, and they viewed differences between them not as problems to be solved, but as facts of life to be accepted. They *believed* they could have a good sex life, they *wanted* one, and they were *committed* to their own and each other's sexual happiness.

The secrets of sexual happiness for these couples can be summarized in six principles that presented themselves over and over again in our discussions. They seem to me to be both necessary and sufficient for any couple to maintain a long and happy sex life together.

1. They experience sex as an integral part of their love.
2. They accept their sexual experience just as it is.
3. They know and incorporate into their lovemaking the differences between what men and women enjoy in sex.
4. They talk about their sex life; in particular, they are willing to ask for what they like.
5. They balance giving and receiving during sex.
6. They deliberately find ways to stimulate their sex lives.

1. Sex Is an Integral Part of Their Love

Shifts in societal norms occur, not in accord with our individual chronological ages, but by decades. Thus, for example, we all changed our attitudes about sexuality during the sixties and seventies, whether we were in our twenties or our forties at that time.

The couples I interviewed had retained the best of what the sexual revolution achieved for us and had rejected its excesses. In delivering sex from repressive Victorian taboos, the sexual revolution went too far, these couples felt, by attempting to separate sex from love or intimacy. "Sexual freedom" had been appealing to some of these individuals at one time, but it now felt to them like a trivialization of something they felt to be mystical and sacred. When sex lost its sacredness, it was missing the very quality that made it so pleasurable; when sex became as common as a handshake, it could no longer convey special adoration and respect.

During the sexual revolution, sex was simply a predominantly physical affair. It was strictly erotic. In the nineties, in sex and in other areas of our lives, the heart is regaining its rightful position in the center of our lives.

First and foremost for the couples I interviewed, sex is an expression of their love for each other. It is pleasurable because it expresses a couple's mutual adoration for one another. Sex allows them to experience their love, to express it, and to feel it. Sex is a form of communication for them, not simply an erotic high. It is their relationship that makes their sex special, not the other way around.

Very few of the couples I spoke with even mentioned sexual "techniques," and when I brought it up, they felt it was trivial. Marne told me

> Every lovemaking session we have is very different. But we probably have only about six or seven "techniques." The variety comes in our moods, our conversations, the amount of time we spend, how turned on we happen to be — stuff like that. It's not some kind of a gymnastics routine that we have to *learn*. I've never even read *The Joy of Sex*, and I have no interest in it. . . . Don't get me wrong — we play around a lot. But we already know what we like to do. We don't have to look in a book.

"Great sex begins with all of life," Jeff told me. "I make love all day long to Gail — when I tell her how beautiful she looks, or how great she is, or when I squeeze her arm or kiss her cheek."

Other couples also emphasized the importance of both verbal lovemaking and "nonsexual" touching and tenderness. Nancy was one of them:

> In my first marriage, my husband never touched me except when he wanted to make love. It just didn't occur to him I guess. He thought the only way he could get caring from me was to get sexual. Sometimes he wanted sex, but sometimes, all he wanted was caring and affection. I used to ask him to get affectionate sometimes when we *weren't* going to make love. He'd do it once and then forget all about it again. George is the total opposite of him. We are all over each other all the time. Now, I will admit, I initiate a lot of it. But George always seems to love it. And when he does spontaneously grab me up in his arms, or come up behind me in the kitchen and hug me, oooooh, I love it so much.

Sex usually reflects whatever else is going on in a relationship. If times are stressful, or if a couple is at odds or a bit withdrawn from each other, their sex life will reflect this. Sometimes an improvement in the relationship or in the outside conditions that are creating stress will brighten the sexual relationship. But other times, a wonderful sexual experience can brighten their moods: they might have an especially warm or exciting lovemaking experience and find that the distance has evaporated.

While these couples emphasized the integral connection between their love for each other, that is, their entire relationship, and their sex lives, they also agreed that it was important for them to start out with a partner who was sexually compatible.

> MICHAEL: Before I met Julie, I dated a lot of women. I was one of those hard-to-please bachelors — no one was good enough for me. My friends all wrote me off as hopeless because I found a flaw in every woman I dated. But I really feel vindicated now because no one was just right for me sexually. Or if they were, there was some other major deal-breaker. But mainly, I needed to feel really turned on to a woman, and I needed to *love* sex with her. And if it wasn't there, no matter how bright and kind the woman was, I just couldn't do it. I was right! Julie and I have an amazing amount of things going for us, but one of them, definitely, is sex. It had to be there.

THE TWO SEXUAL FEELINGS: LOVE AND EROTIC PLEASURE

Couples who are close and in long-term relationships experience two discrete aspects of sex: their connection to each other, and their own erotic pleasure. Women spoke about this separation more than men. Usually they feel these two separate aspects of the sexual experience at different times.

> HANNAH: When I first start getting turned on, I feel these warm, gushy feelings — romantic, sentimental, almost nostalgic. They are all directed at my partner. I feel devoted to him, I cherish him, I feel close and connected to him, it's like I want to merge with him. The more turned on I get, the stronger the feelings become. It's passionate and romantic, and exciting — but it is not exactly erotic. Then I almost have to shift gears deliberately to get more tuned in to my own erotic feelings. I have to think specific sexual fantasies — and only then do I start getting interested in having an orgasm. Then it switches to my own intense pleasure, the building excitement.
>
> Sometimes it's the other way around. Sometimes, I get erotically turned on first — if we've been watching a sexy movie or something. I can get really carried away at those times. [She rolls her eyes.] Then, it's

only *after* an orgasm that I get all affectionate and passionate feeling.

In any case, after we have both had climaxes, and we go into deep, deep relaxation in each other's arms, the warm, close, connected feelings come back. I absolutely love that part of lovemaking. It's so close and so satisfying and so comfortable. It has a timeless quality. I love the feeling that I never want to move again. I feel perfectly secure in his arms.

I can remember I used to get hints of that feeling when I made love with people I was going with before I got married, and I used to long desperately to feel that way with someone I really did love — and wasn't just pretending to love. And now I have that experience, and I feel unbelievably grateful — every time. I'm home.

Several women mentioned that they go through phases when they are experiencing the connection side of sex more, and phases when they are feeling more erotic. But both men and women agreed that sex was comfortable, free, and exciting because the relationship itself was a joy to begin with.

2. Great Sex Starts with Acceptance

Many couples sabotage their sexual happiness by worrying that things ought to be other than what they are. We should make love more often. I should have more orgasms, or better ones. We should talk more, or less, during sex. I should get turned on faster. My wife should be more responsive. My husband shouldn't want sex so often. We should be enjoying sex more than we do. Sex isn't as good as it used to be. And so on. Take a moment to consider your own "shoulds."

Couples who thrive waste no time on such thoughts. Not because their lovemaking is always perfect, but because they recognize that acceptance of things exactly the way they are is the only sensible alternative. Of course if there is something they think they can get help with or improve, they take action. A dozen or more women told me they had consulted with their gynecology nurse practitioners or doctors about sexual issues, such as dryness, painful intercourse, or lack of responsiveness. Three couples had participated in sex therapy, of whom two felt they had received great help from it.

But a general lack of anxiety around sexual issues was most apparent among these couples. They were happy to accept whatever life had dealt them. For example, one man who had had an active and varied sex life before he was married had finally settled down with a woman who followed an Indian spiritual teacher. She was a warm, happy woman who was conservative about her sexual practices. She did not use contraceptives, and she engaged in a very limited range of sexual activities. But her husband was so delighted to be with her and so adoring of her that, even when I spoke with him in private, he brushed off these limitations.

> Sex with her is very special, and that makes it wonderful. I'm glad I got around a bit before I met her, but she's the best thing that ever happened to me, and we have a great sex life. It's different for me, but different in a very wonderful way. I'm learning so much from her — about how much variety and pleasure there can be from exploring one or two types of activities in more depth. Her preferences around sex are just part of who she is. It would be absurd for me to try to persuade her to change.

One contribution of the sexual revolution was to free us to try a wider range of sexual activities. But the negative side of this contribution has been to make us feel that we "should" enjoy sex all the time, and that we "should" try a wide range of sexual activities. Genuine sexual freedom is recognizing that, at the same time you are *free to* enjoy sex in more ways, you are also *free from* having to do anything you don't genuinely want to do. Being "liberated" does not mean that you have to be tyrannized by sex manuals showing new positions and equipment, or suggesting novel behaviors. Sexual freedom means figuring out your own sexual preferences and accepting them.

Many sexual "problems" will disappear if you can simply make an internal shift from viewing them as problems that you have to do something about to viewing them as fine just the way they are. There is no right way for sex to be. This point was brought home to me dramatically years ago when my colleagues and I conducted women's sexuality groups at the University of California in Berkeley. The women in these groups shared with each other in great detail what types of touching, what activities, what fantasies, and what movements turned them on. I may have worked with some two hundred women, and I never heard the same combination of "turn-ons" twice!

People's preferences and experiences were all so different, there was clearly no right or wrong, no better or lesser experience. You — and your sexual experiences — are unique. It's just a question of figuring out what brings you and your partner pleasure and doing that. Your own frequency of sex, your own method of achieving orgasm or of being sexual without orgasm, your own pleasurable activities whatever they are, are right *for you*.

Couples who thrive accept their own bodies and their own sexuality, their partner's body and sexual preferences, and the variations and changes that occur over their months and years together. Hannah told me a rather touching story:

> I've been getting lots of menopausal symptoms. It's kind of a drag, but one thing that has alarmed me and that I never expected is that I seem to take much longer to have an orgasm — once I'm headed in that direction. After this had been going on for a while — you know how you don't really notice something until you notice it, and then when you do, it has been there for a while? — I started to worry that it might be sort of annoying for Marty. So I mentioned it. He was so sweet. He said that he hadn't even noticed it, and that he was never in a hurry anyway, and that the longer things went on the happier he was. I mean he just made me feel so wonderful. And I completely let go of worrying about it.

All couples reported that they had lots of different kinds of sexual encounters with each other, everything from "quickies" to long, leisurely afternoons or weekends away. Sometimes they are in perfect sync with each other, and they have really passionate, heightened pleasure and feel absolutely wonderful. Other times their moods are mixed or low and they just go through the motions and don't get especially turned on. They go through periods of time when they are making love often, and other periods when they suddenly realize they have gone a month or more without making love. These flush or dry spells can last a few months or even a few years, but inevitably, the tide turns and a new era emerges. But the quality that made all these couples say that they are happy with their sex lives is that they did not worry about all these shifts and evolutions. Sex ebbs and flows in many ways, and that's okay.

Elaine's attitude was a good example of this acceptance:

When we first met, we were like rabbits. We were totally hot for each other's bodies. I mean we were in bed all the time. I'd say for the first three or four years, we had really wonderful sex all the time. Now, I'll tell you, it's really different. Neither one of us is very interested. It's like we've run out of steam. Maybe we make love once a month, I don't know. But our relationship has never been better. We're in a great place with each other. We just aren't very interested in sex. And it's just fine with both of us.

It is, of course, more of a challenge simply to "accept what is" when there is a difference between the two of you than when you are in sync. A common example is when one person is in the mood and the other isn't. What I noticed about these couples is that *they did not take these differences personally* — unless they knew it was a reflection of some tension going on between them. For example, Carolyn and Eddie were in a "dry period" when I interviewed them.

CAROLYN: I know Eddie is under an enormous amount of stress right now. He just started a new job, and it isn't going very well. He's just not in the mood for sex. Besides, both of us have had colds. I'm getting a bit "horny," but I'm not at all worried about this. I'm doing all I can to support him. I've been hinting around, and trying to get him turned on, but I'm totally patient. I know it's not going to go on forever. After all, we have fourteen years of history I can draw on.

Perhaps partly from the media and movies, we are led to believe that sexual experiences are all alike. They are not. Just as your face, your fingerprints, and your accent are different from everyone else's, so are your sexual feelings and preferences. Your uniqueness makes you rare and special. Couples who thrive do not attempt to conform to an elusive sexual standard. They accept and enjoy what they have with each other.

3. Thriving Couples Accommodate the Differences Between Them

Men's chief complaint about women is that they aren't responsive enough and aren't interested enough in sex. Women's chief complaint about men is that they proceed too fast. (Why do women fake orgasm? Because men fake foreplay.)

Couples who thrive discuss these basic tendencies too, but because their relationships are dominated by a spirit of goodwill and generosity toward each other, they have found ways to work with these ongoing issues so that, much of the time, they meet both their own and each other's needs and desires.

The clichéd woman's line, "I have a headache, not tonight," seems to have a grain of truth in it among the women I spoke with. Several told me they sometimes have an *initial* resistance to having sex when the invitation is offered, verbally or nonverbally. "I'm not in the mood at that time," one woman told me. "I'm in my head, thinking about the children or some committee meeting." But women in successful relationships have learned that if they pay very little heed to that strong message, "Oh no, not now," the resistance fades. They are motivated to *ignore the initial urge to withdraw* because a) they have enough experience to know that if they give themselves a chance, they will get turned on and enjoy themselves; b) they *want* an active sex life because they believe that it is an important component in their relationship; and c) they want to make their husbands happy and to accommodate their desires. Several women spoke about this:

> In the very early stages of our relationship — maybe we'd only been going together six weeks or something, Darrell said something to me like, "I just love that you always want to make love, that you never turn away. My ex-wife — and the women I've been going with — said no a lot. They had a headache or they weren't in the mood. I hated that. I just love that you never say no." The comment made a big impression on me. I wanted to give him that. The first time I *wasn't* in the mood, I didn't want to disappoint him, so I went with it anyway, and I found out that I did get really into it if I gave myself time. If we always waited until I was in the mood, we wouldn't make love very often, and we'd be missing a lot of pleasure and connection. But Darrell plays his part in this, too: He *knows* that he has to get me in the mood, and he's patient and gentle and does all the things he knows I respond to.

> A lot of times Jim will start giving me signals early on and then we'll brush our teeth and hang out for a while — or if it's Sunday morning, he'll go get the paper and start the coffee so we'll have it there when we are ready. This gives me a chance to start shifting gears. I have to make a deliberate effort to stop thinking about all the other things on my mind and think erotic thoughts, and I start touching myself and getting

myself turned on. Sometimes he's not aware of this, but when he is, it is a real turn-on for him.

When I'm not in the mood, I let David know it in a sort of teasy way. I'll say, "You have to do all the work tonight," or "I'm not going to get turned on, I'm too tired." He knows I'm half kidding. I'm not saying no, but it takes all the pressure off me. I've given myself permission to be the passive partner this time, and he has a little challenge. Sometimes I don't get very turned on, but often I do — if I just let myself relax into it, and let go of my other thoughts.

Of course men aren't always in the mood for sex either. Adrienne and Clen, the couple who have the policy they call "mood schmood," made an important point:

> CLEN: I realized that sexual desire can be just an *idea*. It's not always going to appear as full-blown lust. Even if I'm not feeling sexy, but I think I might want to have sex that night, that's sexual desire — the desire to have sex. That's enough. Especially after our daughter came along — and we are both working full-time — if we waited until we felt physical desire, we might hardly ever have sex.

Your most important sex organ is your brain. If you are thinking about all of the other things in your busy life, or you are worried about something and feeling anxious, you won't be feeling very sexy. But you are not at the mercy of your thoughts; you can control them. It may help you to make a few notes about whatever is occupying your mind at the moment. Make a list, or a short journal entry so that you can let go of your busy thoughts and come back to them later. If there is no time for an interruption like this, make a mental list, or just remember what you want to come back and think about — or worry about — later. Then start thinking about some lovely sexual fantasy. Relax. Let your partner know in some teasing way that you need a little time and a little help to get in the mood. Don't worry if your mind is on other things besides him and sex. Let it wander around if it wants to. Just don't get invested in your other thoughts, and, as in a meditation, keep coming back to your sexual fantasies. Give yourself time to get turned on, and it will happen — more some-times, less others.

Sometimes resistance to sex may be more than just the traditional

female role in the mating dance. Sherry found that her lack of responsiveness signaled other problems:

> I can usually get in the mood for sex pretty easily. I'm very grateful
> that Tom initiates sex as often as he does. I just love that he is so turned
> on by me and that he wants to make love a lot.
>
> Recently I got into a period where the sex just wasn't going well. I
> wasn't enjoying it. I wasn't letting myself get turned on. It seemed like
> it must be obvious to Tom, but I didn't say anything for a while. Then
> finally I did, and it opened the floodgates. I realized that he had been
> helping with the kids less and less and had been kind of off doing his
> own thing and that I had been feeling left out and resentful. We had
> this huge talk, and as we began to work this stuff out, our sexual close-
> ness returned. I was kind of amazed at how this resentment had built
> up in me without my realizing it, and that it was what was going on
> sexually that rang the bell for me.

In general I found that women in thriving relationships were concerned as much about meeting their partner's needs as their own. They
wanted to be interested in sex, and they actively worked at being eager
and appealing sexual partners.

And they had lots of cooperation from their lovers.

Men told me that they had had to learn to slow down for women
and to learn the special ways in which they like to be touched, and
that even though they resisted this at first and sometimes still wanted
to have fast, furious sex, in general their efforts were greatly rewarded.
Brad and Alice talked very specifically about their experience:

> BRAD: Alice had to tell me — probably dozens of times at first, and
> she still has to remind me sometimes — about what she likes. I feel like
> I was very thickheaded about it, because it is so different from what I
> like in sex. I mean I just didn't get it for a long time. But she was patient
> and persistent.
>
> ALICE: I knew he wasn't failing to come through for me because he
> was dumb or selfish or malicious. I knew I just had to get his attention
> sort of.
>
> BRAD: What really turns Alice on is the anticipation of being
> touched in her special places. It is *not* a turn-on to her to be touched
> there right away — even gently. It is a turn-on for her to be teased
> about being touched there, to be touched close to and all around her
> special places, and now that I know how to do it, of course I get the

rewards. The longer I hold off on touching her special places, the more turned on she gets — 'til she's finally crying out for me to touch her.

But also, variety is important. If something works one time and then I just automatically go back and do exactly the same thing the next time, she doesn't like that. She doesn't want to feel like she is a machine and if I just touch the right buttons, she'll operate. It has to be varied and have a quality of spontaneity. (How am I doing, Alice?)

ALICE: Fantastic! You know, what means so much to me now is that you so obviously care about what I want. And if it isn't happening for a while and it seems like you forget and I remind you, you don't get defensive or feel criticized. You make light of it.

When men and women in thriving marriages take care of each other sexually, they both get their needs met. When men take a long time to tease women and build their anticipation, women become responsive and involved in sex. And the more responsive women are, the happier men are to move slowly and to tease. On the other hand, if men and women focus only on getting their own needs met, no one wins. Men move too fast, and women get turned off rather then on. What makes all this happen successfully among couples who thrive is that they talk to each other.

4. If You Ask for What You Want, You Are Much More Likely to Get It

Asking for what you want sexually is not always easy. It can be awkward or embarrassing — even, I found, for couples who have been happily married for many years. Some felt it takes the romance out of sex to get all clinical about it. As one woman said, "When I ask for something, and he does it, all I can think about is, 'Oh, now he's doing what I asked for. I better respond.'" Others found it hard to ask in a way that didn't imply criticism. "I'm afraid when I ask, he'll think I'm not happy with what we have, that I'm unappreciative or critical." And some felt that they were supposed to know already and shouldn't have to ask, or that their partner should know already and shouldn't have to be told. Hannah told us earlier about waiting a long, long time to ask for what she wanted sexually. Sarah had a similar experience:

I feel really silly about this, but it took me years to tell Tim about a particular fantasy I had for us. I ran the conversation in my head many times, and I would tell myself the right moment would arrive. I have no idea, really, why I let it go so long. I guess I thought he would think it was silly or that it would destroy the whole idea to talk about it. But one day out of a clear blue sky when we were just hanging out — not when we were being sexual — I just mentioned it. He loved that I told him, and we tried it right away, and it has been a really wonderful addition to our sex lives ever since. I can't really believe I waited so long. I don't know, I think it is just some deep, old irrational taboo to talk about sex.

Jenny identified another reason it might be harder for women to ask for what they want in sex:

> You know men can get a lot more of what they want in sex without having to ask because they are more in control of their own pleasure. Women are more dependent on men for their pleasure than vice versa. If a man wants a certain kind of pleasure, he can just do it. But a woman has to get a man to cooperate, and it is not so easy for her to communicate what she wants nonverbally. I mean, I don't let this stop me, but I just notice it a lot. Will hardly ever asks me for anything. If he wants it, he just does it.

The couples I spoke with seemed to understand instinctively that they had to take responsibility for getting what they wanted in sex, even if it was difficult. They did not expect their partners to be mind readers. Sarah continued:

> I think communication in sex involves a lot of trust. If I can trust that Tim will ask for what he wants and that he will say no if I ask for something he doesn't want to do, then I can always feel free to ask for everything I want. In order for it to work, I have to trust that Tim will take care of himself. But if he said yes to everything I wanted and just hoped I'd figure out what he likes, then I'd have to worry that I was asking for too much or that I wasn't doing enough to meet his needs. In order to take care of myself and not feel guilty, I have to trust that Tim will take care of himself.

Janet and Carl have "sex talks." Whenever either one wants to ask for something or just talk about their sex life in general, he or she announces, "Let's have a sex talk." They have long since established the ground rule that asking for something new does *not* imply that there was anything wrong with the old way. This enables them not to get defensive or to feel criticized.

Cory and Lou are in the habit of writing each other letters, because they enjoyed it so much for a four-month period when they were apart. They sometimes write about sex in their letters, everything from requests to expressions of appreciation to sharing sexual fantasies.

Your partner will probably never be successful in guessing what you like sexually. Finding a way to ask for what you want in your lovemaking is critical if you are to get what you want. Couples who thrive say that their good communication about sex has increased both their sexual pleasure and their closeness.

5. The Best Sex Involves a Balance of Giving and Receiving

Sex works well when a woman can let herself go completely, receiving pleasure, and a man can get thoroughly involved in giving his partner pleasure. Women enjoy relinquishing control. It can be heavenly for a woman to trust a man enough to say, verbally or nonverbally, "I'm completely yours. I give myself over totally to you." A woman needs to be allowed to receive pleasure without feeling guilt. Her partner's reassurance can help this to occur.

> MARNE: I love it when Rick takes my hands and puts them gently up over my head and holds them there. It's a way of saying, "Relax. Don't worry about giving back anything right now. I'm in charge. Just take in all this pleasure. I'm enjoying it too." I think it's one of the sexiest things there is.

But it is also true for most women that they have to feel they are giving enough overall in order to be completely comfortable receiving. And of course, men like to relax and be pleasured too. So the giving and receiving has to balance out eventually. I found that most thriving couples "kept score" over a period of weeks or months, not within one sexual encounter. And they said they had few problems because they were both fair-minded and concerned about keeping the balance and because they both enjoyed both giving and receiving.

> EARL: I don't think we have ever discussed this balance thing in our lives until right now. It has never come up between us. But now that

you mention it, it is certainly true that, looked at over a period of time, we do both give and receive — sometimes at the same time or one after the other. Sometimes, we get into one pattern for a while, then we switch. . . . I'll tell you one thing though: I love it when Karen initiates sex. It doesn't happen too often — just often enough. But I really love that. It make me feel so desired.

The thriving couples I spoke with didn't worry about balancing the giving and receiving in their lovemaking but seemed to achieve a balance naturally. They all agreed this balance was important.

6. Couples Who Stay Excited About Each Other Deliberately Stimulate Their Sex Lives

The affectionate and adoring feelings between couples are sustained by their everyday activities with each other and their general "aliveness." But erotic feelings feed on renewed stimulation. Many of the couples I interviewed mentioned a wide variety of activities that they deliberately practice to keep their erotic feelings fresh and exciting. Some did these kinds of things often, some rarely, and some never. And of course, different things are erotic for different individuals. What turns one person on may bore another. But I heard about all of the following erotically stimulating activities: Reading erotic literature, especially D. H. Lawrence and Anaïs Nin; nude dancing together; stripteasing for each other; viewing adult videos together or separately; trying new ideas from sex manuals; sharing or acting out new sex fantasies; doing erotic dances for each other; playing strip poker; and bathing or showering together.

CARL: Janet is the best erotic stimulation I could want. After twenty years, it still feels exciting to make love with her. I love how well we know each other, how comfortable we are with each other, how familiar. She's a beautiful and exciting person, and she gets more that way all the time.

In the end, it is the spirit of goodwill and generosity that makes sex a delicious treat for couples who thrive. They don't buy into the myth that good sex fades with time, and they don't waste their time worrying about it. Instead, they put their energy into making certain that they are doing all they can to keep their own sex life exciting.

Happy, functional couples do not allow resentments to last very long between them without working them through. Sex is not a weapon or symbol for them. They don't find themselves withholding sex because of unexpressed anger from some other area of their life.

They are as eager to meet the needs of their partner as they are to meet their own needs. They understand, accept, and cooperate with each other. They are not critical or judgmental. They stay in touch with each other. And they give attention to their sex lives.

It is their goodwill and sense of fair play that leads them to make certain that they balance giving and receiving and that they talk about what is going on in their sex lives, even if they find it difficult.

Experiment #26

1. Set aside an hour for a conversation with your partner and discuss each of the six major points in this chapter.
2. Each of you write a letter to the other about your sex life. Mention all the things you like, any concerns you have, and ask for everything you want. Read the letters in each other's presence and discuss them.

Magazine articles and talk show debates about sex often cause more problems than they solve, for whether they are discussing better orgasms, frequency of sex, amazing new erotic spots, or even solutions for "sexual dysfunction," their underlying message is, you could do better. They make us worry that someone else may be having a better sex life than we are. That anxiety will kill sexual pleasure.

You are the expert on your own sexual pleasure. If an article gives you an idea to explore and you have fun with it and then either take it or leave it, great. But if something you read or hear starts making you insecure, just accept that *you* are a greater authority than this other "expert" (because you are), and, in your head, write your own article. Pretend that your readers can have a good sex life if they follow your advice to do exactly what you and your partner do. What would your own "six guidelines for good sex" be?

You can have a perfect love life — if you simply define as perfect exactly what you have. I wish you and your partner a lifetime of fun, relaxing, close, erotic, and varied lovemaking — as often as is right for you.

Chapter 10

TRAIT 8: PLEASURE
Part B: Passion

D O YOU BELIEVE that a couple can sustain passion and excitement in their relationship over a period of many years?" Ever since I began working with couples more than twenty years ago, I have been interested in their answers to this question. For seven years, I kept track of people's responses. Fully 85 percent of them answered no. These were typical comments:

> Passion and longevity are incompatible. Real passion cannot be sustained. That initial hit of passion is not supposed to go on forever. It's just nature's way of getting you together.

> Sex is more exciting when it is new.

> When you fall in love, you start seeing the whole world through rose-colored glasses. Everything's really exciting. Then, the excitement's over. Life falls into a routine. After the honeymoon, *you never get to have that feeling again!* Instead, you have to start dealing with all the conflicts and disappointments you have with each other.

> Romantic love is a brand-new invention in human history. Other cultures don't have it, and we have had it in Western Society only since the Middle Ages. And then the knights didn't have sex with the women

they loved. Hollywood feeds this thing about romantic love, but it's not real life.

In a casual conversation, a woman who had been married for twenty-eight years told me,

> I like my husband okay. We live together just fine. We have our separate lives, and we still play bridge together every week. But we rarely have sex. I don't feel "in love." I haven't for years. There's nothing wrong. I wouldn't leave him. I just figure that's the way marriage is. Nobody could be all that excited after twenty-eight years.

Couples who thrive disagree with all of these comments. They love to talk about how much they love each other, how excited they are to be together. They are affectionate, they have sparkle, they talk effusively about each other. They can sometimes be caught acting like newlyweds. In fact Mary and Wes told me that on a recent airplane flight, the flight attendant gave them free champagne because she thought they really were on their honeymoon.

Couples who thrive don't live in a constant state of heightened excitement, of course. They have ups and downs. Their relationship goes through periods of being distant or in conflict and plateau periods where not much is happening between the couple. But the happy couples I spoke with all reported that they still felt excited about their relationship and that, *periodically, they tap back into the excited closeness and passion that they felt at the very beginning of their connection.*

To be sure, the passion that couples who thrive keep in their relationship for many years is not the same as the infatuation that two people may feel when they first meet. But the common belief that sexual and romantic excitement must inevitably fade with time is just not true.

In this chapter, we will look first at infatuation to see what it really is, and what sort of a role it plays in love. Then we will look at the period of time during which a couple comes down off cloud nine and begins to ground their relationship in a more everyday world.

The transition from the lofty heights of total obsession with love is always experienced as somewhat of a loss, and the more prepared a couple is for this transition, the better they handle it. We will examine the quality of the passion that does live on for years and years in couples who thrive. We will see that many couples deliberately create "peak experiences" for themselves. And finally, we will see how a couple's passion spills over to other parts of their lives and to other people, and we'll see what these couples do when they become attracted to someone other than their spouse.

The Honeymoon Phase

The excitement of new love is like a natural drug high. In fact, as we now know, it actually *is* a drug high because a strong attraction to another person causes hormonal and chemical changes in our bodies. When two people are in love, all the regular rules of life get suspended. The obsession to be together can be almost unmanageable. It causes people to neglect their work or other responsibilities. Their bodies are flush with excitement all the time. They bask in each other's presence.

Being in love is a truly beautiful experience. It is one of nature's great gifts to us, a natural human event that lets us feel a sustained "high," or "peak experience."

But is nature betraying us? Is infatuation a cruel joke, because it will always eventually be taken away?

No. Infatuation is supposed to be temporary. Its transience doesn't invalidate it. George Bernard Shaw pointed out the absurdity of the idea that "when two people are under the influence of the most violent, most insane, most delusive and most transient of passions, they be required to swear that they will remain in that excited, abnormal, exhausting condition continuously until death do them part."

Apart from being an absolutely glorious experience, what contributions does this period of unmitigated bliss make to a couple when it is the beginning of their lifelong journey together? And what are its liabilities?

The benefits of infatuation are substantial. The first is that it gives us a glimpse of Heaven.

Our human souls cry out for two things: We want a special connection with another human being, specifically, intimacy, closeness, and unconditional love. And on another level, we long for a connection with something greater than ourselves and our fellow humans, something that reaches beyond even the vastness of human life to give it meaning. We want a vision of wholeness, a connection with the deepest inner truths of the universe. We come into this world, in Wordsworth's stirring words, "trailing clouds of glory," seeing all things "apparelled in celestial light," and we long to reconnect with that glory, that celestial light.

Falling in love is like taking a cog railway to the top of a mountain. You get a chance to see what it is like up there, and once you have been up there, and you know how exquisite it is, your life is forever changed, because you now know you can return there.

As you *climb* up the mountain of life, you can never know what is above the highest point to which you have climbed; you can only know what is below you. If you take a cog railway to the top, you haven't climbed there, so you may not know how to get back on your own, but you have seen it, you know it is possible. So if you are someone who wants to experience life fully, now that you have glimpsed the heights, you will want to find a way to get up there on your own.

One of the great values of the ecstasy of new love is that it motivates you. It creates the desire in you for lifelong happiness through love. And this is motivation you will need when the veil is lifted and you begin to see life as it usually is. Infatuation entices you to come along on the journey of love. Ken Keyes says falling in love is "nature's way of luring you into a relationship." Once you are enticed, you need motivation to stay there, because along with bringing you great treasures, love will raise up from dormancy your "issues," your "stuff," as we say in my women's group, "your material." A new relationship will *create* fresh challenges, and you need to be highly motivated to work through them.

As we have learned from the thriving couples in this book, the secret to success in working through the challenges that arise in a new relationship is to view them not as problems but as grist for the mill, as opportunities for growth and learning. The mill needs grist in order to get results. You need conflicts, issues, dilemmas, differences in order to grow both personally and in your relationship. Fortunately, the bond you have created in the early ecstatic phase of your relationship gives you the motivation you need to proceed through the challenges.

Of course the down side of infatuation is that it is easy to fall in love with a person who is not an appropriate lifelong mate for you. It is common for people to get strong signals from their intuition, but, smitten by Cupid's arrow, to ignore them — at the risk of great personal anguish. Infatuation alone is not a solid foundation for a lifetime of love and partnership.

The End of the Honeymoon Phase

Inevitably, the heady bliss, the charged excitement and delirious pleasure of new love does not last, for it is not the same as the deeper, more enduring passion that replaces it. As appealing as it may seem at the time, we can't live our whole lives at a fevered pitch. Nevertheless, we never let go of infatuation happily; its disappearance is almost always accompanied by disappointment, sadness, and grief.

And the loss is made more difficult still because, after you have seen heaven, earth can look more limited than it did before. You felt whole; now you can once again see the fragmentation. You thought that the holes in your own life had been filled by your lover; now you see that they are still there, and you are thrust back into the reality that you have to fill them yourself.

Besides, you can get addicted to bliss.

But the thriving couples who had a period of infatuation at the beginning of their relationship talked far more about what they gained from the experience than about the pain of its loss. For one thing, they will always have the memory of their mutual euphoria, a little treasure that no one can ever take from them, and beautiful memories *are* an important part of your inner life. They help you feel good about yourself. They help to define who you are and are a part of what makes you unique.

More important, a couple's honeymoon experience is a part of the distinctive shared history that makes them a couple. No one else was there. No one but the two of them knows exactly what it felt like. The heightened passion they felt is something they can continue to draw upon throughout their lives for inspiration, motivation, and renewed love.

Passion has been awakened in them, or has been lifted to new heights. Their bodies have been loosened up to allow them to experience their full capacity for pleasure. This awakening will spill over into other areas of their lives and other people. For the more passion you feel, the more you are capable of feeling.

So thriving couples let themselves mourn their loss, but they also savor what they have gained.

One woman told me about her experience with the transition from the honeymoon phase of her new relationship.

MICHELLE: In previous relationships, I was with men who wouldn't get close to me at all. So when I met Conrad and he was so emotionally available and so intimate, I was ecstatic. But I kept having the feeling it was too good to be true. I kept talking about it, and getting him to reassure me that he wouldn't change. After we had been together about six months, we went to a yoga retreat together. It was a gorgeous setting, and we had lots of free time. I wanted it to be a time when we would get all close and lovey-dovey — you know, intense. Conrad was really enjoying himself, but he was kind of spaced out. He wanted to read and relax. I mentioned that he seemed sort of distant and preoccupied, and he got annoyed. He said I was worrying far too much about this, that he loved me totally and completely, and that it was okay for us just to relax together. The whole thing kind of shocked me. I just didn't want that change. I loved the intensity. I knew things had to settle down, but I kept thinking, not yet, not yet. But I got the message. Even though I didn't really agree with Conrad, something in me decided to behave as though he were right. I didn't have much choice really, I guess. I felt really sad, but I started to relax and read, too. And guess what. By the end of the week, we had reached a new level of closeness. We spent this idyllic day together walking up a mountain stream. We were in heaven. And that night our lovemaking reached new heights.

It is human nature to want to hang on dearly to something wonderful. But it is one of life's paradoxes that if you cling desperately to something that you want, you will annihilate it. Knowing when and how to let go graciously of something that isn't going to last anyway is one of the marks of a mature, self-loving person. No one says it better than William Blake:

> *He who binds to himself a joy,*
> *Doth the wingèd life destroy.*
> *But he who kisses the joy as it flies*
> *Lives in eternity's sunrise.*

Couples who thrive are masters at kissing the joy as it flies. They let go of what they can't have and focus on the richness in their relationship. Rather than grasping for abundance, they let it flow into their lives. Although I spoke with couples in a wide variety of circumstances, they all experienced their lives as exciting and abundant. Because they weren't grasping for passion; they trusted that it would be there.

A marriage therapist I know told me of a couple she was working with. Linda talked continually about how she wanted more from her husband, Jim, and about how inattentive he was. Finally the therapist said, "I'm going to take a position here. I think Jim needs a bit of space. Linda, let me suggest that you back off just a bit from stating your needs." Linda agreed to do this. At that moment, Jim reached over and took her hand, looked her in the eyes, smiled, and thanked her. And Linda melted. It was the closest moment they had had in some time.

Letting go of something that you dearly want to keep can seem like an impossible task — because you really want it. How can you pretend that you don't?

The secret is this: you don't have to let go of wanting what you want; you only have to let go of your anxiety about it. Relax. Trust that however this thing turns out, it will be "right." It will be good. Let go graciously of the frenzied first phase of love and allow yourself to ease gracefully and quietly into the next phase. It is quite natural to mourn the loss of the "peak experience" phase of new love. Let yourself feel the sadness. But also know that when you close a gate behind you and keep moving forward, you have undiscovered universes before you. Keep walking. As thriving couples know, the best is yet to come.

The Unfolding Begins

"The honeymoon phase doesn't fade — it blossoms!"

After discussing passion with several couples one day, I heard myself making this comment to Mayer. I was thinking about the magnolia tree in our front yard when I was a child. Every spring before its leaves sprouted, the tree became loaded with beautiful buds. I used to look up through the bright pink buds so I could see the bent shapes of the bud-bearing twigs with only the blue sky behind them. The buds were slightly open, just waiting to burst into full flower. It was a spectacular sight. Some years a late frost would spoil everything: the buds would freeze and then they would turn brown and fall off. It was a crushing disappointment after the anticipation. But most years the buds would burst into full gorgeous flowers. Our tree was so spectacular that people would drive out of their way to see it.

The common stereotype about honeymoon periods is that when they are over, they die or fade away — like the buds in a year with a late freeze. But in fact, the honeymoon phase is exciting precisely because it augurs so much potential, and when it is over, it doesn't fade; it blossoms into the full flower that was its promise. The bud is full of urgency, ready to explode. The full flower is free and relaxed. It has nothing to decide or do. It can just enjoy its own beauty.

The thriving couples I interviewed were like full, relaxed blossoms enjoying their own beauty with no feeling of urgency. Their passion had not faded, but rather had unfolded into a comfortable, easy love. These couples had become accustomed to feeling happy.

A jet airplane from San Francisco to New York uses 80 percent of its fuel taking off. But the takeoff is not an end in itself; the reason for all the energy is to get the plane launched so that it can reach a cruising altitude. The cruise is the important part of the journey, and it requires a different kind of energy: even, sustained, always making minor adjustments to stay on course. Thriving couples know that the intensity of infatuation is just the beginning of their journey together.

So if it is true that a relationship's early intensity does not fade but is transformed instead into an enduring passion, what is the nature of this "passion" that couples who thrive nurture and enjoy for years and years together?

I asked the couples I interviewed to respond to the widespread belief that passion cannot be sustained in a relationship over many years.

JULIE: Let me describe last Saturday morning to you, and you tell me whether this is passion. We both worked really hard all week. Saturday morning we slept until we woke up on our own. We slowly started making love when we were half awake. We let it build really slowly and took a long time. Then we just lay there in each other's arms, totally secure, content, at peace. We never even spoke for a long time. Finally, we decided to go out to breakfast and talk about an article we are thinking about writing together, and we got all excited about it. There is a huge area between infatuation and dull, boring routine. A huge area, and that's where we live our lives.

ALICE: Physical touching — hugging, holding, all that — just feels so good. Like think about the pleasure of holding an infant. I never get tired of hugging Brad, of having him hold me — and of kissing. We love to kiss. It always feels sexy. Brad and I have each other to hold on to. I never realized how literal that phrase in the marriage ceremony is, "to have and to hold."

KAREN: I think one reason people *think* they run out of passion is that what they really run out of is language to talk about their passion. After a while, you feel like you've said "I love you" so many times, it becomes routine. But we find ways. We tell each other specifically what we love about each other, and nonverbal stuff. And "I love you" is still a pleasure to say and to hear.

ADRIENNE: I feel the height of romance is when Clen comes up behind me when I am doing dishes and kisses me on the back of the neck and holds me. Every once in a while, we can be in the bedroom, and he will just throw me on the bed, jump on top of me, and shower me with kisses — just playing around.

SARAH: When I think of passion, I think of exquisite tenderness. Soft, gentle touch. Tim makes me feel that I am so special and fragile. When I read *The Bridges of Madison County*, I didn't have to feel envious; Tim and I can make each other feel that way. [She quotes from memory:] "In a universe of ambiguity, this kind of certainty comes only once, and never again, no matter how many lifetimes you live."

MARTY: We are passionate about each other because we are passionate about our lives. I don't think you can isolate passion. If we were bored with what we were doing, we might be more bored with each other. . . . But actually, I know it is also true that I wouldn't have as much passion about my work if I didn't have Hannah to share it all with. . . . Yes, we have times that are just comfortable and content. But I don't see how anyone could ever get tired of feeling close and secure and at peace.

Marty is right that passion is usually not isolated. The two experiences in life that are most likely to give rise to passion are love and creativity. Being in love can stimulate a person's creativity, and the joy that is the result of any successful creative endeavor can heighten and stimulate love. It is not a coincidence that many of the thriving couples with whom I spoke are extremely creative people. Their passion is fueled by their creativity as well as by their love.

The themes that emerged as couples attempted to describe their passion were being best friends and enjoying activities together; excitement at seeing each other after a break; desire to share specific news; affection; physical closeness, touching and holding; sex;

relaxing together; knowing each other increasingly well; variety and change within their relationship; and passion that was not restricted to each other but that spilled over into other areas of their lives. Basically, they love what they have with each other so much that they can't imagine ever getting tired of it.

Passion can mean experiencing flush, tingly, extremely pleasurable sensations in the body. It can mean thinking exciting, exuberant thoughts, or having feelings that are especially intense and powerful. Couples who thrive *like* experiencing these sensations, they *believe* they are possible on an ongoing basis, and they are *committed* to maintaining them in their life together. They let the passion that brought them together blossom for many seasons.

Keeping Passion Alive

Everyone wants to know, what are the secrets to maintaining long-term passion in a relationship? Answers we often hear are:

- pay attention to the relationship; focus on what you love
- talk, spend time with each other
- always tell the complete truth; don't withhold facts or feelings
- surprise each other with flowers, notes, romantic dinners, gifts, etc.
- plan weekends away

These are reasonable suggestions. Couples who thrive certainly follow them. And couples who have lost their spark, who take each other for granted, or who have some antagonism or distance between them can probably use them to good advantage to reconnect, and to get their passion moving again.

In fact, however, passion comes from deep within and can't be replaced like a burned-out light bulb when it goes dark. Focusing directly on passion as a way to revive or sustain it will be of limited value. Couples who thrive feel passion because they love each other and they love their life together.

The real formula for sustaining passion — if you first truly *desire* it and *believe* it is possible — is to cultivate your goodwill toward your partner; commit yourself to the value of time together and a feeling of adventure and aliveness; work on clarifying your boundaries and improving your communication skills; and become more self-disclosing and intimate. Focus on your partner. How can you be more loving to him or her? What can you do to heal any rifts between you? Focus on your relationship. What can you change so that each of you will be happy and can feel grateful for what you have together?

Couples who thrive don't need formulas to sustain their passion. They do pay attention to their relationship, focus on the positive aspects of it, tell the truth, and talk and spend time together, but not as techniques for maintaining passion so much as a result of the passion they already experience. Then in turn their conduct enhances and builds their passion.

Peak Experiences

From scientific studies of love and passion we know that an amphetaminelike substance is released by the brain of a person who is newly "in love," causing a natural drug–induced high. Evidence also reveals that the conditions that created this chemical reaction once can be re-created.

More than half of the couples with whom I spoke told me about episodes of heightened passion during which they were intensely focused on each other — much like the way they felt when they were first in love. In many cases, they deliberately created these experiences by going away to a mountain or beach cabin, or setting aside an evening with candlelight and music. Sometimes the episodes arose spontaneously.

Bonnie told me this story:

> Mike [her husband of seven years] and I had a wonderful experience. The kids were both at camp. He had barbecued salmon, and we decided to open a bottle of champagne that we still had from our anniversary. It was just a lovely evening, and we got to talking about the way I sometimes get so scared when he's out of town, even though I know it is irrational. And he just sat there and listened and really understood me. He never has taken me seriously about this before. But it was as though I got his attention finally. And I just felt this shell inside me cracking away. It was a timeless moment. We felt so close. I can't even describe what was happening. We were both totally aware of each other and our love and how incredibly lucky we feel to be with each other. When we made love, I almost felt I had never made love before. . . . This morning when I left for work, I just sat in the car for a while. I was feeling so happy, tears came to my eyes. I feel like my cup runneth over.

As I asked couples to talk about their "peak experiences," it became clear that the couples were talking about the same types of passionate episodes. These times provide a context for the entire relationship. The partners become focused entirely on each other and have a feeling of "knowing" with absolute certainty that the other is "there" too; their connection is deeply secure and utterly satisfying. They have a sense that says, "Here we are again in that special place that only you and I have ever shared." They are relaxed, spontaneous, and willing to trust their own feelings. All of the characteristics of intimacy are heightened: the couples are open and without barriers between them; they experience sharpened self-awareness and self-love; they are completely honest and share even the most difficult and painful things, for their mutual trust is without doubt or hesitation; they bask in each other's presence; each experiences an outpouring of love and affection and is able to take in the fullness of love from the other.

Intensely close moments that are based on years of shared history are very different from the urgency of new love. The pleasure of sustained love has a depth and brilliance only time can create; yet we overlook the reciprocal relationship between depth and longevity. We forget that ecstasy is heightened if it is rooted in the firm, trustworthy soil of a long-term love.

Imagine being with someone over a period of years who is patient enough to wait as your fears surface and evaporate, as you begin to let this person's love affect you, and as you learn to let go of your struggles and love yourself. Imagine the continuity of achieving clarity about something that has troubled you for years with the person who has been with you for all those years at your side. Participating in the struggle and then sharing the triumph — this is ecstasy.

An intense, intimate sharing is not verbal *or* physical; the two become indistinguishable. Both the body and soul are awakened during feelings of extreme closeness. In his book about his own thriving marriage, Sheldon Van Auken illustrates this mingling of physical and spiritual when he describes an experience he had with his wife of many years. They were cruising on their own small sailing vessel, and were anchored for the night.

> Davy had crept near to me still crouching and I put my arm about her, and she snuggled close. Neither of us spoke, not so much as a whispered word. We were together, we were close, we were overwhelmed by a great beauty. I know that it seemed to us both that we were

completely one: we had no need to speak. We remained so in timeless loveliness — was it hours? We never knew. All about us was the extraordinary beauty of the seafire and the glittering stars overhead. We were full of wonder — and joy. Our boat was alive, lifting to the little waves, and the tall dark masts were penciling across the stars. The moment was utterly timeless: We didn't know that time existed; and it contained, therefore, some foretaste, it may be, of eternity. At last, still with no words spoken, we went below again and, in comfort and a great peace, slept.

One quality that characterizes intense experiences of intimacy, perhaps more than any other, is lack of restraint. The partners, in giving themselves to such an experience, hold nothing back from each other. Both of them are 100 percent available to each other — their bodies, their attention, their willingness to be honest, their capacity to feel, their ability to communicate completely. Neither person is constrained by fears, social expectations, embarrassment, commitments to other people, or worries about each other's loyalty. They do not modify or impede the flow between them in any way. It's easy. Rather than making it happen, they let go and allow it to happen.

Passion That Overflows

As we have seen, the passion that couples who thrive feel about each other does not limit itself to their little world of two. If they are excited about each other, they are usually also excited about their work, their hobbies, their lives in general, and of course — about other people too. How does their passion express itself in other areas? And what do they do when they get turned on to friends, colleagues, or acquaintances of the opposite sex?

VOCATION

Thriving couples feel compelled to spread around the blessings they feel have been bestowed upon them. They are as passionate about their work, their children, their friendships, and their causes as they are about each other. These are people who feel a responsibility to become involved with the world around them. They find a need that they believe their special talents can address, and then become passionate about making an impact in that area.

A thriving relationship is like a reservoir. It is fed by streams and rivers — love, mutual support, and goodwill, and when it becomes full, it overflows, offering its abundance to others who need it. This subject came up numerous times in my interviews. As a professional speaker told me,

> Sometimes my wife is the *focus* of my passion, but more often, she is the *source* of it. I feel safe in the world and empowered and can bring passion to my work because she is there for me. She quite literally inspires my work.

If a love were focused only on itself, it would soon shrivel up. The nature of passion is that it expands, grows, spills over and rushes out like a teaming river into the world around it, enlivening all that it comes in contact with. People who are passionate about their love and their work empassion others with their very presence. Enthusiasm is contageous. Deep feelings tap into other deep feelings.

EXTRAMARITAL RELATIONSHIPS

Many of the happy couples I interviewed said that the matter of outside relationships was a non-issue for them. I frequently heard comments like these:

It never comes up.

It's not anything we've ever discussed, but I'm sure we'll tell you exactly the same thing about it.

We have total fidelity, not because we "agreed" to it, but because we love each other. There is no way either of us would ever look twice at anyone else.

Other couples felt it was a sign of the strength of their relationship that they could be honest about feelings they get for other people.

> CORY: I get crushes on men pretty often. And I enjoy it. I think if you are afraid of it, or you feel guilty, it can get you into trouble. But I know I'm not going to do anything I'll regret. I don't give mixed signals; I'm very clear about my limits. I mean, most of these men don't know I find them a turn-on. For example, a while ago, I got smitten by this guy at work. I was working on a project with him. Well I loved it.

It brightened up my day whenever we got together. He liked me a lot, too, and we flirted a little — just in fun. I see no problem in this. Of course I told Lou about him. Because it was part of what was going on in my life. I wouldn't keep anything like that from Lou. And Lou understands that I'm just enjoying the vibes. Eventually, we had him and his wife over for dinner, and the four of us have become friends. At first, I had incredible fantasies about him. Fantasy life is wonderful, because you can do anything you want in a fantasy and there is no harm done to anyone. But what happened — and what always happens if you just hang in there long enough — is that the attraction faded. I find if I don't try to suppress it, and I don't do anything to act on it, the attraction will run its course. I've had this happen maybe three times over the course of our marriage. I think it is a sign of the strength of our relationship that we can allow feelings about other people to come in. It's obvious no one needs to be threatened by it. It's just a thing that happens sometimes. No big deal.

LOU: I find it a pleasure when other men are attracted to Cory. After all, she chose me.

It is probably unrealistic to assume that, just because you are now part of a thriving marriage, you will never get turned on to other people. But couples who thrive are clear that they are never going to act on feelings toward another person. As Rick put it, "I use my turn-on to other women to get all the more turned on to Marne."

Thriving couples have such confidence in their own relationships that they are not afraid of their feelings for other people.

ALICE: We've been friends with one couple for ten years. I find the guy very hot. I still don't know whether he has ever had that kind of attraction to me. But we are all good friends, and it doesn't matter. I enjoy it. Sometimes I fantasize about him. I always look forward to seeing them. Brad knows I'm turned on to him. Big deal. I'm much more turned on to Brad, and Brad knows that, and that is all that matters.

JENNY: You know what helps me? When I was single I dated so many men who turned out to be not at all right for me. When I get turned on to someone now, I just think, "Don't worry Jen. After two dates with him, you'd be ready to move on. There's no way he could ever match what you have now." And I know this is true.

With two exceptions, all the couples I interviewed told me they were monogamous and wouldn't consider any other lifestyle. Two couples came to monogamy after experimenting with open relationships. Their comments are interesting because they are so similar, and because they represent people who have tried a variety of lifestyles.

PETER: We've been married twenty-eight years. In the sixties, we "opened" our marriage because we bought the whole line that went with it: "You'll grow. Your own relationship will be strengthened." Well, we went through some very painful and stressful years — working hard to convince ourselves that jealousy was immature and old-fashioned. Our marriage survived because we really are right for each other. On our twelfth anniversary, we got married all over again and gave up all our "extra-curricular" activities. Being monogamous is a lot more than just whom you sleep with. It has to do with focus. The focus of my life now is my wife. Before, it was as though we were standing in the same house but each gazing out a different window. Actually, I have to say I think each of us is richer because of those years. We learned a lot — and we got our curiosity satisfied. But it would have been a tragedy if our marriage hadn't survived.

ANNE: I've been in both kinds of relationships — open and monogamous — each for a lot of years. I'm very happy with monogamy now, but I think there's a big key to it — maybe two big keys: one is that I think my husband is a truly wonderful man. I mean, if I had big doubts about him, I might always be looking. But now, I meet a man I like a lot but I'm just not available. I've found my man!

The other key is, both of us dated a whole lot before we met, and we were both married before. Jim twice. We know what we are missing, and we are glad to be missing the rat race and half-hearted relationships. We are happy to have all that behind us and to be able to get on with our lives. I'm not sure I could be so content about monogamy if I hadn't explored the world first.

The thriving couples I spoke with *feel* the excitement and beauty of their love for each other. They experience desire for each other; enthusiasm about each other; deep affection toward each other; and powerful, compelling emotions — in other words, passion. Whether or not their relationship started with infatuation, their adventure together keeps this passion alive and lets it emerge over and over, sometimes overflowing into peak experiences.

1. Do you believe that it is possible for a couple to sustain the passion in their relationship for many years? Write a paragraph in answer to this question.
2. Give your relationship a "passion rating" on a scale from 1 to 10, with 10 being the most passionate. Do this separately from your partner and then compare.
3. If your rating is 6 or below, together brainstorm a list of factors you think diminish the passion in your relationship.
4. Together brainstorm a list of things that might stimulate and enhance the passion in your relationship. (Any of the techniques at the end of chapter 7 would be a good place to start.)
5. If your rating was 7 or above, discuss together, when was the last time you had a "peak experience"? What might you do to create one sometime soon?

Reviewing the Eight Essential Traits of Couples Who Thrive

Liz was four months pregnant when I first met her and her husband, Ted. Liz wanted Ted to take childbirth classes with her, but Ted was reluctant. His friends at work told him that the classes were pointless and that there was little for the man to do.

Over several weeks I saw Liz and Ted exhibit most of the Eight Essential Traits of Couples Who Thrive.

They very much *wanted* and *believed* they could have a happy relationship together — that's why they came to talk with me. Ted talked disparagingly of a couple he knew who fought all the time, and he felt very clear he didn't want to be like them. And he was devoted to Liz. When he saw her unhappy and he felt helpless, he wanted to get help.

Many nonthriving couples have the same fights over and over for years because their motivation to be happy is not high enough to get them to any source of help. The excuse nonthriving couples use is "We can solve our problems on our own. We don't need an objective third party." But these couples don't end up solving their problems because they don't know how; instead, they learn to live with them.

Ted and Liz were clearly *committed* to each other. Ted had already been through an unpleasant previous marriage, and he made it obvious he was grateful to be with Liz. Also, they were willing to find the *time* they needed to work through this decision and to do the homework I suggested — even though they were both working, had relatives visiting, and were generally quite busy.

Nonthriving couples find ways to put off problem solving. They may think, "We'll do it when we get around to it," but they never do.

When I encouraged Liz to ask Ted for what she wanted and to explain why it was important to her, she made her request simply and without blaming Ted. She seemed to understand that he had a legitimate point of view, too. Then, with no prompting from me, Ted said, "I can see this means a lot to you." This was a fine example of *relationship-enhancing communication*. Ted was conveying that he understood Liz before he started in on his own reasons for not wanting to attend the classes.

Nonthriving couples defend their own position first. They may never genuinely listen to or acknowledge each other.

Ted and Liz had enormous *goodwill* toward each other, as was apparent throughout our discussions. Ted wanted to find a way to make Liz happy without having to do something that was obviously uncomfortable for him. And Liz regretted that she had tó make a request that was hard for Ted. Neither of them was being selfish or inconsiderate.

Nonthriving couples are sometimes willing to meet their own needs at the expense of their partner.

Liz's *boundaries* were especially clear. She seemed quite aware that it was not her job to "fix" Ted's discomfort, and she was not going to drop her fond desire and simply acquiesce to his reluctance. She stood her ground about what she wanted.

In a nonthriving couple, the wife might have given in to her husband but remained disappointed and angry. She would complain to her mother and her friends about how selfish her husband was, they would all concur, and a wall would begin to build between husband and wife.

In the end, it was Ted's curiosity — his commitment to *aliveness* — that solved their dilemma. He talked with some men who had attended childbirth classes and began to feel that, even though it felt like a big risk to him, he could see the possibility that he might be missing out on something quite wonderful. In the end, that was the risk he didn't want to take. He agreed to take the classes and only then decide whether he wanted to attend the birth. Liz was thrilled with this plan.

Nonthriving couples often take the "safe" alternative. They would rather be comfortable than excited. They back off from challenges and opportunities.

Ted and Liz approached their problem as a couple. They saw that until both of them were happy, neither would be happy. Neither was willing to act selfishly or independently of the other. Their ability to share all their feelings — disappointment, hurt, fear — with each other on the way to solving their problem showed me how trusting, close, and intimate they were.

Nonintimate couples, who are not able to share feelings, have to think and act independent of each other — even on matters that affect them both. They endure their painful feelings alone. Then they harbor resentments toward each other that they are also not able to share. These private negative feelings make it hard for them to be open and free with each other sexually, and they erode the potential for passion and the easy, comfortable pleasure of being together.

After Ted and Liz solved their problem, they were able to see that the strife and anger between them was a result of their disagreement, not a sign that they were falling out of love or that they were going to be a couple who would fight a lot — something they both dreaded. They felt great relief to know that they could get through a difficult problem and feel close and excited again. Also, Ted learned that he did not have to be stopped by his fears. Even though he felt fear, he had a choice about what to do. And he saw that his courage to face this problem rather than solve it his own way at the expense of Liz's happiness led him to new discoveries about himself. Ted and Liz both gained valuable *perspective* from their experience of facing their problem directly and moving beyond it.

Nonthriving couples ignore problems or live with them for years. They never learn that problems have solutions you can't see before you try to solve them, or that if you are willing to face and move through the bad times, the good times follow.

*   *   *

As you read through Ted and Liz's story, did you identify with them?

Here is an opportunity for you to think about yourself and your partner with regard to the traits we have been discussing.

Experiment #28

STEP 1. Slowly and thoughtfully, list the Essential Traits of Couples Who Thrive down the left side of a page in your notebook as follows:

Desire for happiness
Belief that we can be happy together
Commitment to our happiness
Goodwill toward my spouse
Focus on positive aspects of my spouse
    and our relationship
Gratitude that we are together
Acceptance of each other as we are
Trust and respect
Generosity
Valuing time together
Valuing a feeling of aliveness
Maintaining my boundaries
Belief that good times follow bad
Belief that I will learn and grow
    by facing problems directly
Listening to and acknowledging my partner *first*
Asking for what I want
Honoring our gender differences
Affirming my spouse regularly
Sharing feelings, especially difficult personal ones
    and feelings about my spouse
Accepting our sexuality just as it is
Taking initiative to rekindle our passion

STEP 2. Draw two columns to the right of your list; label the first "Before" and the second "Now."

STEP 3. Identify an ongoing problem or disagreement you have with your spouse or a challenge you face. Now for each trait on the list, think about this trait in relationship to the way you have dealt with your ongoing problem. If you can't recall exactly what a trait involves, refer back to the chapter about that trait. In the first column, give yourself a grade: from A for excellent to F for total failure. With a different colored ink, give your spouse a grade.

Don't take this experiment too seriously. There is probably no couple anywhere that would get straight A's. If you think you failed miserably at one of the traits, it doesn't mean you are a failure at life or love; it just means you have identified an area in which you can improve.

STEP 4. Now that you have seen how thriving couples behave, spend some time discussing your problem, disagreement, or challenge — for at least one full hour.

STEP 5. In the second column, grade yourself and your spouse on the conversation you have just had.

If you are like other couples who have tried this experiment after completing my workshop, you will see dramatic improvement in some of the categories. And you will be able to see in what areas you can still grow — *if* you want to become a truly happy, thriving couple.

That desire — as I said in the opening pages of this book — is where it all begins.

Part Two

THE CHALLENGE

Chapter 11

CREATING A PERFECT MARRIAGE
IN AN IMPERFECT WORLD

D URING MY RESEARCH for this book, I asked my mother the secret of her wonderful fifty-six-year marriage to my father. Without hesitation she replied, "The secret of our success is that we were married in 1937 and not 1993!"

My mother is appalled at the obstacles we face in our marriages that were never an issue in hers. Just the idea that two people would choose to live apart from extended family, both work full-time *and* raise children seems impossible to her. Add to that the hurried pace that technology (which was supposed to give us more leisure time) has engendered; the economic pressures most families face; raised expectations about what it means to be "intimate"; the upheaval in gender roles; the rapid value shifts that occur almost every decade now from the Free Decade to the Me Decade to the Decade of Greed and now the Decade of Meaning; and general societal problems that affect families, such as drugs, crime, and environmental problems, and my mother is not the only one who wonders how couples make it these days let alone manage to have beautiful, abundant love lives.

Creating a thriving marriage is a challenge because of certain persistent obstacles that stand in the way. It is important to look squarely at these challenges, for as you undertake to build your own thriving marriage, these are the impediments you will face. Many — but not all of them — are within you and within your power to change. Some are imposed from outside and you must first recognize them and then find a way to act in spite of them, for they won't go away.

The obstacles to thriving marriage are these:

1. deep internal wounds, usually from childhood (acquired externally, now internal);
2. inappropriate expectations (internal);
3. pressure to divorce (internal or external);
4. cultural values (external);
5. apathy (internal).

1. Deep Internal Wounds

Family history plays a big role in every relationship. What couples who thrive have in common is not that they came from unusually "functional" families, but that they, in one way or another, have made peace with their past. They are not enslaved to it. They recognize that they can't necessarily change the deeply ingrained beliefs and behavior patterns that they inherited from their parental and sibling relationships, but they are familiar with these beliefs and patterns, and they are able to make choices about them when they show up in their marriage.

Psychological theories about marriage abound. One is that you marry a person who has both the positive and the negative qualities of your opposite-sex parent in the subconscious hope that you can complete your unfinished business with that parent. For example, if your parent consistently withheld approval from you, you may marry a spouse who is also withholding in order to win from him or her the approval you so crave.

Another theory is that you carry within you an image of an ideal lover, and that you project that image onto a real person and marry him or her. Eventually you discover that your spouse is not the personification of your own ideal image, but a real person with a personality of his or her own.

It is widely believed that your basic personality is formed when you are very young, and that you carry your reaction to your primary caregivers into adulthood. For example, if your mother was invasive and you learned very early how to protect your privacy, you may still have trouble letting anyone get close to you. If your parents divorced, you may still be terrified of being abandoned. If your parents abused you, you may fear intimacy because you associate it with pain. If your parents were alcoholic and you were the only one left to manage your chaotic family, you may feel that you always have to be in total control.

All of these theories have truth in them. Whichever ones help you to gain the most insight about your present beliefs and behavioral patterns are the ones you should use. These simple questions will help you apply these theories to your own life:

1. How do I (or did I) feel and behave toward each parent? Do any of those feelings and behaviors show up in the way I think about or behave toward my spouse?

2. What is my picture of the ideal spouse? In what ways does my spouse match or not match this ideal picture?

3. What are my primary personality characteristics? Can I attribute these to the situation in my family as I was growing up?

The insights you gain from studying the origins of the person you are today can be extremely interesting, but they won't be *useful* in helping you to move beyond dysfunctional behavior unless you resolve to do something about them. You can't change your past, but you can overcome it — if you want to, if you believe you can, and if you commit yourself to doing so.

Resolving to learn about and overcome your deep, old wounds requires great courage. Opening up old wounds from childhood can be painful, and changing deeply ingrained attitudes and behavior requires tenacity, patience, and support from the people who love you. But your wounds from the past are givens, so your only other choice is to live at their mercy, to continue to let them run your life. You are far more likely to have a thriving marriage if you take your life over and run it yourself. This means understanding and overcoming the debilitating parts of your past that are an impediment to your happiness and the happiness of your spouse.

Experiment #29

Ask yourself the three questions in this section. First write your answers in your own notebook. Then ask your spouse for his or her response, and compare your answers.

2. *Inappropriate Expectations*

Your expectations greatly affect the quality of your experience.

Consider this: If you expect to get $50 and you get $500, you will be delighted. If you expect $5,000 and you get $500, you will be crushed. It is the same $500; all that changed was your expectations.

We all carry around ideas about what marriage should be, and we measure our experience against these expectations. One of the big keys to happy marriage is finding out what expectations about marriage are buried in your psyche and freeing yourself from their influence. It could be that all you have to do to have a happier marriage is to change, not your marriage or your partner, but your ideas. If you can change your thoughts, you can change your experience.

When I first moved to California, my then husband and I were living in a tiny apartment. Although he had been accepted into the school of his choice, I had been rejected by my first choice and was attending my second choice. I very much wanted a job that was open at Planned Parenthood but was edged out by someone else. I was discouraged.

Then one night in a conversation with friends, I began to recount the process by which we had decided to move to California. It had been a dream for me — one I very recently hadn't believed I would ever achieve. Yet here I was! That night, falling asleep, I played a game with myself. I pretended I was still back in New York just thinking about moving to California. I began to plan the details of my dream. "We'll find a great, cheap little apartment right in the heart of Berkeley's most active neighborhood. We'll both be in school, making friends from both schools. I'll get turned down for a job I want, but this will end up giving me more time to write, and I'll get some things published. We'll have time to take great little trips almost every weekend, to Mendocino, Big Sur, Napa, the Gold Country, Tahoe." I continued to fantasize — as though it were a dream off in the future — exactly what I already actually had. My mood turned around dramatically. I began to be excited about what I had rather than discouraged about what I didn't have.

Try this game yourself. It is a simple illustration of the principle that changing your thoughts can actually change your experience.

Experiment #30

For just a moment, pretend you are fifteen years old, dreaming about your future. Make the dream exactly what you have right now, as though your whole life as it is now is a prize you are longing for when you are fifteen years old. Include in your fantasy some of the things you are not so happy with just now along with the successful resolution of these "areas for improvement."

If your expectations for your marriage are inappropriate, you may be damaging an otherwise quite wonderful relationship. Let's review several of the common debilitating expectations about marriage:

1. *The "peak experience" quality of your honeymoon will last forever.* It won't. It isn't supposed to. The honeymoon will blossom into an abiding passion that you can sustain for many years.

2. *Marriage will solve all of your problems.* A great marriage gives you a wonderful companion. It solves the problem of loneliness, of unpredictability in your sex life, of uncertainty about your relationship future. It provides you with security in love.

But that's all.

Marriage will not provide you with high self-esteem if you don't have it already. It will not give your life meaning and direction if you are still searching. It cannot relieve your existential isolation if you are a habitual loner. Your marriage partner cannot make you happy all the time.

In short, it is inappropriate to expect your marriage partner to provide you with anything that you should be providing for yourself.

Not only will marriage fail to fix personal flaws or problems, but it will probably magnify them. If you are habitually late, you are inflicting this behavior only on yourself if you are alone, but when you get married, you will be making two people late. Similarly, if you tend to fly off the handle or complain about small things, or if you feel insecure at times, these tendencies will get magnified in marriage. When you are living closely with someone, you have more opportunity to be "triggered" into your habitual behavior, and the person with whom you are living is more likely to find the recurring behavior annoying.

Rather than fixing these problems, marriage will exacerbate them.

Yet too often we go into marriage expecting that it will be a universal cure. If you have that expectation, let go of it. Instead, ask your partner to support you as *you* begin to make the changes you want for yourself.

3. *My spouse should be able to meet all my needs.* Most married people have had the experience of being disappointed to learn that their spouse is simply not going to meet all of their needs. "I wish he enjoyed dancing." "I wish she would learn to play golf." "He never wants to discuss movies after we've seen them." "She hates entertaining my business associates." "If only she would learn to sail."

If we could start out with the expectation that our spouse is supposed to meet only a certain number of our needs and not all of them, and that it is entirely appropriate to go outside of marriage in order to get certain needs met, we would not have to experience disappointment. For example, the fact that Willy doesn't have two-hour-long discussions with Beth is not a problem as long as Beth has other places to get her need for long discussions met. But if Beth believed that there was something wrong with her marriage because she and Willy didn't have long talks, this could create tension for the two of them. It is easier and more appropriate for Beth to change her beliefs about the marriage than for Willy to change his behavior.

4. *Marriage will change me — or my spouse.* Unwitting magical thinking leads some people to believe that they — or their spouse — will become a different person after they marry. When they learn that they have brought their same old selves with them into the marriage, they are bitterly disappointed.

Elaine has a tendency to become depressed. She believed that her depression was related to her single status and that if she could only get married, this would end her depressive episodes. After she got married, she became twice as depressed when she found that marriage did not cure her. Only when she was able to let go of her inappropriate expectations about her marriage was she able to tackle the real source of her depression and get some lasting help.

Elaine had to do this work for herself. Neither her husband nor her marriage could do it for her.

5. *I can have everything I want in my marriage.* Carla described herself to me as "greedy" in her marriage, a tendency many of us have:

> I have a wonderful relationship, but I want more. I'm glad John loves
> me, is financially stable, does all the cooking, is hilarious, and is great

in bed, but I want him to go to more movies, enjoy my family, worry less about money, and not be so uptight about new people. I want everything!

The expectation that you can have everything you want in your marriage will always be frustrated. If you can accept your spouse, be grateful for what you have, and be gracious about the things you don't get from your spouse, you are more likely to thrive as a couple.

6. *There is no such thing as a truly happy marriage.* Far more debilitating than expectations that are inappropriately high are expectations that are inappropriately low. You have to believe in happy marriage in order to have one. If you believe you can have a happy marriage, you will desire one, and if you desire one, you will commit yourself to making it happen. Everything in your marriage flows from your belief that you and your spouse can be truly happy together.

3. Pressure to Divorce

Most people who feel that everything isn't perfect in their own marriage believe that they and their partner are not a good enough match. "People who have great marriages are lucky," they believe, "because they found really suitable partners. We can't have a thriving marriage because we just aren't right enough for each other." Or, "I want a thriving marriage, but my partner doesn't."

Couples who thrive did make an appropriate choice when they decided upon each other as marriage partners. But their relationship continues to be a great pleasure for them, not only because they are compatible with each other. Their relationship is thriving because they make it thrive. They have cultivated the qualities in themselves as individuals that make them good marriage partners. While most people think that thriving couples have a good marriage because they are so right for each other, the causal connection actually goes in the other direction: they seem so right for each other because they both adhere to principles that make their marriage work. They want a wonderful relationship with each other; they are fully committed to making it happen on a continuing basis; they pay attention to what they love about each other; they have an abundance of goodwill toward each other; they make certain they spend plenty of good, quality time together; they know how to handle conflicts and challenges and to keep these in perspective; and they value closeness.

Among couples who are not thriving, these qualities and these principles of living and relating will not be found to any great extent.

So the real question is not "Are you with the right partner?," but "Are you the right partner?" Far more important than choosing an appropriate partner is being an appropriate partner.

There are very few circumstances where divorce is genuinely the best answer. If you married very young or very quickly, you have been married a short time and have no children, and you realize you weren't using good judgment and simply made a mistake, maybe divorce will not be terribly traumatic and you can make a wiser decision if you try again.

If your spouse is someone who is abusive to you; genuinely mean-spirited; utterly uninterested in you and in your relationship; or hopelessly addicted to drugs or alcohol, you may indeed be acting in your own and your family's best interest to get out of the situation altogether.

But apart from extreme situations like these, even though divorce may seem like an easy out, it is rarely the best solution. It's easy to believe that divorce will give you the opportunity for personal growth, the chance to see where you went wrong and do it differently the next time. But realize this: if you don't make any *personal* changes, you will take your same old self with you into your next marriage and very likely repeat your self-defeating patterns. And if you are prepared to make some personal changes, how much more sensible and rewarding it is to change within your present marriage, to build upon the history you share and the qualities you do love about each other.

An impasse in a marriage is an opportunity for personal growth. In particular, it is an opportunity to grow in the understanding and experience of love. If your partner were the perfect embodiment of your dreams, your marriage would not reach into the deepest recesses of your being. You would not tap into each other's dark sides and bring up the parts of yourselves that need to be healed. It is the impediments to intimacy that allow you to experience the strength of your love and that push it to new heights. You love each other so that you can heal each other's old wounds, so that you can each become more self-loving. Your acceptance of your imperfect partner is the greatest gift you can give, and one of the most momentous learning experiences you can give yourself.

Thriving couples are merely imperfect partners who are committed to their journey.

You need two things in a love relationship: an emotional connection and the ability to solve problems, to work with each other. If between the two of you you can find the barest spark of each of these basic needs, you have enormous potential to have a fully loving, pleasurable, and fulfilling life together. The literature from marriage therapists is rife with stories of marriages that had gone dead being fully revitalized.

If the two of you were once romantic and happy together, you can find the place inside you that cares for your partner. Everyone needs to be loved and nurtured. If you have stopped behaving in a loving, nurturing way toward your spouse, you may be amazed at how he or she will respond if you resume that kind of behavior. Begin to view yourself as the kind of person described in this book. Look for the qualities in your partner that you do like and mention them. Think about the connection you feel with this person. You like your hometown, or your early childhood friend whom you still know, or even a sibling — not because they are so wonderful, but because they are in your life, they are a part of you. Your spouse is connected to you even more deeply. Find that connection and nurture it.

THE COST OF DIVORCE

Divorce is far more devastating than most people who go into it realize it will be. "When no-fault divorce was ushered in twenty years ago," writes Fred Moody in the *Seattle Weekly*, "it was hailed as a quick and easy solution to relationships gone sour. Now, a generation later, legions of divorced parents and their children are emerging to paint a far different picture: one of financial travail, psychological devastation, and endless emotional turmoil."

Divorce is forever. Years after the actual separation, children continue to live out the emotional scars of their parents' lack of motivation to stay together and work on becoming happier people. Women who retain custody of their children suffer, on the average, a 33 percent decline in their standard of living after divorce, adding to their feeling of bitterness and their general stress. While divorce is supposed to free the parties emotionally, more often it ties them up for years with feelings of anger, despair, loneliness, and the fear of risking love again.

Becoming the right partner for your mate — so that your mate will again become the right partner for you — is far more growth-producing and satisfying than divorce. It is harder to imagine changing yourself than it is to imagine simply leaving, but in many cases changing yourself is in fact easier and far more rewarding in the end than divorce. Rather than changing the external world, change your internal world. Don't feel you have to make a huge shift all at once. If you are unhappy with your marriage right now, it will be impossible for you to imagine that you could ever feel any different. But don't give up until you have genuinely tried to make a change within yourself. Choose a tiny internal shift to start with, such as giving your spouse one compliment, one positive, loving comment today. Start small and be genuinely open to what will happen. After you have reestablished your goodwill, there will be plenty of time and opportunity for you to ask for changes, according to the guidelines discussed earlier in this book. But for now, try to become the spouse you want your spouse to be to you. One tiny step in that direction could be the best thing you ever did — for yourself, for your spouse, and for your marriage.

4. Cultural Values

Our cultural values are inhospitable to intimacy. Building a happy marriage in our culture is like trying to grow fat, ripe tomatoes in the desert. For as a society, in our race to achieve material abundance, human and emotional values are often neglected — or even maligned.

We value money. If you want to be happy, our culture tells us, buy something. Whether it is floor wax or a fancy car, products are the avenue to abundance, peace of mind, and well-being.

It is not true. The real avenue to happiness is deeply satisfying human relationships. As individuals, many of us know this. But we are helpless to create a cultural climate that supports love. Instead, we must try to create loving relationships in a society that subordinates love to "success." As long ago as 1956, psychologist and writer Erich Fromm made this observation:

> In spite of the deep-seated craving for love, almost everything else is considered to be more important than love: success, prestige, money, power — almost all our energy is used for the learning of how to achieve these aims, and almost none to learn the art of loving.

Americans who want to form intimate connections, have families, and build deeply pleasurable human relationships are on a crash course with their own culture. For a society that trains its members to produce and achieve, to accumulate and consume, must systematically and deliberately destroy their ability to love. The two value systems are incompatible.

Efforts to soften the clash between human-oriented values and production-oriented values have emerged in recent years, as we shall see in a moment. But these changes remain the exception rather than the rule and serve to underscore the presence of a value clash more than to indicate that it is disappearing on any widespread scale.

Our culture provides rewards for those who make progress or make money, but you can't get rich or famous by having a good intimate relationship. This is not an accident or oversight; corporate and bureaucratic America needs people who are competitive, achievement-oriented, capable of living fragmented lives, and not overly concerned with pleasure or intimacy. The skills required to succeed in the workplace are diametrically opposed to the skills that are needed to build successful human relationships. It is tough to operate as an efficient, guarded, aggressive bureaucrat all day and then at night and on weekends transform yourself into an open, trusting, caring, expressive, sensitive, intimate partner.

We are having difficulty in our love lives, not because we are failing, but because we are succeeding in a system that is not only indifferent to love, but that systematically precludes it. Because we accurately perceive that the rewards go to those who win the competitive games, we learn to play these games, not realizing the toll they take on our personal lives.

It is no accident that we have popular magazines entitled *Time, Money, Fortune, People,* and *Success.* (There is also a magazine called *Marriage**; it has a circulation of 7,500.) Our mass media both reflect and perpetuate our cultural values.

A glaring example of America's trivialization of personal growth and quality relationships is the remarkable fact that psychology and self-help books are treated by mainstream media as somewhat less than "legitimate" nonfiction. The *New York Times* lists them in a separate category along with cookbooks! Talk show hosts are reluctant to engage self-help authors, implying that their topics are not substantive — unlike such topics as politics, war, money, business, sports, and entertainment. Even though major political and corporate problems can often be traced back to some individual who has used

---

*For information on *Marriage* magazine, call (612) 454-6434.

poor judgment or has abused power, professionals who might give such people genuine help with overcoming their personal liabilities and motivating them to higher purpose are trivialized.

In the same vein, political figures dare not admit that they have sought the help of therapists or counselors, that is, that they have shown any interest in expanding their self-knowledge (for good therapy is like getting a Ph.D. in yourself. You don't have to be sick to get better!)

When one of the most visible political pioneers of our time, feminist writer and activist Gloria Steinem, dared to describe the staggering impact of self-esteem on every other aspect of our lives, she was greeted by the mainstream press with such derision that it was almost possible to feel the fear that drove her detractors. A "squishy exercise in feeling better," one reviewer called it, as though feeling better is not a legitimate goal.

Steinem's is a radical proposition indeed, that in the end, we can't solve our collective problems until we each feel good about ourselves and love each other. The "system," and the corporate system in particular, is threatened by ideas like these. It needs us to believe that happiness comes from the tangible comforts of life, the things that money can buy.

Our cultural aversion to intimacy is also undermined by bars and nightclubs. If as a culture we were going to make a place for genuine human interactions, it would be in our leisure time activities, the places where we go to relax and be sociable. But rather than creating settings that encourage intimate conversations, we make sure the decibel level of ambient noise is so high that any conversation will be impossible, let alone any honest or personal interaction.

Freud was the first to point out that every healthy life requires a balance between work and intimacy. As a nation, we have not achieved this balance. It is no accident, as writer George Leonard pointed out, that Valentine's Day is a minor national holiday. No banks or government offices close and nobody parades down Fifth Avenue. A much greater fuss is made over Labor Day, which honors work, and Memorial Day, which honors war.

Business before pleasure. How thoroughly we abide by this idea as a nation! We may be the first people ever who have the ability to seek the highest forms of human fulfillment but who eschew them in favor of filling lesser needs.

Psychologist Robert Johnson points out:

[Western people] amass riches on an unprecedented scale. But few of us, very few indeed, are at peace with ourselves, secure in our relationships, content in our loves, or at home in the world. Most of us cry out for meaning in life, for values we can live by, for love and relationship.

SIGNS OF PROGRESS

According to a 1990 study at the University of Maryland, eight out of ten workers today would sacrifice rapid career advancement in order to have more time with their families. If money was the driving force of the eighties, our need for a sense of meaning is beginning to drive the nineties. Success has been redefined from "having it all" to "having yourself," from achieving the most to experiencing the most. Suddenly we are moving from big cities with their high-speed energy to small, human-scale towns. In significant numbers, former corporate climbers are "downshifting," eschewing the Peter Principle in favor of the pleasure principle. Quietly, when we weren't looking, money became something you need a certain amount of in order to enjoy an easy journey along the back roads of life, rather than the prize at the end of the fast lane. More than anything, we want control over our lives. We see the tragedy of spending our lives as modern-day slaves to work that is, in the end, someone else's pursuit. We are no longer willing to delay our quest for meaning. And meaning, we are learning, boils down to connecting with each other. Whereas, in the eighties, *Money* magazine featured families who had achieved prosperity, now more often it gives us stories about people who are forsaking great wealth to pursue something that does good for others.

At its height, the Sexual Revolution trivialized sex and severed it from love; now, for most people, sex is inseparable from love. For yuppies, glitz was more important than heart; a showy partner was just one more element in the flashy package. Now, former yuppies can be found on weekend outings with their children or volunteering for worthy causes. Or again, in the eighties, feminist women who elected to stay home with their children had to endure put-downs from their career-bound sisters; now, parenting is a respected option among feminists. Even the business world is embracing what used to be viewed as "personal skills." Managers now "empower" their subordinates rather than "supervising" them, and salespeople sell by serving their clients and by establishing relationships with their customers. Wherever we look, heart is taking its rightful position at the center of our lives as we continue to move toward balanced values and human-oriented priorities.

THE REBEL: MOVING AGAINST THE MAINSTREAM

So here's the dilemma. Some of us are trying to live enlightened, people-centered lives in a system that was set up to achieve other goals and that, for the most part, continues to pursue them. It will take institutions a very long time to catch up with the current values revolution.

Don't wait. If you want a truly thriving, abundant love relationship in your life, you will have to become something of a rebel. Don't expect society to support you. Our culture doesn't understand thriving love relationships, doesn't believe in them, and doesn't value them.

Happy, flourishing marriages are still a novel concept. So be aware, as you pursue delight in your life, that you may confront societal obstacles: people who are threatened by your values or institutions that will try to thwart your efforts. You may have to make professional or business "sacrifices," trade-offs that will puzzle or intimidate others. You may even feel confused yourself at times, for you won't fit in as you used to, and that can be disorienting for a time.

But be tenacious. The rewards to be gained from the unswerving pursuit of a thriving marriage are worth any swimming upstream that you may need to do. Don't let obsolete cultural values deter you from opening your heart to love — and to thriving marriage.

Remember, rebels are not so much people who *behave* differently as people who *believe* differently. If you buy the American myth that you are what you accomplish, then you will do whatever is necessary to succeed and to surround yourself with evidence of your success. If, on the other hand, you see that wealth and status are sometimes achieved at the expense of things you value more — such as truly joyous human relationships — then you will find your own private ways to rebel. You will allow yourself to discover your deepest inner desires, and to be motivated by them rather than by social pressures.

An active and successful eighty-four-year-old man who had lost his wife of many years fourteen months before told me: "The most important thing there is is to love another person. There is nothing else, really, in life. And to love a lot of people. In as many ways as you can. But people don't get this. They are so busy running around, you can see they don't love."

In the movie *Always*, a character died in a crash. He returned as a ghost to tell the woman he loved, "I love you. I should have said the words. I should have told you I love you, because I know now that *the love we hold back is the only pain that follows us here.*"

But the most unlikely source of comments like these was conservative politician Lee Atwater:

> I acquired more [wealth, power, and prestige] than most. But you can acquire all you want, and still feel empty. It took a deadly illness to put me eye to eye with that truth, but it is a truth that the country, caught up in its ruthless ambitions and moral decay, can learn on my dime. [Whoever leads us through the nineties must] speak to the spiritual vacuum at the heart of American society. . . . What is missing in society is what was missing in me: a little heart.

HOW TO COPE WITH ADVERSE CULTURAL VALUES

Couples who thrive aren't waiting to put their hearts at the center of their lives. They aren't waiting for corporations and government policies to become more enlightened about the importance of human happiness and love. Thriving, joyful couples recognize that achievement and material abundance at the expense of richly satisfying love is not abundance at all, but a cover for emptiness. They know that real success is having control over their own lives, being able to do what they truly want to do for themselves, and being free to support the happiness of the people they love.

Our era is one of limitless opportunity for marital quality *and* staggering societal challenges to marriage. We have a bigger vision of love and more resources to achieve it than ever before, but we are confronted with a tough world as a context for our efforts.

Couples who thrive do not waste energy grumbling or whining about the state of the universe. Many of them are actively involved in trying to bring about a better world, but they do not let society's ills keep them from thriving themselves.

If you determine that the impediments to happiness in your own marriage are related to external pressures, then your focus should be on figuring out a way to thrive in spite of the problems, for they are not likely to disappear quickly. This may require creative problem solving and may mean that you will need to make big changes. If you need both of your incomes, you can't find adequate child care, and your workplaces won't allow you to work part-time or on flex schedules, maybe one of you will need to change jobs. Maybe you will need to move. Maybe you will need to organize a day-care center or lobby your company to provide on-site child care.

If you face economic pressures, force yourselves to find creative ways to scale back. Mayer and I once took a car-camping trip across country with our son and budgeted $7 per person per day for food. We had to be creative, but we treated our goal as a game and were quite pleased with ourselves for succeeding.

If your work schedule is overwhelming or your work is unsatisfying, don't wait to make a move. Consider downshifting, moving to a job that will give you less money or status but also reduced stress and more quality time with your family.

My point here is not to imply that solutions to external pressures are easy, but to remind you that the societal problems won't go away. If you are reeling under their influence and you want to become a happier couple, you will have to become proactive and make a change in your response to the societal problems. Either that, or continue to let them oppress you. Those are your only two choices.

It's not a perfect world; nevertheless, you can have your own perfect marriage. There is nothing extraordinary about the couples in this book except their desire for, belief in, and commitment to thriving marriage. If they could do it, so can you.

5. Apathy

The greatest enemy of thriving marriage is apathy and procrastination.

You feel something is a little wrong, but you ignore it or push it to the back of your mind. You find yourself complaining to your friends about your spouse, but you never take any of the actions they suggest. You tell yourself you will speak with your spouse about something, but you never do it. You know you want to spend more time with each other, but the press of your schedules never lets it happen.

Talk to your partner. Set aside times to be together. Choose several of the experiments in this book that interest you most and do them together. Gather your courage and ask your partner for what you want. For if you don't put positive energy into your marriage, who will? And if not now, when?

There is no impediment to thriving marriage that you cannot overcome if you are highly enough motivated. There is no reason you cannot be part of a relationship like the ones described in these pages if you want one enough.

Romantic love between two people who are equals and who share both intimacy *and* commitment was an experiment. Now the news is out: it works. Romantic love's potential to allow deep, sustained intimacy has been realized by many happy couples. If you aren't one of them yet, I hope this book has inspired you to become one.

If you do nothing else suggested in this book, try this final experiment. It requires very little time, and can open the doors to greater happiness for both of you.

Experiment #31

Ask each other, "What do you need from me to feel loved by me?" Each of you answer honestly, and then put genuine effort into giving your partner what he or she needs to feel loved.

Your marriage is an extraordinary opportunity for you to deepen the richness of your life. Great love between two people will transform them and then reach beyond the two of them to everyone they touch. The deeper and more passionate your love is, the more concern you will feel for other people and for the world we inhabit. Love is the beginning of the cure for the world's ills, and love is the end, for what more can we desire for the entire planet but that we all have a love so great that we are no longer interested in destroying each other and our planet, but only in deepening and expanding the experience of love for all people — toward each other and toward the earth that sustains us.

You will be making a contribution to the transformation of the planet by turning your marriage into a thriving romance. For yourself and for everyone around you, think right now about your spouse and the qualities you adore. Take the time to say something lovely that you have never said before. Offer to do a favor. Think up a fun surprise. Enjoy each other, right now, for you will never have this moment again.

I wish you love in great abundance for many, many years.

Bibliography

Bloomfield, Harold, M.D., et al. *Lifemates*. New York: New American Library, 1992.

Branden, Nathaniel. *The Psychology of Romantic Love*. New York: Bantam, 1981.

——— and E. Devers Branden. *The Romantic Love Question and Answer Book*. New York: Bantam, 1987.

Cohen, Sherry Suib. *The Secrets of a Very Good Marriage*. New York: Carol Southern, 1993.

Covey, Stephen R. *The 7 Habits of Highly Effective People*. New York: Simon & Schuster, 1989.

Farrell, Warren. *Why Men Are the Way They Are*. New York: McGraw-Hill, 1986.

Ferguson, Marilyn. *The Aquarian Conspiracy*. Los Angeles: J. P. Tarcher, 1980.

Gaylin, Willard, M.D. *Rediscovering Love*. New York: Viking, 1986.

Godek, Gregory. *1001 Ways to Be Romantic*. Weymouth, Mass.: Casablanca Press, 1991.

Gordon, Thomas. *P.E.T.: Parent Effectiveness Training*. New York: Penguin, 1975.

Gray, John. *Men Are from Mars, Women Are from Venus*. New York: HarperCollins, 1992.

Hendricks, Gay, and Kathlyn Hendricks. *Conscious Loving: The Journey to Co-Commitment*. New York: Bantam, 1990.

Hendrix, Harville. *Getting the Love You Want: A Guide for Couples*. New York: HarperPerennial, 1988.

Hochschild, Arlie Russell. *The Second Shift*. New York: Viking, 1989.

Hume, David. "A Treatise of Human Nature." In *The Philosophical Works*. Vol. 2. Evanston, Ill.: Adlers Foreign Books, 1974.

Johnson, Catherine. *Lucky in Love*. New York: Viking, 1992.

Johnson, Robert A. *WE: Understanding the Psychology of Romantic Love*. San Francisco: Harper & Row, 1983.

Keen, Sam. *The Passionate Life: Stages of Loving*. San Francisco: Harper & Row, 1983.

Keyes, Ken, Jr. *Your Heart's Desire*. Coos Bay, Oreg.: Living Love Publications, 1983.

Kingma, Daphne Rose. *The Men We Never Knew*. Berkeley, Calif.: Conari Press, 1993.

Lewis, C. S. *The Four Loves*. New York: Harcourt Brace Jovanovich, 1960.

Livermore, Beth. "The Lessons of Love." In *Psychology Today*. March-April 1993.

Lowen, Alexander, M.D. *Depression and the Body*. Baltimore, Md.: Penguin, 1972.

Luks, Allan, and Peggy Payne. *The Healing Power of Doing Good*. New York: Fawcett, 1992.

Martz, Sandra H., ed. *If I Had My Life to Live Over*. Watsonville, Calif.: Papier-Mache Press.

Meiers, Mildred, and Jack Knapp. *5600 Jokes for All Occasions*. New York: Avenel, 1980.

Mornell, Perre, M.D. *Passive Men, Wild Women*. New York: Ballantine, 1979.

Moyers, Bill. *Healing and the Mind*. New York: Doubleday, 1993.

Oden, Thomas C. *Game Free: A Guide to the Meaning of Intimacy*. New York: Harper & Row, 1974.

Peck, M. Scott. *The Road Less Traveled*. New York: Simon & Schuster, 1980.

Pransky, George S. *Divorce Is Not the Answer*. Blue Ridge Summit, Penn.: Tab Books, 1990.

Roszak, Theodore. *Making of a Counter-Culture*. Garden City, N.Y.: Doubleday, 1969.

Rubin, Lillian B. *Intimate Strangers: Men and Women Together*. New York: Harper & Row, 1983.

Rubin, Theodore Isaac, M.D. *Reconciliations; Inner Peace in an Age of Anxiety*. New York: Berkley Books, 1980.

Saltzman, Amy. *Downshifting*. New York: HarperCollins, 1991.

Scarf, Maggie. *Intimate Partners: Patterns in Love and Marriage*. New York: Random House, 1987.

Schaef, Anne Wilson. *Women's Reality*. Minneapolis, Minn.: Weston Press, 1981.

Skolnick, Arlene S. *The Intimate Environment: Exploring Marriage and the Family*. Boston: Little, Brown, 1987.

Starhawk. *Truth or Dare*. San Francisco: Harper & Row, 1978.

Tanenbaum, Joe. *Male and Female Realities: Understanding the Opposite Sex*. Sugar Land, Tex.: Candle Publishing, 1989.

Tannen, Deborah. *You Just Don't Understand: Women and Men in Conversation*. New York: William Morrow, 1990.

Van Auken, Sheldon. *A Severe Mercy*. San Francisco: Harper San Francisco, 1980.

Watzlawick, Paul, et al. *Change*. New York: W. W. Norton, 1974.

Welwood, John. *Journey of the Heart*. New York: HarperPerennial, 1990.

Yanagi, Soetsu. *The Unknown Craftsman*. New York: Harper & Row, 1972.

Young-Eisendrath, Polly. *You're Not What I Expected*. New York: William Morrow, 1993.

About the Author

Susan Page, M.Div., is the former Director of Women's Programs at the University of California in Berkeley. She began her career as a Protestant campus minister at Washington University in St. Louis and Columbia University in New York. She also served as the Executive Director of a Child Abuse Prevention Agency, helped to found a Shelter for Battered Women, and has had a private practice in management consulting and training. Susan began her now famous relationship workshops in 1980. A much sought-after keynote speaker, she is a member of the National Speakers Association. She has been happily married since 1981 and lives in Berkeley, California.

Susan Page welcomes your comments and especially your success stories. To correspond with her, or for information about her tapes, lectures, and workshops, write to

1941 Oregon Street
Berkeley, California 94703